Crowdfund Investing
FOR
DUMMIES®

**by Sherwood Neiss, Jason W. Best, and
Zak Cassady-Dorion**

WILEY

John Wiley & Sons, Inc.

Crowdfund Investing For Dummies®

Published by
John Wiley & Sons, Inc.
111 River St.
Hoboken, NJ 07030-5774
www.wiley.com

WILEY

About the Authors

Sherwood Neiss: Sherwood Neiss is a co-founder of Crowdfund Capital Advisors (CCA). He is an expert at building successful businesses. He is a three-time Inc. 500 winner whose company won E&Y's Entrepreneur of the Year. As a serial entrepreneur and investor during the credit crunch, Sherwood saw a need for a change in outdated securities laws and did something about it — as a co-founding member of Startup Exemption, Sherwood co-authored the crowdfund investing framework used in the JOBS Act that was signed into law by President Obama on April 5, 2012. CCA advises angel groups, venture capital, private equity, investment banks, and hedge funds on understanding how to profit in what expert VC Fred Wilson claims will be a $300 billion per year market. He produces comprehensive crowdfund investing educational materials so that investors can decide whether crowdfunding is appropriate for their portfolios, as well as help them access the essential tools to invest safely, legally, and successfully. Sherwood co-founded and sits on the board of the Crowdfunding Professional Association (CfPA) and Crowdfund Intermediary Regulatory Advocates (CFIRA), where he leads the fight to ensure that investors are protected while entrepreneurs have access to the capital they need to start and grow promising companies. He also sits on the boards of advisors for several crowdfunding portals and industry players, as well as on the boards of Invest Crowdfund Canada and the European Crowdfunding Network. An avid public speaker, Sherwood speaks at congressional hearings, universities, and seminars around the world discussing crowdfunding. Some of his appearances include testifying in front of Congress, the MIT Global Startup Workshop in Istanbul, and the 2013 SXSW Conference in Austin, Texas. He is a contributing author to TechCrunch, VentureBeat, Forbes, and The Huffington Post. Sherwood is a recipient of the first Crowdfund Visionary Award. He holds an International MBA from Thunderbird and a BA from Tulane University.

Jason Best: As a co-founder of Startup Exemption, Jason Best co-authored the crowdfund investing framework that was used in the JOBS Act to legalize equity- and debt-based crowdfunding in the United States. The JOBS Act was one of the largest changes in U.S. investment laws in over 30 years; it allows private companies to raise capital via their online social networks. Jason has provided U.S. Congressional testimony on crowdfunding and was honored to attend the White House ceremony when President Obama signed this legislation into law on April 5, 2012. He is also a frequent speaker both domestically and internationally, including speaking at the 2012 White House Global Entrepreneurship Celebration; TEDx San Miguel de Allende, Mexico; and the Global Innovation Symposium and Globe Forum in Stockholm, Sweden. As a co-founder and principal at Crowdfund Capital Advisors (CCA), Jason works with angel groups, venture capital firms, and family offices, as well as the World Bank, governments, and NGOs, to understand crowdfunding and to create successful strategies for maximizing the value of this emerging asset class and its ecosystem. Jason is a co-founder of the Crowdfunding Professional Association (CfPA) and the Crowdfund Intermediary Regulatory Advocates (CFIRA), which is the global industry advocacy organization for crowdfunding. Additionally, he is a board member of the European Crowdfunding Network and the Canadian Technology Alliance. CCA also participates in the U.S. State Department's Global Entrepreneurship Program.

Jason is a co-founder and serves on the leadership team of the UC Berkeley Program on Innovation in Entrepreneurial and Social Finance, in addition to serving as an Entrepreneur-in-Residence at the Center for Entrepreneurship and Technology at UC Berkeley. As a successful investor and entrepreneur, Jason brings over a decade of executive leadership experience at two SaaS companies, one of which earned an Inc. 500 Award two years in a row. This award is given annually by *Inc. Magazine* to the 500 fastest growing private companies in the United States. As part of the leadership teams of those two companies, he helped raise over $40 million in private capital. Jason contributes to publications including TechCrunch, The Huffington Post, and VentureBeat. He is a recipient of the first Crowdfund Visionary Award.

Jason earned his master's degree from the Thunderbird School of Global Management, the world's top international MBA program, and also holds a bachelor's degree from William Jewell College.

Zak Cassady-Dorion: Zak is currently the CEO and co-founder of Pure Mountain Olive Oil, LLC, a chain of olive oil and balsamic vinegar tasting shops in the Northeast United States. He is also a co-founder of Startup Exemption, where he led the effort to legalize debt- and equity-based crowdfunding. He co-authored the crowdfund investing framework that was used in the JOBS Act to legalize equity- and debt-based crowdfunding in the United States. In the campaign to legalize crowdfunding, Zak provided U.S. Congressional testimony on crowdfunding. He was honored with an invitation to the White House on April 5, 2012, when President Obama signed the JOBS Act into law. He is a recipient of the first Crowdfund Visionary Award.

Zak is a partner of Crowdfund Capital Advisors (CCA), where he works with angel groups, venture capital firms, and government organizations consulting on crowdfunding. Zak speaks regularly across North America about crowdfunding to entrepreneurial groups and universities.

Zak has successful entrepreneurial experience in Latin America and Southeast Asia, in addition to a successful business development career with Wyndham Worldwide. He earned his MBA from Thunderbird School of Global Management, ranked as the world's top international MBA program, and a BS from the University of Vermont. Zak has worked, lived, and traveled in over 35 countries and is fluent in English, Spanish, and Portuguese. When not working, Zak can be found playing an adventure sport in the wilderness, such as rock climbing, hiking, skiing, paragliding, kayaking, or skydiving.

Dedication

This book is dedicated to unreasonable people who question the status quo, create solutions, and make rational positive change. When we began the fight to legalize crowdfund investing, people told us we were crazy. Sometimes good timing, good luck, optimism, and hard work come together to make change happen. Be unreasonable in pursuing what you believe in.

This book is also dedicated to our parents, family, loved ones, and friends, who have been and continue to be unreasonable in their love and belief in us as we pursue what we're passionate about.

Authors' Acknowledgments

This book is a team effort. Our teams started with our parents (Gertrude and Edward Neiss, Sulin and Roger Best, and Trisha Cassady and Pablo Dorion) who ignited in each of us the passion to pursue a master's degree in business from Thunderbird, the American Graduate School of International Management. Our paths wouldn't have crossed if it weren't for this fortunate circumstance. Our families gave us the support and critical feedback we needed along the way to pursue our passions and to do so with integrity and optimism.

We couldn't have done this without the opportunities we've had in business that taught us the fundamentals of taking an idea, seeding it with capital, and growing successful companies. The lessons we learned there were critical to our being able to translate the needs of startups and small businesses into a framework that would reside on the principles of crowdfunding.

And we couldn't have done this without a bipartisan Washington, D.C., that understood that the Internet and social media could allow us to update securities laws to match the way we live our lives today and will do so in the future. Our thanks go to Karen Kerrigan, who was our champion through the entire process in Washington. Deep gratitude goes to President Obama for his early leadership on crowdfunding and for the opportunity to attend the JOBS Act signing ceremony in the Rose Garden of the White House on April 5, 2012. We thank Representative Patrick McHenry (R-NC) for his bipartisan leadership in drafting the first bill in the U.S. House of Representatives on crowdfund investing and for its passage with over 400 votes. Thank you to Senator Jeff Merkley (D-OR), Senator Scott Brown (R-MA), and Senator Michael Bennett (D-CO), for taking the leadership in driving a bipartisan compromise in the U.S. Senate.

Of course, this book wouldn't have been as wonderful as it is without the awesome input of Joan Friedman. Thank you, Joan!

With the passage of the law, we've had the good fortune to become friends and compatriots with people who will lead the crowdfunding industry into the future: Doug Ellenoff, Judy Robinett, Whitney Johnson, Davis Jones, Richard Swart, Vince Molinari, Chance Barnett, DJ Paul, Ryan Feit, Ruth Hedges, Luan Cox, Chris Tyrrell, Candace Klein, Joy Schoffler, Kim Wales, Chris Reed, Dan Meader, Carl Esposti, Kevin Grell, Brian Tsuchiya, Alejandro Cremades, Tanya Prive, Mike Norman, Maurice Lopes, Dara Albright, Steve Yin, Freeman White, Sara Hanks, Brad Thatcher, and iLona Major. Thank you also to David A. Saltzman for being the first securities attorney to patiently listen to our crazy idea and to provide important early feedback.

In Washington D.C., we thank all the dedicated, hard-working people we met with and who believed in crowdfund investing. Specifically, we would like to thank Doug Rand, Andy Green, Kunal Punwah, Ryan Minto, Marne Marotta, Nat Hoopes, Brian Murphy, Brian Appel, and Shelley Porges.

From Woodie: Thank you to the following people for helping me along my journey: Chris Bookfield, Andy Buyting, Marc Casey, Shelli Coleman, Tom Coleman, Colin Denney, Levi Downs, Joe Freeman, Scott Giersch, Matt Hagan, Keith Harris, Alex Jacobs, Ray Janssen, Bryan Kilpatrick, Scott King, Andrew Kranis, Frank LaRocco, Maria Helena Lopes, Nancy Maveety, Patrick Menasco, Kevin Miller, Marvin Miller, Roy Morris, Todd Pearsall, Diana Perez, Brian Petro, Bud Russell, Kerry Shahan, Steven Stralser, Craig Thomsen, Marc Wallace, Ricardo Zapata, and my brothers and sisters: Shelley, Marc (and Carolyn), David, Gary (and Amy), and Heidi.

From Jason and Woodie: Thanks to Trent Blanchard, Karin Brandenburg, Guy Chetwyn, Whoopi Goldberg, Verne Harnish, Tom Leonardis, Todd Malensek, Neil Malik, Alix and Susan Shaer, and the entire Thunderbird Crew: Rob Mitchell and Jay Cabalquinto, Kellie and Chedo Vugrincic, Laura and Francis Santora, Rich Gardner and Kiko Kas, Kya and Neil Sainsbury-Carter, Amanda and Sami Eden-Fox, Stephanie Marcone, Julie Smith and Taylor Rabbetz, Arpana and Raj Jain, Alexine Hazarian, Tomas Soto, Meredith Tolan, Kristine and Bryan McCabe, and Doug and Karmei Morin.

From Jason: Thank you K-Tjen for believing in me; I can't wait to see what's next. Thank you to Andrew, Misti, Hunter, and Lara Best; David Law; Darin Barker; Luke Cassady-Dorion; Michael Wykoff; Thapanont (Tae) Phithakrattanayothin; Joel and Mary Werner; Julie Goins; Debbie Ramirez; Victoria Hernandez; Chris and Arron Hester; Scott and Krista Hester; Keith Davis; Richard Chisenhall; Jenna Daly; Bruce Jenett; Greg Horowitt; Sen Luo; Denmark West; Sang Lee and Michael Ellis; Doug Vu; Gary Manalus; Greg Millard; Michelle and Mark Karma; Joyce Reitman; Ken Singer; Greg Slamowitz; Al Watkins; Nima Adelkhani; David Arronson; Leslie Yuan; John Rowe; Draven Lee; Nacho and Lloyd and Judy Jenkins.

From Zak: Thanks to my wonderful and supportive family: my brother, Luke Cassady-Dorion, who is my best friend and mentor; my mother, Trisha Cassady, and father, Pablo Dorion, for their endless support and encouragement in everything that I do; and my stepfather, Earl Dworkin, and step-mother, Nancy Gilman. Thank you Erin Marie Freund for all that you do for me. And thank you to Thapanont (Tae) Phithakrattanayothin, Marc and Meg Laurent, Shaun Miller, Charlie Ruehr, Wolfgang Foust, David Law, Mike Caplice, Zach Glaser, Donnel Much, Michael Welch, and to all my other friends without whom I wouldn't be where I am today.

Publisher's Acknowledgments

We're proud of this book; please send us your comments at http://dummies.custhelp.com. For other comments, please contact our Customer Care Department within the U.S. at 877-762-2974, outside the U.S. at 317-572-3993, or fax 317-572-4002.

Some of the people who helped bring this book to market include the following:

Acquisitions, Editorial, and Vertical Websites

Contributor: Joan Friedman

Project Editor: Elizabeth Kuball

Acquisitions Editor: Tracy Boggier

Copy Editor: Elizabeth Kuball

Assistant Editor: David Lutton

Editorial Program Coordinator: Joe Niesen

Technical Editor: Mark D. Svejda

Senior Editorial Manager: Jennifer Ehrlich

Editorial Manager: Carmen Krikorian

Editorial Assistant: Rachelle Amick, Alexa Koschier

Cover Photos: John Wiley & Sons, Inc.

Cartoons: Rich Tennant (www.the5thwave.com)

Composition Services

Project Coordinator: Sheree Montgomery

Layout and Graphics: Joyce Haughey, Andrea Hornberger

Proofreaders: Lauren Mandelbaum, The Well-Chosen Word

Indexer: Claudia Bourbeau

Publishing and Editorial for Consumer Dummies

> **Kathleen Nebenhaus,** Vice President and Executive Publisher
>
> **David Palmer,** Associate Publisher
>
> **Kristin Ferguson-Wagstaffe,** Product Development Director

Publishing for Technology Dummies

> **Andy Cummings,** Vice President and Publisher

Composition Services

> **Debbie Stailey,** Director of Composition Services

Contents at a Glance

Table of Contents

Introduction

● ●

Crowdfund investing is an exciting new business financing opportunity created by the JOBS Act that President Obama signed into law in 2012. It taps into the power of the crowd by connecting entrepreneurs and small business owners with investors via LinkedIn, Facebook, Twitter, and other social media networks. And it offers small investors the chance to purchase an equity stake (or to fund debt) in small, private businesses run by people they know and trust.

Regulated by the U.S. Securities and Exchange Commission (SEC), crowdfund investing occurs via online funding portals — websites that host investment campaigns and collect investor pledges. An individual can invest only a limited amount each year in these campaigns (to mitigate investor risk), and a campaign must be funded completely in order for the business to receive investor dollars.

Is crowdfund investing a funding source you should consider for your startup or small business? That's a big question, and it requires some serious consideration. Asking for crowd support can produce amazing results; you can benefit not only from the money but also from the talents, skills, and collective wisdom of your crowd. But using this funding source is a big responsibility. If you decide to sell equity shares of your company to the crowd, your investors become your business owners. In doing so, you must be prepared to be a master communicator (because crowds don't like silence and will fill it with speculation) and to spend every dollar with your crowd's best interests in mind.

If you've got a great concept, a solid business plan, and vibrant social networks, you may find that crowdfund investing is a great fit for you. Reading this book is your first step to figuring out if that's the case.

About This Book

In this book, we address two separate audiences:

- ✔ Small business owners and entrepreneurs looking for capital
- ✔ People with capital — even very modest amounts — who may be interested in investing via this new funding resource

If you're in either camp, you've come to the right place!

For both audiences, we've done our best to outline what we envision the crowdfund investing industry will look like based on the parameters set by JOBS Act. For the small business owner or entrepreneur, that includes how a crowdfund investing campaign will proceed, what services an online funding portal will provide, and how your investment crowd influences the way you conduct business post-funding. For the potential crowdfund investor, that includes how you find the necessary information to become educated about various investment opportunities, how you actually commit funds to a startup or small business, and what role you play in the venture post-funding.

The word *envision* in the previous paragraph should tip you off that we're discussing a subject that's emerging as we write this book. The three of us were involved from day one in developing the crowdfund investing framework that served as a model for the part of the JOBS Act that addresses this subject. We're not outsiders making predictions based on our hopes and dreams; we're intimately familiar with how the legislation was crafted and how SEC regulations are being developed to support it. However, we fully realize that the law remains subject to change or interpretation after SEC regulations are adopted in 2013. Until the SEC adopts such regulations, the sale of securities through crowdfund investing is prohibited, and the new regulations may affect the accuracy of this book's content.

We do our best here to offer you a broad introduction to this subject and to show you why crowdfund investing has the potential to ignite our economy, create jobs, and promote investment at the community level. But we strongly encourage you not to take this text as gospel because all new laws and regulations are works in progress. Therefore, before you take any action to start a crowdfund investing campaign or to invest in such a campaign, you should read the most up-to-date information you can find about industry regulations. The SEC website (www.sec.gov) is the best place to start, and you can also visit the website for the Crowdfunding Professional Association (www.crowdfunding professional.org), an industry trade organization that we helped to launch.

We cannot emphasize this enough: **If you're a business considering offering equity buy-in to crowd investors, you should consult legal counsel before making any such securities offering.** And if you're considering selling debt instead, or if you're a potential investor intrigued by the crowdfund investing concept, you must undertake due diligence to make sure you're educated and up to date on the SEC regulations at play.

Conventions Used in This Book

To help you navigate the text as easily as possible, we use the following conventions:

- ✔ Whenever we introduce a new term, it appears in *italic*. You can find a definition or explanation nearby.

✔ If we want to share interesting information that isn't essential to your success with crowdfund investing, we place it in a gray box called a *sidebar.*

✔ All web addresses are clearly formatted in `monofont` so they're easy to pick out if you need to go back and find them.

Keep in mind that when this book was printed, some web addresses may have needed to break across two lines of text. Wherever that's the case, rest assured that we haven't put in any extra characters (such as hyphens) to indicate the break. So, when using one of these web addresses, just type in exactly what you see in this book. Pretend as if the line break doesn't exist.

What You're Not to Read

Because we have two distinct audiences for this book, you may find that not every chapter presents information that's crucial to you. We encourage you to peruse the chapters in Part I no matter what perspective you're coming from. If you're a business owner or entrepreneur, Parts II, III, and IV are written for you. (Investors and curious onlookers, you may or may not find that the chapters in these parts are essential reading.) Investors, you'll get coziest with the chapters in Part V. (Business owners and entrepreneurs, we suggest that you at least skim these chapters as well, because understanding the investor's perspective can only help you to succeed.) Part VI is a fun one that's written for every reader to enjoy — feel free to skip ahead to it if you want to get a taste of what this book is about.

Also, as we mention in the previous section, sidebars are not essential reading, so feel free to fly by them if you're in a hurry.

Foolish Assumptions

If you're approaching this book from the businessperson/entrepreneur perspective, we assume that you're bringing at least a little business acumen. Maybe you're already running a company, or you at least have a draft of a business plan in hand and know a bit about how companies are traditionally funded. With that said, we avoid jargon and focus on the fundamentals here, so even if this is the first book you read about business financing, you won't have any trouble following along.

If you're a potential investor, we likewise skip the jargon and stick to the basics here. That means you should have no trouble understanding what we're saying, but it also means that you should supplement your investment education with more in-depth reading. The latest edition of *Investing For Dummies,* by Eric Tyson (Wiley), is a good place to start if you're an investment novice, and we encourage you to heed our repeated warnings throughout this book that investing in small businesses or startups is really risky business. Crowdfund investments should make up only a small percentage of your portfolio. If you have more acumen, we assume you have some portfolio construction experience and/or work with a financial advisor to make sure any new investments you make are logical in terms of risk and potential reward.

How This Book Is Organized

Here's a broad overview of what you'll see in the coming pages.

Part 1: Tapping the Potential of Crowdfund Investing

This is where you discover what crowdfund investing is all about. In Chapter 1, we give you an overview of how this form of private equity or debt investment works and what the potential benefits are to entrepreneurs, small businesses, and investors. Chapter 2 explains how the crowdfund investing concept evolved, why it gained bipartisan support in Washington, D.C., and was included in the JOBS Act in 2012, and how it was one of the largest changes to the business financing landscape in over 77 years.

For entrepreneurs or small business owners, Chapter 3 offers a great overview of how crowdfund investing campaigns work, including the types of businesses that are the best candidates and the risks involved with this funding source. It ends with some wise words from the lawyers. Chapter 4 is a great resource for potential investors, outlining why and how you may want to become part of a company's investment crowd.

Part 11: Planning Your Crowdfund Investing Campaign

If you're an entrepreneur or small business owner, you don't want to miss this part. The chapters here provide the foundational information you need to begin developing a crowdfund investing campaign.

When you plan to seek business funding of any kind, you have to present a solid business plan and define your financial needs. If you need help accomplishing these important first steps, Chapter 5 gives you a quick overview. Chapters 6 and 7 outline the next steps involved when preparing for a crowdfund investing campaign: picturing how large your crowd will be and who will be in it, and choosing an online funding platform to host your campaign. In Chapter 8, we provide a guide for how to create and mobilize your crowd — a necessity for crowdfund investing.

Part III: Managing Your Crowdfund Investing Campaign

The chapters in this part are a crash course for an entrepreneur or small business owner looking to launch and run an online crowdfund investing campaign. In Chapter 9, you find out how to market your pitch, how to tap into your social networks for maximum effect, and what to expect when your campaign gets started. We devote Chapter 10 to helping you prepare for potential problems related to your campaign, and in Chapter 11 we explain what to expect — and what actions you should plan to take — after you successfully complete a crowdfund investing campaign.

Part IV: Running Your Business with Your Investors in Mind

Inviting a crowd of investors to support your startup or small business is no small matter; when you take this step, you accept a fiduciary responsibility to your crowd. We know you want to do the right thing by your investors, and this part can help. In Chapter 12, we demonstrate how to communicate clearly and regularly with your crowd so they're always informed about the status of their investment. Chapter 13 advises how to avoid mistakes that could lead your investors to revolt and shows you how to win them over again if they do. And Chapter 14 recognizes that even the best laid business plans can experience hiccups (or major detours), so we offer advice for keeping your investors happy even when your plans are delayed or your goals need to change.

Part V: Becoming a Crowdfund Investor

This part is written with the investor in mind. The JOBS Act that legalized crowdfund investing opened the door for many people to have the opportunity to invest in small, private companies for the first time. But before you invest a dollar, you need to read this part.

The risks inherent in investing in small businesses and startups are extremely high, and you have to make sure that this type of investment makes sense as a small part of your financial portfolio. You also have to make sure that you do your homework and study thoroughly the investment opportunities available to you, as well as the investment limits established by the legislation. Chapter 15 can help you work through all these steps. In Chapter 16, we explain how you actually commit your capital by interacting with the online funding portal that supports the crowdfund investing campaign.

Chapter 17 focuses on how to be a valuable asset to any company you support (without becoming a nuisance). And finally, Chapter 18 encourages you to map out your investment exit strategy well in advance so you aren't making any rash decisions.

Part VI: The Part of Tens

Here, we offer short-and-sweet chapters that present the best practices for a crowdfund investing campaign and the reasons that we believe every nation should be noticing what the United States is doing with crowdfund investing. We then turn our attention to some case studies: ten examples from the crowdfunding world that illustrate the power of collective investments, as well as ten crowdfunding stories that will tug at your heartstrings.

Icons Used in This Book

Throughout this book you'll notice small graphics in the margins, called *icons.* These symbols are meant to draw your attention to particular ideas.

This icon denotes information that can ease your efforts when starting a crowdfund investing campaign or making an investment decision.

To avoid a common misstep, heed the advice offered in a paragraph accompanied by this icon.

These tidbits are worth tucking into your mental filing cabinet for future use.

Where to Go from Here

This book is designed to allow you to open to any chapter and understand what's being discussed, so you shouldn't feel obliged to start with Chapter 1 and read straight through. However, we strongly encourage you to spend time with the chapters in Part I because they offer such a helpful overview of what crowdfund investing is about and how it takes place. Then, if you're a business owner or entrepreneur, look for the chapters in Part II, III, or IV that best address your questions or concerns. If you're an investor, you may want to head straight to Part V to get the scoop on issues related to making investment decisions.

No matter where you start, we hope you catch just a bit of the excitement we feel about this new industry! And we encourage you to stay up to date with the regulatory changes that come from the SEC by visiting www.sec.gov.

Part I

Tapping the Potential of Crowdfund Investing

The 5th Wave   By Rich Tennant

"I'm guessing, but I suspect our funding came through."

In this part . . .

Here you find out the basics about this fresh opportunity called *crowdfund investing*. Chapter 1 provides a quick overview of how this form of private equity or debt investment works and how businesses and investors stand to benefit from it. In Chapter 2, you find out how the concept of crowdfund investing evolved and why it gained such rapid and fervent support in Washington, D.C.

If you're an entrepreneur or small business owner, don't miss Chapter 3, which offers a great overview of how crowdfund investing campaigns function, including which types of businesses are the best candidates and what risks are involved with this funding source. It ends with some wise words from the lawyers. If you're coming to this topic as a potential investor, turn to Chapter 4, which outlines why and how you may become part of a company's investment crowd.

Chapter 1

The Crowd's in Your Corner: Funding or Investing in a Business

....

....

*T*here are very few instances in history when we've had a start date for an entire industry that will disrupt the way the world looks at business. This is one of them. For the first time in 80 years, the average Jane and Joe have the ability to start a business with the help of the crowd or own a part of a friend's American dream.

Communities will come together to look at business ideas, fund those they believe in, rally around entrepreneurs with knowledge and experience, and help create millions of jobs. Welcome to the emergence of Web 3.0, where the social network meets seed/early-stage financing — and where you become an active participant instead of a passive investor. It merges the principles of crowdfunding, where a large group of people pool small dollar amounts to help someone bring an idea to fruition, with early-stage financing and growth capital for startups and small businesses. What is it? Crowdfund investing. In this chapter, we offer an introduction to why this new industry exists and what it's capable of accomplishing.

Sharing Our Hopes and Themes

Unreasonable, disruption, and *hope:* These words summarize the themes of this book. Although this book is meant to provide a road map to crowdfund investing from either an entrepreneur's or an investor's point of view, we hope it also serves as a motivational tool to show you how laws that have been in existence for 80+ years don't have to govern our future if they no longer serve society due to sociological and technological change.

It's **unreasonable** to believe that three entrepreneurs, who are not lobbyists or lawyers with blank checks, could show up in Washington, D.C., and change a law in 460 days. But that's what we did. We showed up when our country was suffering from the worst recession since the Great Depression. When millions of jobs were lost and hundreds of thousands of businesses were closing. When the financial markets had seized up and capital had stopped flowing to the people responsible for getting us out of prior recessions — small businesses.

We brought a solution to get money flowing to startups and small businesses so that they can grow and hire employees. In doing so, we **disrupted** the way in which the financial markets will forever operate. For over 80 years, we've lived under laws written in the 1930s that governed how businesses could raise capital. Although those laws were prudent for the times when they were written, they proved to be crippling in the aftermath of the collapse of the world financial markets in 2008.

In this book, you see how crowdfund investing takes us back to our roots, where communities come together to fund and support local businesses. It leverages the power of community to decide which businesses are worthy of funding and which entrepreneurs should be trusted. It provides the mechanism for the funding to happen and a framework to carry the business forward.

We're **hopeful** because anytime you disrupt a large institution or system, you create fear and uncertainty — but you also create opportunity. That's why we've worked so hard to put together this book: to provide guidance and clarity around this new way to raise capital so that you can take advantage of this opportunity whether you're a businessperson looking for capital or an investor seeking good investments. We hope that the information we share will provide the knowledge you need to become an entrepreneur or to support one that you know, love, and trust! Crowdfund investing isn't something new; it's an old way of financing companies that's facilitated by the power of technology. We have the power; now is the time to use it!

Packing a Punch: The Power of the Online Crowd

When governments in the Middle East start to topple because of a tweet, you begin to understand the power of social media. Never before have we had a tool so powerful that a small group with no resources can rally thousands of people together via Twitter to promote an idea (Occupy Wall Street) or protest a government (Egypt). Never before have we had a tool to provide fact checking in real time, and never before have we been so connected because of technology. Social media creates transparency and accountability. Businesses of the future will use this transparency and accountability to build trust and loyalty. Why? Because social media is the conduit to allow us to do what we love to do as humans: engage.

But although the world is operating more and more as one global community, we still rely on our local communities for our bare necessities. That's what this book is about. Our goal is to show you how to rally your online crowd to conquer your own part of the world. It's about connecting people at a local level to create businesses that will benefit communities. And instead of doing it at city hall, you'll be doing it online where most of us spend our days.

In this section, we briefly tour the rapid evolution of online crowd activity, from crowdsourcing to crowdfunding to crowdfund investing.

Sparking the revolution with crowdsourcing

Part of this revolution we can credit to *crowdsourcing:* the online gathering of a group of people to share knowledge and wisdom to build a better product. Crowdsourcing first gained prominence in the world of programming in what was called *open source.* Open-sourced programming was a way for companies to leverage the collective coding power of essentially freelance programmers so that they could deliver a great product (code). By opening it up to other programmers, people were allowed to clean up, fix, and/or improve the code. The theory was that opening up the proprietary code to the crowd wouldn't make competitors but compatriots. The crowd would work together to make it better.

Most recently, we've seen this concept expand into online collaboration through mediums like Wikipedia, an online encyclopedia of sorts, where the crowd's wisdom fills the pages. Anyone is free to edit it, and together the information is more powerful than any one person could create.

Shifting toward finances: Crowdfunding

It was only a matter of time before this community involvement moved into the financial arena. And in reality, it already had. Going to the crowd for funding is nothing new; keep reading for examples of how we've been doing this for decades, and turn to Chapter 2 for more details about the emergence of crowdfunding.

Donation-based efforts

The American Cancer Society (ACS) has been crowdfunding for decades. It hosts events like Making Strides Against Breast Cancer, in which teams form to raise money to fight cancer. Large groups of people pool donations together for a good cause — in the case of ACS, to the tune of half a billion dollars since 1994! However, any charitable giving, whether to a church, National Public Radio, or AIDS walks, is really crowdfunding.

And the crowdfunding concept doesn't apply just to charity. Politicians crowdfund their re-election campaigns all the time. The theory is, if they can actively engage voters with campaign contributions, those voters will have a vested interest in the success of the candidate. Unfortunately, this can also be seen as one of the biggest problems with politics. Politicians are constantly out there looking for capital to fund their campaigns . . . so much that they aren't always focused on policy. (Mind you, we didn't have that experience in Washington, D.C. Both sides of the aisle took plenty of time to sit down with us, understand our crowdfund investing framework, and help us pass the law. But that's a story for Chapter 2!)

One of the reasons for President Obama's 2008 success was his ability to harness the power of crowd donations. His campaign was able to raise over $50 million from over a million passionate followers. These people spoke not only with their voices but also with their wallets. Instead of relying on individual large contributors, the Obama campaign went to hundreds of thousands of Americans and asked them for small contributions. It was the difference between winning and losing for Obama. It also shows you the power of pooling small dollar contributions together.

Most recently, we've seen people use crowdfunding to raise money for art-related projects. Probably the most well-known platform for doing so is Kickstarter (www.kickstarter.com). Started by a guy who wanted to raise money to put on a concert, Kickstarter has become a crowdfunding phenomenon where people from all over the world are helping to fund mainly art-related projects — to the tune of $250 million in 2012!

Microfinance projects

Back in 1983, a man by the name of Muhammad Yunus started the Grameen Bank. The goal was to leverage the undeveloped skills of the poor by providing the money to entrepreneurs to create businesses. The unique feature was that there was no collateral. The bank would provide micro-loans to borrowers (98 percent of them being women). Peer pressure would ensure that borrowers followed through with repayments. It was so successful that Yunus went on to win a Nobel Peace Prize. (See Chapter 2 for a bit more detail about his story.)

Although Yunus's efforts were funded by microfinance organizations and community development banks, individuals like Matt Flannery and Jessica Jackley saw the ability to expand the opportunity by allowing the crowd to step in and pool their resources in the same way to help entrepreneurs in the developing world. Their story led to Kiva (www.kiva.org). Kiva allows people in developing countries to lend money via the Internet to people in developing countries. Kiva doesn't pay out any interest on the loans it facilitates. People do it to help others around the world, to be a part of something other than themselves, and to build a stronger global community. (Kiva gets a bit more discussion in Chapter 2 as well.)

Embracing the equity world: Crowdfund investing

Which brings us to today. Over time, we've become comfortable giving to causes we believe in or entrepreneurs in the developing world who need financial assistance to create their own jobs. Now we're bringing these concepts to our shores. Instead of just giving your money away because it feels good or is the right thing to do, now you can do so and own shares of stock in that business! For decades we've been used to investing in Fortune 500 stocks listed on public exchanges. Now you'll be able to invest in businesses in your own backyard. Although some of these businesses may have the potential to be high-growth businesses, not all of them will have the ability to make you rich. They will, however, provide tangible benefits that money invested in a Fortune 500 company can't provide — benefits like convenience, service, and a sense of community.

Why People Care: Appreciating the Appeal of Being Part of the Crowd

The heart is a powerful thing. Emotional impulses drive people to make decisions. Coupling those impulses with logic can be powerful, and that combination is the main force behind what will drive crowds to become part of crowdfund investment opportunities. People aren't just wallets — they're users of products and services — and no one knows better what solutions they need than those who live in communities under the same circumstances.

Thanks to the advances in technology, we can solve problems faster and cheaper than at any other point in history. No longer does it take a Fortune 500 company to deliver a local solution that can be tailored to the needs of a community; an entrepreneur with initiative can do the job.

If you can appreciate these facts, then you understand the desire of the crowd to step in where they see a solution to a local problem and to fund it. Thanks to technology, we now have a medium to allow crowd solutions to take place. And thanks to the advances in the law, people now have the choice to be active participants in the growth of a business, to reap rewards for doing so, or to see their returns tied in with those of entrepreneurs over the long term. In this section, we touch on some of the key reasons that crowds will quickly get onboard with quality crowdfund investing campaigns.

Using the technology at your fingertips

Thirty years ago, it would have been very difficult for crowdfund investing to occur on a massive scale. Today, however, the technology you need to raise capital for your business is at your fingertips. All you need is a computer, a video camera (or a built-in camera on your computer), vibrant social networks, and the passion to create or expand your business. This book details how you can use technology to make a successful crowdfund investing pitch and raise the money you need to launch or grow the business of your dreams.

As an investor, you'll be able to find businesses that people in your social networks are launching, and you'll be able to support them with your dollars and your expertise. We all like being part of something that's bigger than ourselves, and crowdfund investing allows us to do exactly that. From the comfort of your own living room, you can help your nephew or former roommate or co-worker get a new company off the ground.

Reaping rewards through perks

Through websites such as Kickstarter, crowdfunding has allowed people to pursue their passions through direct support from their online networks and beyond. People have gained support in the form of dollars and through expertise from the crowd. Many people have launched crowdfunding projects and been blown away by the support that they found. (See Chapter 21 for a description of ten such projects.) Oftentimes, people think that they're alone in their passions, but after they create an online campaign requesting financial support, they're happily surprised. This type of support goes a long way toward energizing people into building something great.

Before we led the fight to legalize equity- or debt-based crowdfund investing, all crowdfunding was perks- or rewards-based. That meant that, as an investor, you would get small perks in exchange for your dollars. Sometimes the perk took the form of presales of a product. For example, the entrepreneur developed a prototype, but in order to build the product on a larger scale, she needed more capital to make it a reality. This direct support of the entrepreneur's passion has allowed many projects to come to fruition that otherwise would not have happened.

Consider another example: If an artist wanted to raise money to make a new music album, he might give people a sticker for a $5 contribution, give them a digital copy of the completed album for $10, give them a hard copy for $30, list the supporter's name on the album as a co-producer for $100, and for $1,000 offer backstage passes to the band's concert. Bands have even offered to do private shows for their supporters above a certain level of contribution.

The way that the security laws were written before the passage of the JOBS Act in 2012, people who raised the money could not legally give back any financial return, including even giving back the original investment. What they could give, however, were perks.

Perks-based crowdfunding has been a huge game changer for a lot of manufacturing companies that wouldn't have been able to secure the capital to build their products without it. It has been a win-win for everyone involved: "Investors" have received products that they really wanted, and companies have received the capital they need to make these products.

In the case of artists, fans have been able to reap the rewards by helping their favorite bands or documentarians find the needed capital to create their projects. Fan "investors" receive the product they've helped create and also get the satisfaction of being part of something bigger than themselves. Individually, a $25 investment wouldn't get the receiver very far. When pooled together with the rest of the crowd, however, each $25 investment goes a long way.

The new frontier: Entering the equity realm

When President Obama signed our crowdfund investing bill into law on April 5, 2012, as part of the JOBS Act, he said that it was game changing for the American economy. With the financial collapse of 2008, the flow of capital dried up for entrepreneurs and small businesses that needed the cash to start and grow their companies. We saw this problem and took it upon ourselves to find a solution. Capital still existed after the collapse, but it wasn't moving from the people who had it to the people who could use it to start businesses and create jobs.

That has changed. All the great benefits of crowdfunding still exist, but the perks that investors stand to receive now also include financial gain. People may put money into crowdfund investment campaigns for many reasons: to help out a friend or family member, to support a business that provides a service they desire, to be part of something bigger than themselves, or to reap success through a financial return.

As we mention repeatedly in this book (including in Chapter 4), investing in a startup company is very risky. Your risky investments should occupy only a small portion of your overall portfolio, and your crowdfunded investments should be considered some of your riskiest investments. The chances of your investing in the next Facebook are very slim, but at least you now have the opportunity to make investments that were previously reserved for only the wealthiest Americans. (See Chapter 2 for an explanation of accredited and unaccredited investors.) With that opportunity comes a great deal of responsibility to be a well-informed investor.

With the legalization of equity- and debt-based crowdfund investing, we've broken down the barriers for the small investor to be able to invest in startup companies. When federal securities laws were written more than 80 years ago, information was slow moving, often through word of mouth. Less than 5 percent of the population invested their money in stocks and bonds. Today, more than 50 percent of the population have these types of investments, and with the Internet, any information we desire is only a Google search away. The securities regulations have finally started catching up with the changing times.

Spotting the Business Beneficiaries of Crowdfund Investing

There are many business beneficiaries of crowdfund investing. The obvious beneficiaries are the businesses receiving the capital, but equity- and debt-based crowdfund investing has created a brand-new industry, and many people will make a lot of money from it. (For example, check out Chapter 7, where we introduce the types of online funding portals that will host crowdfund investing campaigns.)

In Chapter 3, we identify and describe the types of businesses most likely to benefit from crowdfund investing: startups, small businesses (including technology companies, bricks-and-mortar retail shops, and service companies), and anyone else who doesn't easily qualify for traditional financing. The term used in the JOBS Act for such entities is *emerging growth companies*.

Launching and growing a successful business isn't easy — and it never has been. Entrepreneurs and small business owners need the support of as many people as possible to be successful. Large, publicly traded companies have long had the support of many successful people; they have vast resources to pay experienced people to help guide them through the many complications of running a business. Now, crowdfund investors can support growing companies and entrepreneurs in ways that before were not possible, with both financial support and expertise.

How does crowd expertise benefit a business? As we explain throughout the book (including in Chapter 17), crowdfund investing should be an active investment. If you buy stock in Apple or General Motors, all you give is your money. But when you engage in a crowdfund investing campaign, you can also support a company with your knowledge and skills.

For a business, the collective knowledge of the crowd is much greater than the knowledge of any group of experts. If you're heading a startup company and you raise money from a venture capital group, you also get their knowledge support (from a small group of people). In a crowdfunded company, your pool of investors may number 200, 300, or even higher. The collective knowledge of the crowd will be game changing for many small businesses. Of course, dealing with so much input may be overwhelming if you don't handle it in an organized fashion. Check out Chapter 12 for tips on communicating with your investors, including setting parameters for receiving and responding to your crowd's advice.

Keep in mind that the biggest beneficiaries of crowdfund investing are the American people. With more businesses being launched, more jobs will be created. The more jobs that are created, the more capital will flow through the U.S. economy.

Figuring Out How Businesses and Investors Find Each Other

With the advent of crowdfund investing, we have the classic two-sided market problem: How do you match demand and supply? How do you help businesses that need funding find willing investors who are looking to make investments in Main Street businesses or startups?

Prior to the passage of the JOBS Act in 2012, making such connections was difficult or even impossible. The laws governing how private businesses could seek capital from individual investors were written in 1933 and 1934 and were set up to protect people from scams and rip-off schemes. These laws created the Securities and Exchange Commission (SEC) and determined how stocks and securities were sold in the United States. Read Chapter 2 to find out more about what these laws said and how they restricted investment in private companies.

The JOBS Act permits private companies to *generally solicit* for equity and debt offerings, meaning they can publically advertise and discuss such offerings (subject to certain restrictions). Also, it makes crowdfund investing possible by enabling business owners to communicate with anyone via their social networks (such as LinkedIn, Facebook, and Twitter) to find potential investors for their business or startup ideas.

However, you must be aware that general solicitation and communication regarding equity and debt offerings can take place *only* in very specific ways that are regulated by the SEC. Therefore, businesses must make sure they're clear on how to do this and what they need to do to protect themselves, their investors, and their customers from fraud, as well as to stay compliant with SEC regulations.

This book provides you with the information and resources you need so that you can organize and execute an effective campaign. We can't guarantee success, but we can give you best practices and insights to use as you work to create a successful business.

In this section, we briefly discuss two key ways that companies position themselves to find crowdfund investors: by crafting excellent business plans and by posting their offerings on SEC-registered online funding portals. We also briefly explain how potential investors should start the process of evaluating crowdfund investing campaigns.

Creating a business plan that involves crowdfund investing

One of the most important steps you can take before launching a crowdfund investing campaign is creating your business plan (a topic we detail in Chapter 5). You may have the world's greatest business idea, but investors and lenders need to understand what you're going to do with their money and how it will deliver a return on their investment; otherwise, you'll never get off the ground. A business plan forces you to get specific about your ideas, test your assumptions, and answer questions that potential investors will likely have. For investors, your business plan provides a standards-based way to evaluate your business versus others.

As you construct a business plan that includes crowdfund investment money, you need to take into account the time and process for raising money and, even more important, how you'll communicate with your investors over time. Do you have a strong online social network today? Do you have hundreds of connections on LinkedIn and Facebook and hundreds or thousands of followers on Twitter? If not, you need to build your online presence *before* you start trying to raise money online via crowdfund investing. The vast majority of investors in your business will be people who you know already; they'll find out about your offering via social networks. If you need help building your social networks, turn to Chapter 8.

Posting your campaign on an SEC-approved platform

The SEC, the Financial Industry Regulatory Authority (FINRA), the Crowdfunding Professional Association, and the Crowdfund Intermediary Regulatory Advocates are the key entities focused on creating rules that enable an orderly market to form for crowdfund investing. You'll see these names throughout this book, and you should get familiar with each entity's industry involvement.

As we explain in detail in Chapter 7, you should use only an SEC-approved crowdfund investing funding portal (website) to list your equity or debt offering. (As a potential investor, you should shop for campaigns only via SEC-approved funding portals as well.) You must follow all SEC regulations and ensure that the funding platform you use is also registered with FINRA. Doing so protects your company, your investors, and the industry as a whole.

Identifying investments of interest

We've briefly talked about what companies need to do to attract crowdfund investors. In this section, we switch our focus to potential investors. We devote Part V of this book to the investor's perspective. Here are some key concepts that all potential investors must keep in mind when considering participating in this asset class:

- ✔ **Private businesses and startups are high-risk investments. We repeat:** *These are high-risk investments.* Could you see significant returns? Maybe. But you absolutely *must* proceed with caution.

✔ **You should create a portfolio of investments that has a mix of risk/ return profiles based on your individual situation.** We believe that investments classified as high risk should make up less than 10 percent of your investable capital. You should consult with a qualified professional regarding your individual circumstances and planning.

✔ **Based on your income, you're limited to how much you can invest each year in crowdfund investments.** This limit, which we detail in Chapter 4, helps ensure that no one can lose his entire savings on one bad investment.

✔ **You should plan to make small investments in at least ten crowdfund investing campaigns.** Most professional investors (angel investors and venture capitalists) expect that out of ten investments in private companies and startups, seven will lose money, two will break even or have a small return, and one will have a significant return. Are these numbers guaranteed? Absolutely not! You must do research on each potential investment, talk with people you trust, consider carefully, and then make small investments in people you know, products you use, businesses you trust, or entrepreneurs you believe in.

✔ **Crowdfund investing is an active form of investing.** As an investor, you get to know these businesses much more personally than you know any public company you invest in. As we explain in Chapter 17, you can help the businesses with your expertise, but you must make sure you don't become a nuisance to the business owner.

Predicting the Future of Crowdfund Investing and Crowdfunded Businesses

Crowdfund investing is an entirely new industry and an entirely new asset class for investors to evaluate. We believe that it represents the beginning of Web 3.0, where the social web (or Web 2.0) combines with businesses raising capital. It creates a new way for businesses to get seed funding or growth capital, and it will generate an entirely new ecosystem of businesses, business models, processes, and strategies that can be used in starting or growing a business. Just like the ecosystem that was formed around the social web, we see the formation of an ecosystem of businesses to support and enhance this new, highly innovative industry.

Anticipating new forms of capital creation and financial instruments

Creativity and opportunity generate the possibility for new strategies, tactics, and services to begin. It'll be fascinating to watch as this new way to raise capital creates new business models and ways of thinking.

As society continues its move toward deeper customization of experience, more digital connections will occur, making in-person connections less regular. People will create more experiences, value, and relationships online. We can't wait to see how these sociological changes affect how businesses grow and succeed.

As nations, investors, and business owners become accustomed to these types of relationships and transactions, we believe that more governments will allow cross-border capital flows via crowdfund investing. The regulatory frameworks will need to be revised to allow this, but we believe that, over time, governments will see the benefits and will be able to put reasonable safeguards in place to protect business owners, investors, and communities.

Redefining community

When people discuss crowdfund investing in terms of "community-based financing," you must understand that "community" is not just related to the geography of where you live and work. The web has made it far easier than ever before to create communities online. These communities could be communities of origin, communities of interest, or communities of diaspora. The web can now connect these communities in ways that enable them to support businesses and ideas in convenient and engaged ways. This should be a great benefit for all types of communities. These communities also can assist in crowd vigilance to provide additional security and protection to reduce and eliminate fraud wherever possible.

Building communities and businesses based on the power of crowds

We're at the very beginning of a new chapter in the history of corporate America. Many individuals feel disconnected and disappointed in large corporations. They want to find ways to shop and invest locally, ways to support their own communities and interests. We've already seen a few companies that were unable to get the attention of traditional venture capital and angel investors but have been able to find crowds to invest in them. In some cases, these same companies have gone on to receive investment from angel or venture capital investors because the company had already received the support of the crowd and proved there were customers for their services.

We hope this book helps both businesses and investors understand the risks and rewards of crowdfund investing, plan carefully, execute well, learn lessons, and reap the rewards of their efforts. We understand that crowdfund investing is no cure-all or perfect solution to all funding problems, but we do think that it offers an alternative that will be beneficial to thousands of businesses and investors around the world.

Chapter 2

Tracing the Origins of Crowdfund Investing

• •

In This Chapter

▶ Studying U.S. history for signs of crowd-based investments

▶ Nudging small businesses out of the capital markets

▶ Preparing for a regulatory overhaul

▶ Turning the crowdfund investing concept into legislation

▶ Grasping what the JOBS Act accomplished

• •

*T*he concept of crowdfund investing isn't new. Its origins actually trace back to 3000 B.C.; it was one of the earliest forms of financing. Back then, banks and financial institutions didn't exist, but people with money and people who needed funds did. Deals were made among people who knew each other, and accountability was reinforced through interaction and oversight. The rates of return (interest rates) were determined by how well the individuals knew each other and how much money someone needed. The weaker the connection and/or the more money needed, the riskier the investment was and the higher the return had to be.

In this chapter, we go back to our collective financial roots to understand what happened to this form of financing and why it's now "new all over again" and has become one of the hottest topics in early-stage business financing. We look at the risks that led to changes in U.S. financial laws in the early 20th century and how these laws had the unintended consequence of shutting off capital markets to many startups and small businesses. And we discuss how today, with the Internet and technology advances, we can safely go back to where we started.

Then we walk you through the industry framework we took to Washington and give you a taste of our personal fight to legalize crowdfund investing. This framework enables everyone to use the Internet to gauge the value of people's ideas and use online reputations and their own judgment and experience to make their own decisions about which ideas have the best chance for success.

Looking Way Back: Evidence of the Crowd Concept in Early U.S. History

If you have a tough time imagining life in 3000 B.C., perhaps you have an easier time envisioning life in the United States in the late 19th and early 20th centuries. In this section, we offer some examples of very American institutions and icons that emerged from the crowd.

Building-and-loan associations

Before the Great Depression in the 1930s, banks existed primarily to finance infrastructure and the activities of governments. Farmers also used banks because the Industrial Revolution led to a change in farming techniques that required farmers to take out loans for new equipment. Other individuals and businesses had limited access to bank capital.

To address the lack of capital access, groups of people would deposit their savings into an association — a *building and loan.* When the association gained enough money, it financed activities for its members, mainly through mortgages. This system helped many working-class people to buy homes.

Unlike banks, these associations made their investments based primarily on the interests of their members instead of on the promise of the greatest returns and security. Associations tended to serve small groups or communities and didn't offer many of the services that banks did.

Financing the Statue of Liberty

Most people know that Lady Liberty was a gift from France to the United States to recognize the nation's centennial in 1876. But did you know that this gift wasn't funded by either government, but instead, by the generosity of the crowd? The citizens of France paid for the statue, and the citizens of the United States paid for the pedestal.

How did they do this? Citizens in both countries held meetings, theater performances, art auctions, prizefights, and rallies to raise money. And in some cases, donors were offered perks (just as happens today with rewards-based crowdfunding, as we discuss in the upcoming section "Watching the rise of donation- and rewards-based crowdfunding"). Frédéric Auguste Bartholdi, the Statue of Liberty's architect, offered a miniature version of the statue with the name of the buyer engraved on it in exchange for a donation.

Despite the fundraising efforts, the United States found itself short of the $250,000 needed to create the pedestal. And getting the word out to potential donors back then was a bit difficult. (No text messages or Facebook pages were around to help.) Enter newspaper publisher Joseph Pulitzer. In the early 1880s, he purchased *The World,* a New York City daily newspaper, and he took up the cause of the statue's pedestal. With access to thousands of readers, he used his newspaper to mount an energetic fund drive, promising to print the name of each donor, no matter how small the donation.

Pulitzer's audacious plan worked, and millions of people around the country began donating whatever they could. Even schoolchildren across America donated pennies. A kindergarten class in Iowa sent $1.35 to Pulitzer's fund drive.

Why did they do this? Because these people believed in the project and wanted to give back; they wanted to be a part of history and be a part of something bigger than themselves. These are the same reasons that people enter crowdfund investments today.

Bamboozling the crowd: Snake oil salesmen and other frauds

Investors have been putting money into startups and small businesses since the Industrial Revolution. In the early days, most such investors came from wealthy families (the Morgans, the Vanderbilts, the Rockefellers . . .), but smaller investors got involved, too. Starting in 1911, the process of raising capital from the public was enforced by each state under so-called *blue sky laws.* With these laws, states regulated the offering and sale of stocks to protect the public from fraud. The specific provisions of these laws varied among states, but they all required the registration of all securities offerings and sales, as well as the registration of every stockbroker and brokerage firm.

Unfortunately, the blue sky laws were often ineffective. In 1915, the Investment Bankers Association told its members that they could ignore blue sky laws by making securities offerings across state lines through the mail. Enter the snake oil salesmen. Because the markets weren't regulated at the federal level, shady stockbrokers started to issue stocks in dubious, fictitious, or worthless companies and selling them to people in other states, using the mail as their means of communication.

If you're a movie buff, you may be familiar with the snake oil salesman — a character that appears in many Western films. He's a "doctor" with dubious credentials who travels by covered wagon from town to town. The fast-talking salesman (full of hype and bogus evidence) sells "medicine," such as snake oil, that supposedly cures all sorts of aches and pains. To enhance sales, he always has an accomplice (a shill) who attests to the crowd the marvelous beneficial effects of the snake oil. The salesman tries to leave town before the swindle is discovered. This practice became known as *grifting* and its practitioners, *grifters*. This practice of selling items with little or no real value to unsuspecting buyers then found its way into the stock markets.

Leading up to the Great Depression, which began in 1929, the marketplace was full of exuberance. Stock prices kept going up, reinforced by shady brokers. Tempted by promises of riches and easy credit, many investors started to borrow money to buy essentially worthless stocks. Greed drove them to neglect the risks and believe unreliable information about the securities in which they invested.

During the 1920s, approximately 20 million large and small shareholders set out to make their fortunes in the stock market. Of the $50 billion in new securities offered during this period, approximately half became worthless as a result of the stock market crash in October 1929.

Realizing the Federal Government's Role in Limiting Business Funding

When the stock market crashed in October 1929, public confidence in the markets collapsed. Investors large and small, as well as the banks that had loaned to them, lost great sums of money in the ensuing Great Depression. For the economy to recover, the public's faith in the capital markets needed to be restored, so Congress held hearings to identify the problems and search for solutions. This section offers a quick overview of what happened next.

Creating the SEC and the first securities laws

During the peak year of the Depression, Congress passed the Securities Act of 1933. This law and the Securities Exchange Act of 1934 (which created the Securities and Exchange Commission [SEC]) were designed to increase public trust in the capital markets by requiring uniform disclosure of information about public securities and establishing rules for honest dealings. The main purposes of these laws can be reduced to two common-sense notions:

✔ Companies publicly offering securities for investment dollars must tell the public the truth about their businesses, the securities they're selling, and the risks involved in investing.

✔ People who sell and trade securities — brokers, dealers, and exchanges — must treat investors fairly and honestly, putting investors' interests first.

Monitoring the securities industry requires a highly coordinated effort, so Congress established the SEC to enforce the newly passed securities laws to promote stability in the markets and, most important, to protect investors. The Securities Exchange Act of 1934 requires that issuing companies register distributions of securities (stocks) with the SEC prior to interstate sales of these securities. This way, investors have access to basic financial information about issuing companies and risks involved in investing in the securities in question.

The SEC was founded in an era that was ripe for reform. The 1933 and 1934 laws set the way the capital markets would function for about the next 50 years.

Regulation D: Defining accredited investors

From 1933 to 1982, the way business was conducted in the U.S. capital markets stayed relatively unchanged. In 1982, the SEC adopted Regulation D, which established three exemptions from the registration requirements under the Securities Act of 1933. The term *exemptions* is used because the updates enabled some companies, in certain situations, to issue securities without the requirement to register them with the SEC.

Included within Regulation D's definitions was the term *accredited investor*. The SEC adopted two definitions of the term, one based on net worth and the other based on income:

✔ **Net worth criteria:** Under the net worth test, an accredited investor is someone who, at the time when she purchases a security, has a net worth of $1 million or more, not including the value of her primary residence. (Note that net worth could be the individual's net worth alone or that of herself and her spouse.)

✔ **Income criteria:** Under the income-based definition, an accredited investor is someone with individual income above $200,000 during the two most recent years or with joint income (with a spouse) above $300,000 in each of the two most recent years. (This person also should expect to achieve a similar income in the current year.)

Why do these criteria matter to you? Because prior to the 2012 JOBS Act, a company issuing stock to investors had to restrict the number of *unaccredited* investors it sold to. If you were starting a small business raising less than $5 million in securities in 2010 and wanted equity investors, you could have only 35 unaccredited investors. (You could have an unlimited number of accredited investors.) This structure allowed for your closest supporters (your mom and a handful of other cheerleaders) to become equity owners in your business while preventing you from roping hundreds or thousands of other people into investing in a company that might carry loads of risk.

In the pre-Internet world, sounds reasonable, right? Unfortunately, the side effect of this regulation was that small investors found themselves largely shut out of some of the most lucrative investments (such as technology startups), and small businesses and startups found themselves relatively restricted when trying to raise funds. Plus, the underlying implication of the definition is that small investors are, by virtue of their smallness, less educated, sophisticated, or knowledgeable about risk than larger investors. (We happen to strongly disagree. Just look at how much money accredited investors lost with Bernie Madoff.)

Noting the effects of Sarbanes-Oxley on small businesses

The 1990s and early 2000s saw the rise of a whole new level of *financial engineering:* the creation of financial structures and instruments that allowed corporations greater flexibility (and much greater risk) in their investments. Most of the time, the "flexibility" really was code for *leverage* (the practice of betting on the direction of a stock's, or other financial instrument's, movement). The larger the bet on the direction, the larger the risk (and losses) if the stock moved in the opposite direction. When corporate bets worked as planned, companies showed significant gains. What happened when these bets soured? Let us remind you of two extreme examples of the results.

Enron was an energy, commodities, and services company based in Houston, Texas. Between 1995 and 2000, it was called one of America's most innovative companies. Enron filed for bankruptcy in December 2001, and several of its top corporate officers were later convicted of financial crimes. (A great documentary on this fiasco, called *Enron: The Smartest Guys in the Room,* gives you a front-row seat to what happened.) These executives were hiding huge losses in offshore accounts that were not reported in Enron's financial statements, and their "engineering" finally collapsed. Thousands of employees lost their jobs, and millions of Enron shareholders lost billions of dollars. At the time, it was the largest corporate failure in U.S. history, and it was all due to a handful of executives playing fast and loose with company money to enrich themselves.

In July 2002, just seven months after Enron's demise, WorldCom also declared bankruptcy after using fraudulent accounting and finance practices to hide losses and inflate revenues. Again, the company's collapse led to thousands of job losses and billions of dollars of stockholder losses.

With back-to-back, multi-billion-dollar business failures that were based on accounting and finance fraud, the federal government was pressed to enact significantly enhanced financial regulations. As a result, the Sarbanes-Oxley Act of 2002 (commonly referred to as SOX) was the largest overhaul of federal securities laws since the 1930s. It covered a wide range of corporate governance, accounting, industry analyst relations, and financial reporting issues.

Although well intentioned, SOX had enormous unintended consequences for all businesses and the public capital markets. These negative consequences were most profound for small businesses that were interested in going public to raise capital. Because SOX treated all companies (regardless of size, industry, geography, or market) exactly the same, all companies faced a similar burden related to regulatory costs. This setup may seem reasonable at first blush, but imagine a mom-and-pop store trying to achieve the same reporting and accounting standards followed by a Fortune 500 company; it can't be done.

Effectively, SOX ensured that if your business is worth less than $100 million, it makes zero financial sense to go public. That's because, in order to execute an initial public offering (IPO), you'd spend millions of dollars, and then your annual compliance fees would be well over $1 million. That fact effectively closed the IPO market for all but the largest corporations and dramatically reduced small businesses' access to capital.

Continuing to tighten capital access with Dodd-Frank

The financial crisis of 2008 was rooted largely in real estate and sub-prime mortgages (and financial engineering and leverage). The financial regulation that responded to it was called the Dodd-Frank Act. Among its consequences, Dodd-Frank significantly limited homeowners' ability to use credit cards or lines of credit on their homes to finance new businesses. Granted, many people had been getting into trouble because they used such lines of credit like free ATMs, so regulation seemed necessary. But prior to Dodd-Frank, equity lines of credit and credit cards were very common (and in some cases viable) ways to access capital to start or grow a business.

Laying the Groundwork for the JOBS Act

Much of the groundwork for the JOBS Act, which (among other things) opened the door to crowdfund investment, was laid with the 2008 financial collapse. After past recessions, small businesses got the country back on track. But this time around, they couldn't do so because all the typical ways that small businesses gained access to capital had dried up. Banks weren't lending, credit card companies slashed credit limits and hiked interest rates, and private equity and venture capital firms (which we explain in Chapter 3) invest money in less than 2 percent of companies that approach them. Many people and organizations still had cash after the 2008 collapse, but that money wasn't flowing to the entrepreneurs who could use it to start businesses and to small businesses that could create jobs.

The three of us could see the problem clearly, and we offered a solution. We had zero political experience at the time, yet we were able to get a crowdfund investing bill passed in the U.S. Congress in 460 days — from the creation of our Startup Exemption Regulatory Framework to the day we attended the presidential signing ceremony in the Rose Garden of the White House. That's largely because, when jobs are scarce in the United States, everyone in Washington is talking about the problem. If you approach them from a nonpartisan perspective, with a tangible and actionable solution, they listen. In this case, people from both sides of the aisle jumped onboard and helped to push this legislation through.

In this section, we briefly explain why we were (and are) so bullish on crowdfund investing and why the time was exactly right for the U.S. financial regulatory system to allow it to happen.

The technology equation: Internet + social media = easy crowd access

The changes in how people communicate made the time ripe for crowdfund investing. In the past decade or so, people have largely moved their conversations and friendships online. We communicate with our friends and loved ones on the Internet and via social media, and doing so allows for easier access to crowds. Instead of having to make dozens of phone calls to tell your friends that you're starting a new venture, now you can spend ten seconds updating your Facebook profile and let all your contacts know at once.

Virtually every business today has to have an online presence. People spend an increasing amount of their time online, and that includes time they spend shopping, investing, and making other business-related decisions. Therefore, it just made sense to introduce the means for entrepreneurs and small businesses to raise funds online and for individual investors to locate such investment opportunities via their online social networks.

The other major change that has occurred courtesy of the Internet and social media is unparalleled transparency that has never before been available in the finance world. A company that dares to play games with its financial reporting is much more likely to have that fraud broadcasted far and wide by investors who share their horror stories online.

Watching small business funding dry up

After the financial collapse of 2008, small business funding dried up. If you were a small business owner or entrepreneur and you went into a bank for a loan, the bank would require three years of financial statements, as well as enough assets to back your loan. If you were trying to fund a startup, meeting these requirements was impossible. (As a brand-new business, where would the financial statements come from?) And even if you were a going concern, the asset requirement likely took you out of the running for the size of loan you really needed.

Credit card financing was no longer a readily accessible option either. Credit card interest rates were raised to extremes, and credit limits were slashed. (You can argue all day about whether this was a good or bad thing, given how addicted our nation was to easy credit, but it had a net negative effect on even successful small business owners.)

With traditional financing out of reach and access to private equity and venture capital extremely limited, something had to give for small businesses and startups.

Recognizing that investors want other options

Before the JOBS Act, the average small investor didn't fund small businesses and startups. Federal financial regulations made doing so tough, and unless your nephew or college roommate or another close contact was the one opening the business, chances are, you would have no way of hearing about this type of investment opportunity.

But after 2008, many people lost trust in the traditional financial systems. They stopped putting blind faith in big companies, big banks, and Wall Street. They still wanted to invest their money in businesses (it's what Americans do!), but they didn't want the people responsible for the global meltdown to take a cut of the pie.

With the advent of crowdfund investing, the average small investor today can sit in her living room anywhere in the world, study 20 different pitches from 20 different entrepreneurs or small business owners, decide which of them make sense for her, and fund them with the click of a mouse. And she can feel assured that, when doing so, her funds are directly supporting the individual making the pitch — not a multinational financial conglomerate that couldn't care less about the $100 or $500 or whatever amount she's investing.

Crowdfund investing is essentially creating a new set of investors: micro-angel investors. Before the JOBS Act, accepting $100 from a small investor was way too complicated to have been worth it. (The regulations just didn't allow for it.) Now, a business owner has a platform for raising funds in such increments, and every $100 or $500 or $1,000 investment can have a big impact on that business's success.

Following in the footsteps of microfinance

In many ways, Muhammad Yunus, the father of microfinance, laid the foundation for crowdfund investing. *Microfinance* focuses on small (micro) loans, typically in the $300 to $500 range, to entrepreneurs (mainly women) in the developing world. The core tenets of microfinance and crowdfund investing are similar: Both systems are about getting capital in the hands of people who have trouble raising it via traditional means, so those people can start and grow their businesses. Yunus made his first microfinance loan in 1976, and shortly afterward he started the Grameen Bank, the world's first microfinance organization. (He and the bank won the Nobel Peace Prize in 2006.) Microfinance has since grown to be a factor in almost every developing country in the world and has had an amazing impact on alleviating poverty.

Following the path blazed by Yunus, in 2005, Matt Flannery and Jessica Jackley launched Kiva (www.kiva.org), which allows someone with as little as $25 to make a loan to an entrepreneur in the developing world. Kiva connects with microfinance organizations in the developing world, which locate entrepreneurs and help write their stories and explain why they need the money. Then it allows donors to become part of a crowd that supports an entrepreneur's mission. Since Kiva began, it has funded over $300 million in loans with a 98 percent repayment rate — far better than credit card companies have in the developed world. (Because the organization is a 503(c), the SEC allows for the principal of the loan to be repaid.) The site is a platform where anyone with an Internet connection and a debit card can sign on and make a loan.

Watching the rise of donation- and rewards-based crowdfunding

Out of microfinance and Kiva sprouted donation-based crowdfunding websites. When they first began, these sites mainly supported art-related projects. If a band wanted to make a new album, for example, it created a profile on a crowdfunding website, posted some of its past music, and talked about its plans for the new album. Then it listed how much money it needed and how it planned to use the money. The band created a bundle of rewards that donors/investors would receive upon giving money. For instance, if someone gave $25, she'd get a CD of the new album; for $100, she'd get her name on the album cover; and for $500, she'd get backstage passes to the band's next concert.

The wild success of these websites (which are currently funding over $10 million a month) led to other campaigns that focused on crowdfunding via presales of products. One such success was an iPod Nano watch kit. Scott Wilson created a watch into which you could plug your iPod Nano. He didn't have the upfront capital to manufacture the watch, so he put his concept on Kickstarter (www.kickstarter.com). Wilson wanted to raise $15,000 to buy material. For $25, someone would receive one of the watch kits in the mail. He ended up getting 13,512 backers and raised a whopping $942,578.

Success stories like these demonstrated that the concept of crowdfund investing had traction. They proved that people will invest money online through crowdfund and crowdfund investing portals. From a business plan perspective (see Chapter 5), donation-based crowdfunding was akin to a proof of concept for crowdfund investing.

Striking a chord: Crowdfunding pioneers

It appears that the first time electronic crowdfunding was used to support an arts-related project was in 1997, when fans of the English rock band Marillion wanted a tour but the band had no money for it. Fans raised $60,000 — in secret — for the band to tour the United States. (Now those are some dedicated fans!) The band really appreciated that effort and continued to raise money for touring that way. Over time, other bands caught on.

In the early days, crowdfunding efforts were conducted largely by e-mail. Today, the web and social media make it even easier for a band to connect with potential micro-patrons of the arts. It has become standard practice for artists to use a rewards-based platform like Kickstarter (www.kickstarter.com) when they need to raise money for their band, film, book, or other project.

The Startup Exemption: Advocating for Change

The specific idea for crowdfund investing began as many good ideas begin: over drinks with friends. Near the end of 2010, the three of us were talking about the state of the economy (which was horrible) in the wake of the 2008 financial meltdown. Even though it had been two years since the market crashed, the official unemployment figures were still above 9 percent, with estimates of underemployment at similar rates. Most small business financing had evaporated. Other than a few tech startups in the San Francisco Bay Area, New York City, Boston, and Austin, it was nearly impossible for even profitable, successful community businesses to receive the capital they needed for working capital or expansion. And capital to start a new business? Forget about it.

Weekly, we would see announcements from the government and from banks that new programs were available to provide capital to small businesses. But people or businesses that were actually able to access these funds were very difficult to find.

With these problems weighing heavy on our minds, we sat around Jason's dining room table and considered our own options for raising money for several businesses, which were extremely limited despite having collectively raised $87 million through traditional financing for previous projects. At the same time that we were getting shot down by banks and private equity, we were giving away our own money to people on donation-based crowdfunding websites so they could launch art-related projects, and we were investing in entrepreneurs in third-world countries via Kiva.

A light bulb went off. We thought to ourselves, "If we can donate to artistic projects all over the United States and we can lend money to entrepreneurs in other countries, why can't we use the web and social media to raise money for U.S. small businesses we know and entrepreneurs we believe in and give people a slice of equity in return?" We couldn't possibly have scripted what happened next.

Hitting the regulatory barriers

The three of us believed we had a great idea for a business, which was a crowdfund investing website that would allow businesses and entrepreneurs to sell shares (or make revenue-based financing loans) via their social networks. However, when we went to talk with a securities attorney, he politely explained that what we planned to do was illegal based on the Securities Acts of 1933 and 1934. He said that we couldn't publicly solicit the sale of private shares to unaccredited investors. He continued by saying that to change this law would require an act of Congress, and that was unlikely to happen.

We pushed aside the idea for a few weeks but kept coming back to the fact that it was exactly the right thing to do. It didn't make sense that laws written 77 years ago (when the majority of Americans didn't have a telephone!) should govern the sale of securities in the age of the social web. We really believed then, and still believe today, that crowdfund investing is Web 3.0: the social web + capital formation.

The lawyers we spoke with told us to throw in the towel and try something else. However, being the optimistic entrepreneurs that we are (and possibly slightly stubborn and naïve), we set out to change the laws, to get capital flowing, and to get America growing.

Developing a new financial framework

In order to get something passed through Congress, we knew that we had to put investor protection at the forefront. In January 2011, the three of us reviewed the Securities Acts of 1933 and 1934, as well as Regulation D, which governs small, private sales of stock for small business (mainly to accredited investors). We thought about how to balance the capital formation needs of small businesses and entrepreneurs with our desire to protect investors from fraudsters. We created the Startup Exemption Regulatory Framework as a proposal to leverage the power of community financing with social media and small business.

After many drafts and countless edits, we built `www.startupexemption.com` and were ready to take our framework to Washington. We were told that we needed to find a champion in Washington to help us navigate the system, and Karen Kerrigan, president of the Small Business and Entrepreneurship Council, was that person. She fully supported our initiative and helped us to get our framework in front of the right people.

We began to talk about our framework to the media, to members of the U.S. House of Representatives, and to any other insiders who would listen. We were happily surprised at the reception.

The Startup Exemption Regulatory Framework

Here is the framework we developed, upon which Title III of the JOBS Act was largely based. Keep in mind that the legislation does not reflect every aspect of this framework.

✔ **Amount and class of shares:** A "funding window of up to $1 million" for entrepreneurs and small businesses. A *small business* is defined as one with average annual gross revenue of less than $5 million during each of the last three years or since incorporation if the business has existed for less than three years. This definition is consistent with definitions utilized by the Small Business Administration. Straight common shares along with their standard rights, as well as revenue-based financing (RBF), could be used. Common stock is on par with similarly used shares in early-stage rounds of friends-and-family financing, and RBF is a new form of financing where investors own a percent of future revenue for a certain period of time.

✔ **Limit:** Investment from unaccredited investors is capped at $10,000 or 10 percent of their prior year's adjusted gross income (AGI). The $10,000 limit is in line with other established financial disclosure limits like those on banking transfer reporting requirements. Accredited investors are not subject to any limits. (*Note:* The vast majority of individuals who choose to make crowdfund investments will most likely invest less than $500. The current average is approximately $80 on existing crowdfunding platforms.)

✔ **Risk disclosure:** Given that 60 percent of Americans now own stocks or mutual funds, there is a certain level of investor sophistication that is greater today than ever before. (In the 1930s, only 5 percent of the population invested their money.)

In addition, unlike investing in the public markets where individuals rely upon the experience/advice of advisors, people choosing to invest via crowdfunding will often be investing in their social networks with people they know and trust. Hence, accreditation should be attached to investors' understanding of the risks inherent in this type of investment. Prior to using these platforms, investors will have to agree, using current standard verification technology, that they understand there is no guarantee of return, that they could lose their entire investment, and that their liquidity/return is limited to any dividends, sale, public offering, or a merger of the company.

✔ **500-investor rule:** Eliminate the 500-investor limit for crowdfund investing via this window.

✔ **State law:** Exempt these offerings from state law registration requirements based on the limited size of the amount that can be raised, but leave intact a simplified and modified state law notice filing requirement, similar to the way SEC Rule 506 currently works, but less cumbersome.

✔ **General solicitation:** Allow for general solicitation on registered platforms where individuals, companies, and investors can meet virtually, ideas can be vetted by the community as a sort of peer review, and individuals can make informed decisions regarding whether to invest their money.

✔ **Filing and reporting:** Standardized forms (generic term sheets and subscription agreements) based on industry best practices are used to maintain transparency and reduce time and expense for all parties. They're electronically maintained using standardized procedures. Post-funding, standardized and automated reporting for use of proceeds are required on a quarterly basis by entrepreneurs. Platforms provide the SEC monthly offering reports that include information on: deals funded; entrepreneurs' names, Social Security numbers, addresses, and dates of birth; amounts of capital raised; lists of investors; and individual dollar amounts contributed.

✔ **Platform broker/dealer exemption:** Due to the small nature of the dollar amount and the high volume of automated activity, allow facilitation of funding for securities without need for a Financial Industry Regulatory Authority (FINRA) broker/dealer license by the facilitator, where deals facilitated fall within the constraints of this framework.

✔ **Availability:** This exemption is not available to foreign issuers, investment companies, and public companies.

Getting crowdfund investing into the JOBS Act

Our goal was to get someone in the U.S. House of Representatives to introduce a crowdfund investing bill. We had been told that, even if we did get a bill submitted, it could take five to ten years for it to move through the House and Senate to final passage and presidential signature. Even more disturbing were the facts: According to GovTrack.us, around 10,000 bills are introduced a year; on average, a mere 5 percent of them succeed. Our actual time between the creation of the Startup Exemption Regulatory Framework and the president's signing of the JOBS Act was 460 days. Although 460 days feels like a lifetime to an entrepreneur, it's lightning speed in Washington, D.C.

What happened during that time period? The White House took early notice and asked us to send our framework and a summary of our proposal for their review. We took part in three congressional hearings, and President Obama put part of our framework into his jobs speech in August 2011. The big breakthrough came when Congressman Patrick McHenry (R-NC), the chairman of a subcommittee of the Banking Committee, took our framework and wrote it into law. His bill (H.R. 2930) passed through the House in October 2011 with 96 percent approval. Immediately following, in a highly unusual act, the Democratic president issued a Statement of Administration Policy that fully endorsed H.R. 2930 (a Republican bill) and called on the Democrat-controlled Senate to pass it quickly so he could sign it into law.

Next, we turned our attention to the Senate, where we walked the halls and, in November 2011, held a rally on the grounds outside the Senate office buildings early one morning in the freezing rain and driving wind and gained the attention of a bipartisan group of three senators: Sen. Jeff Merkley (D-OR), Sen. Scott Brown (R-MA), and Sen. Michael Bennett (D-CO). We worked with their staffs to craft legislation on the Senate side, and we took language from the three separate bills that emerged and created a common-sense consensus proposal for crowdfund investing.

Around the same time, the JOBS Act (short for Jumpstart Our Business Startups) was created by combining several pieces of proposed legislation with the goal of providing additional ways for small and emerging businesses to access the capital markets so they could grow, create jobs, and spark innovation. The crowdfund-investing bill was rolled into that act, which was passed by overwhelming majorities of both houses of Congress. We were thrilled to be invited to attend the Rose Garden ceremony at the White House to watch President Obama sign the legislation into law on April 5, 2012.

That day, we also created a working group of individuals that had been involved in the legislation and wanted to ensure that the industry was able to form in an orderly fashion. That working group became the Crowdfunding Professional Association (for industry and investor advocacy) and the Crowdfunding Intermediary Regulatory Advocates (to establish strong working relationships with the SEC and FINRA).

Grasping the Regulatory Revolution

So, what exactly did this legislation change in the U.S. financial regulatory system? And how do these changes stand to benefit business owners and investors? In this section, we answer these questions in very broad strokes. Then we devote a good deal of real estate throughout this book to getting more specific about how the JOBS Act changed the investment landscape in the United States.

Promoting emerging growth companies

The JOBS Act created a new category of companies called *emerging growth companies* (EGCs) and gives small, growing companies a five-year window in which to become fully compliant with accounting regulations. To qualify as an EGC, the company must

- ✔ Have less than $1 billion in annual revenue
- ✔ Not have gone public more than five years ago
- ✔ Have issued no more than $1 billion in debt securities
- ✔ Have floated less than $700 million in stock securities

You may find it downright funny to see such high revenue, debt, and stock numbers used in combination with the words *small* and *emerging*. Nonetheless, this provision is important because it allows growing companies to have access to the public markets and not be crushed by the regulatory burdens.

Redefining who can invest in small ventures

Prior to the passage of the JOBS Act, accredited investors often were the only people who could invest in private debt or equity transactions. (See the earlier section "Regulation D: Defining accredited investors" to see how this term is defined in net worth or income.) One of the biggest changes the JOBS Act created was lifting the restriction on soliciting unaccredited investors to purchase stock. This means that companies that use crowdfund investing to raise capital are legally able to solicit people of all net worths and income levels to purchase their shares. You can't solicit anyone and everyone, though. You have to follow SEC regulations that require you to directly solicit only people who are members of your online social networks, and to do so by sending out notices that drive people to the online funding portal hosting your campaign to learn the details of the investment opportunity. We explain this regulation in detail in Chapter 3 and on this book's website, www.dummies.com/go/crowdfundinvesting.

Setting up the structure for online investment

Title III of the JOBS Act largely reflects the Startup Exemption Regulatory Framework that we took to Washington (which appears in a sidebar earlier in this chapter). The JOBS Act spells out, among other things:

- The maximum dollars a business or entrepreneur can seek via crowdfund investing, which is $1 million per year (see Chapter 3).

- The maximum amount an individual can invest via crowdfunded ventures in a year, which may be a flat $2,000, 5 percent of the individual's annual income or net worth, or 10 percent of the individual's annual income or net worth. The limit depends on the person's specific finances (see Chapter 4).

- The means by which a company may seek investments and an individual may make them, which is via SEC-registered online funding portals (the focus of Chapter 7).

The legislation also specifies other parameters that seek to promote the business sector while preventing fraud and protecting the investor. This book's website, www.dummies.com/go/crowdfundinvesting, offers a nice overview of the SEC regulations that have been put in place to enact the legislation.

Chapter 3

Raising Capital for Your Startup or Small Business with Crowdfund Investing

Crowdfund investing is meant to fill a void — to support companies that don't qualify for traditional financing. But if someone doesn't qualify for traditional financing, why should a crowd invest in him?

Different types of investors and lenders have different goals and different needs. Think about it this way: When you walk into a shoe store, you're drawn to certain shoes. For one reason (they don't fit comfortably) or another (they're not the right style), you selectively choose what you want to buy. That doesn't mean the rest of the shoes stink — they just aren't what you're looking for. Traditional sources of business financing go shopping for investments in similar ways. A bank usually lends only to businesses that have been in existence for at least three years. (Startups don't fit comfortably in that box.) A private equity firm may toss an executive summary into the trash because it describes a business in a fairly slow-growing industry. (The business is the wrong style for their type of investing.) That doesn't mean the businesses in question is a bad business — it just isn't what the bank or private equity firm is looking for.

This chapter offers a big-picture view of how an entrepreneur or small business owner can use crowdfund investing and how this type of financing differs from others. We describe some categories of businesses that are the right fit and style for crowdfund investing. We then briefly touch on the statutory requirements that an entrepreneur or business owner must follow to raise funds from the crowd, explain how crowdfund investing differs from other types of financing, sketch the process of raising funds this way (a topic that gets lots more attention later in the book), and describe some risks faced by businesses engaging in this type of financing.

Identifying Businesses Ripe for Crowdfund Investing

Title III of the JOBS Act, which created the opportunity for crowdfund investing (see Chapter 2), uses the term *emerging growth companies* (EGCs) to refer to entities that are most likely to utilize this form of financing. In this section, we introduce you to the key categories of EGCs: startups, small businesses, and other entities that find it difficult or impossible to find traditional financing.

Startups

Startups seem sexy. When you think about a startup, you may envision a bunch of high-tech college kids camped out in a fraternity house or apartment, coding away, living on beer and pizza, and figuring out how to change the world and get rich in the process. In reality, startups emerge from every part of a community, from chambers of commerce to incubators (which we describe in a nearby sidebar) to kitchen tables.

Business incubators

In the context of business finance, an incubator has nothing to do with hatching eggs. It's an office space where startup companies are helped to grow by providing them guidance and counsel in a controlled environment until they're ready to hatch. In recent years, we've seen an explosion of incubators around the United States, many of them sponsored by venture capital groups. Entrepreneurs compete to be accepted into an incubator, and the competition is fierce. In many cases, winning a spot in an incubator is tougher than securing capital. (For example, the Y Combinator incubator in Palo Alto, California, accepted only 2 percent of applicants for its May 2012 class.) The entrepreneur must live in (or move to) the city where the incubator is located and work under the direct guidance of the sponsoring venture capitalists.

The goal of an incubator is to have the entrepreneur hash out the proof of concept, build some customer traction, and start generating revenue so the business can be self-sustaining. The entrepreneurs who participate often are rewarded handsomely. According to Harjeet Taggar of Y Combinator, about 75 percent of that incubator's recent enrollees raised convertible debt, and in a recent class, the capitalization averaged about $10 million.

Essentially, a startup is a pre-revenue company that may be in the "great idea" phase or may have been developed into a business plan complete with marketing and financial ideas. In better cases, a startup has a *proof of concept* (meaning that its feasibility has been proven).

Startups are the riskiest types of investments because so many things can go wrong. Maybe the idea itself proves to be bad. (Turns out that people won't actually buy chocolate-covered gummy bears.) Maybe the revenue model doesn't pan out. (Turns out that people expect information on the Internet to be free.) Maybe the concept wasn't thought through well enough in advance. (Turns out that website you need requires an integrated payment system, which isn't in the budget.) The list of possible pitfalls is long and stress inducing.

So, why do startups ever get off the ground? Because great businesses (the kind that bring innovative products to market, earn lots of revenue, and employ brilliant people) have to start somewhere, and many risk takers want to be involved from day one with the Next Big Thing. From the investors' perspective, the chance of return over the long haul is much greater with a startup than with almost any other type of investment, assuming the startup eventually leads to an initial public offering (IPO). Of course, the chance of losing every penny of your investment is also much greater.

Not all startups are IPO material. For instance, consider someone who wants to start an organic farm to supply produce to local restaurants, or someone who plans to run a home renovation business. Neither one is a highly likely candidate for a future IPO. That doesn't mean these aren't good investments — it just means they aren't the types of startups you see discussed at length in the financial press.

Small businesses

From the perspective of the federal Small Business Administration (SBA), a small business generally has fewer than 500 employees for manufacturing businesses and less than $7 million in annual receipts for most nonmanufacturing businesses. But from the crowdfund investing perspective, a small business probably earns less than $1 million in revenue and has fewer than five employees. Why the much narrower definition? Because companies fitting these criteria are the most in need of crowdfund investing support. Historically, businesses with less than $1 million in revenue have a much harder time qualifying for financing than businesses with more than $1 million in revenue.

Why does crowdfund investing focus on small businesses also? Why not just fund startups? One answer is jobs. According to the entrepreneurial think tank the Kauffman Foundation, over the past 30 years, startups and small businesses combined provided the bulk of net new jobs in the United States. In addition, small businesses that have an operational history may be less risky and more attractive than startups. After all, businesses that have been around a few years usually have a business model that's working.

Small businesses stand to benefit greatly from crowdfund investing because those businesses that haven't been around for three years don't qualify for bank loans (even if they're growing steadily). And businesses that are growing steadily (5 percent to 20 percent per year) likely don't qualify for venture capital (because these funders are interested in big exit strategies that deliver a financial return of at least ten times what was invested).

In the following sections, we explain some specific types of small businesses that may be among the likely candidates for crowdfund investment support: technology companies, bricks-and-mortar retail shops, and service companies.

Crowdfund investing is not the right choice for every funding need. If you're opening or running a small business that likely will never make a significant amount of money, you may not want to get a crowd involved in your business. After all, having financial obligations or expectations and unhappy investors can be extremely stressful, and investors tend to be unhappy if they aren't making any money. That stress is very likely to distract you from creating and running your business and will reduce your future productivity.

Locavesting

Amy Cortese coined the term *locavesting* and literally wrote the book on it: *Locavesting* (Wiley). In the book, she discusses how investing in local economies stimulates those economies. When you take a dollar and invest it in a public company (like Apple) that isn't located in your community, you send that money outside your community, and the money never comes back. (Sure, your money may help make the next version if the iPad even cooler, but it doesn't directly support local jobs or businesses.) Say, instead, that you invest that same money in your local Apple Organic Farm. This farm employs a few people and needs to raise money to plant some more trees, hire a couple more folks, and expand its product lines to apple pies, applesauce, and apple serum to remove wrinkles. (We just made that last one

up, but why not? People use pumpkin butter for the same reason!) Every dollar that you invest into Apple Organic Farm goes directly back into the community. The investment dollars help pay wages for the employees who go out and buy local produce and other products and pay their local mortgages or rents and pay local taxes. The farm also buys products and services, many of which come from local vendors.

Ironically, crowdfund investing, which takes place online (and could easily allow someone from Alabama to invest in an Arizona company), has the opportunity to promote locavesting. If an investor approaches crowdfund opportunities with the goal of strengthening her home community, she can provide financial support to her hometown businesses in ways that were never before possible.

Technology companies

Technology companies cover a broad spectrum of activities, including (but certainly not restricted to) information technology (IT), green technology, and device technology. What most technology companies have in common is the use of computers and telecommunications to retrieve, transmit, or store information. Social media sites, online shopping sites, and pretty much any application you can get for your iPhone, iPad, or Android fall into this business category. Other examples might be a new solar panel that can work on cloudy days or a watch that is attached via Bluetooth to your mobile phone.

We expect that many crowdfund investment opportunities will focus on small technology companies. These types of companies are often easy to understand and may have low startup costs (as an example, IT companies may just have to pay for computers and programmers). Plus, depending on how innovative the idea behind the company is, investors may smell huge growth potential.

Bricks-and-mortar retail shops

These types of businesses have an actual storefront. They can be clothing stores, food retailers, or any other businesses that you would walk into to purchase their wares. Traditionally, these businesses have relied upon banks for their capital. Their growth tends to be slower than that of tech companies, and the owners often are happy with just a few branches. Venture capital and private equity firms don't invest in these companies because they don't hold the promise of a huge exit payoff within a less than five-year timeframe.

Before 2008, banks often extended loans to retail shops and accepted their inventory as collateral in case they couldn't fulfill their debt obligations. But since the financial meltdown of 2008, banks have become much stricter with their loan policies; they require a longer financial history and more collateral. As a result, many bricks-and-mortar shops have been unable to secure financing.

This type of business could be a perfect candidate for crowdfund investing. The risk to investors is much lower than with a tech business, as is the potential payoff. Investments in retail shops or other Main Street businesses may be structured differently from investments in tech businesses as well. For example, a bricks-and-mortar retailer may offer investors *revenue-based financing* (RBF), which means the investors are given a percentage of the revenue for a certain time period for a set number of years. Because the chances of a bricks-and-mortar business going public are very low, RBF is a way that a business can secure the needed capital to grow and the investor can receive a stream of income that varies with the success of the company.

Service companies

The service sector includes people who clean your clothes and serve you meals, as well as lawyers, accountants, doctors, dentists, mechanics, electricians, and so on. Service companies are very likely candidates for crowdfund investment support for two key reasons: They're among the easiest businesses to start and the hardest to fund.

Why is funding in short supply for service companies? The biggest expense in a service company is usually the employees, and human resources are volatile. (If you invest time and money to train someone, and he walks off to take another job, your investment goes with him.) In addition, investors don't always see significant return potential from these companies. (How much money can investing in an electrician return?)

Obviously, crowdfund investors face the same issues if they choose to support a service company. But other factors (including knowing and trusting the individual providing the service — something that doesn't apply to banks and private equity firms) can outweigh the inherent risks involved in financing a service company.

Anyone who doesn't qualify for traditional financing

Many new small businesses can't secure bank loans. That's always been the case, and it's become even more difficult since 2008. Banks require security for their loans and, in most cases, want to see two different ways that a business owner can repay them. (They want a backup plan in case Plan A doesn't pan out — if sales or revenues are lower than expected, for example.) When you're starting a new business, you (and your partners, if you have them) invest everything you've got — financially, physically, and emotionally — into getting your business off the ground. You may not have a Plan B, which means you may not qualify for a bank loan.

What about venture capital or private equity? Well, if you live in the San Francisco Bay Area; Austin; New York City; Washington, D.C.; or Boston, you may be in luck. High concentrations of private capital investors operate in these areas and are looking for great ideas to invest in. Geography is on your side because these investors may be looking to invest locally or may simply be more apt to meet with someone whose business is in town (versus halfway across the continent). If you live in Natchitoches, Louisiana, or Arnold, Nebraska, your access to these investors may be more limited.

In addition, if you're starting or running a company in an industry that isn't hot or new, you probably won't grab the attention of private equity firms even if you live in one of the investment hot spots. (Private capital investors generally don't put money into dry cleaning chains or sports bars unless you have a way to generate 10- or 20-fold returns in less than five years.)

And just in case you aren't discouraged enough, venture capital investors and angel investors are increasingly moving away from what used to be considered "seed-stage investments" and taking a more wait-and-see approach before parting with their money. They now tend to watch an entrepreneur bootstrap his business until he has real deliverables or traction. For example, they want the entrepreneur to build a prototype, launch the service or product, sign a certain number of customers, or maybe even get to break even on a cash flow basis before they're willing to invest. If you've ever started a business, you know that these milestones are big, and reaching them on your own is no easy task.

If you have a legal and legitimate business or idea, just because you haven't been able to qualify for traditional financing doesn't necessarily mean your business or idea can't work. Turning to crowdfund investing may provide you an opportunity to raise the money you need to get the proof that you can achieve milestones, create a track record, and demonstrate to investors or banks that they should work with you.

Working within the Statutory Framework

Crowdfund investing is not the Wild West. (We do *not* want risk to run amok and investors to lose their shirts.) When we first created the Startup Exemption Regulatory Framework (see Chapter 2) and began actively promoting it in January 2011, we knew that rational, common-sense regulations would be critically important to the success of this new investment path. For that reason, we built certain rules into our initial framework and have actively encouraged their implementation with the Securities and Exchange Commission (SEC) and the Financial Industry Regulatory Authority (FINRA).

If you determine that crowdfund investing is right for you (Part II of this book can help you make that decision), you must follow all legal requirements and abide by the terms and conditions of the online platform you select to use when you raise capital (a topic covered in Chapter 7).

The intent of Title III of the JOBS Act is to create an orderly market for crowdfund investing that enables entrepreneurs, small business owners, and potential investors to have the best opportunity for success, while protecting investors from potential fraud. In this section, we explain a few of the statutory requirements set forth in the JOBS Act you need to understand. (You find much more detail about these and additional requirements in Part II, and especially on this book's website, www.dummies.com/go/crowdfund investing.)

Limiting funding to $1 million

Our intent with our legislative framework was to create an asset class that provides targeted tools to enable small businesses to grow. Therefore, we wanted to establish a limit for crowdfund investing that would allow for sufficient seed money or early-stage investment for most businesses, while avoiding the unintended consequence of having larger organizations use this asset class as an ATM. The limit we set is $1 million in crowdfund investing funds per year. Organizations that need to raise more than that amount should seek funding via more traditional means.

Also, we're big believers in *lean startup methodology*. We think that business owners should exercise extreme care in determining how much money they need to raise to achieve their next milestone. Any time you raise capital (whether via crowdfund investing or traditional means), you take on investors who expect a return on their investment. If you take on more capital than you can effectively use at that time, you're potentially reducing their return on investment, diluting your ownership stake unnecessarily, and increasing the risks facing your organization. Setting a cap on crowdfund investing discourages businesses from raising excessive capital. It also keeps the funding vehicle targeted at small businesses.

Realizing why an all-or-nothing funding provision exists

When we were sitting around Jason's dining room table writing the framework for the crowdfund investing bill, we decided early on that an all-or-nothing provision was essential. That decision follows the example of many donation- or perks-based crowdfunding services, which we explain in Chapter 2. This provision means that the entrepreneur or business determines upfront the financial goal for a crowdfund investing campaign, works diligently to accomplish that goal, and either succeeds (and receives the full amount) or fails (and receives nothing, despite whatever investment pledges have been made).

Here are some key reasons that this provision exists:

  ✓ **To be fair to investors:** Business owners must be clear with investors about how much money they require and how that money will be used. (Chapter 5 can walk you through the process of making these decisions.) If a business aims to raise $100,000 and promotes to investors what it will do with that money, it can't possibly accomplish the same goals if it raises only a portion of that amount. An investor who pledges to support the $100,000 project shouldn't be assumed to support a reduced version of it.

✔ **To keep it lean:** We mention *lean startup methodology* in the preceding section. The all-or-nothing provision encourages this kind of thinking because the entrepreneur or business owner doesn't want to think too big (aiming for the maximum of $1 million to open several new locations, for example) and risk getting nothing. Instead, this person is encouraged to think more realistically (aiming for $200,000, perhaps, to open a single new location), so the chances of fundraising and operational success are greater.

With crowdfund investing, you can always go back and raise more money with additional campaigns. The more successful you are with your first effort, the easier it will be for you to raise successive rounds of financing (and the less equity you'll have to give up in return for the capital).

It's a much smarter business decision to go after financing in small tranches, to enable incremental growth, than to go after the capital to fulfill all your business goals at once. The all-or-nothing provision encourages entrepreneurs to set their goals at the smallest level possible to be able to grow their businesses to the next level.

Also, by going after the money in small tranches, you build a pool of investors who believe in you and your business. Investors' confidence in you will grow as you accomplish the things you said you wanted to in your campaign. When you launch a subsequent campaign, your happy investors may be very likely to invest in you again (and to bring new investors to the table).

✔ **To discourage fraud:** If the all-or-nothing provision didn't exist, it could be fairly easy for a fraudster to go online, set up a bogus business pitch, and pocket whatever amount of money he could drive to his crowdfund investing page before being exposed. It could be fairly easy to convince a handful of investors to fork over cash for a bogus business plan. But we believe in the power and intelligence of the crowd, and we expect that the crowd can sniff out fraudsters before they're able to secure significant amounts of investment pledges. If a fraudster is able to get $1,000 in pledges toward a $20,000 campaign before he gets busted, for example, he doesn't get the $1,000; he gets nothing. The all-or-nothing provision essentially grants the crowd time to sniff out the frauds.

Use the all-or-nothing provision to your advantage. It'll force you to take an in-depth look at your cash needs and to be fiscally conservative. And if your initial campaign proves successful, you should be able to raise more money down the road by offering less equity each time for the same amount of money raised.

Avoiding general solicitations

To explain this rule, we should first offer a short history lesson. As we explain in Chapter 2, one of the reasons for the collapse of the stock markets back in 1929 was mass speculation. People were making investments assuming that there was no way to go but up, and this hysteria was fostered by salesmen who sent offers to the public in newspapers, for example.

After the 1929 crash, the way in which investments could be solicited changed. The SEC was created, and it determined that the general public was not well served by investment offerings being so openly promoted. Therefore, a company wanting to raise cash had to be listed on an *exchange* (a market like the New York Stock Exchange). To be listed on the stock exchange, a company would have to disclose lots of information to the SEC, including the risks associated with investing in it.

The same laws have been in existence since 1933, although a few updates have occurred — mainly ones that allow private companies to solicit money from the richest 1 percent of Americans without having to go through a costly public registration. The thinking behind these updates was that the wealthy are more sophisticated about investing than regular folks and can afford to risk more of their assets without incurring catastrophic losses.

With the JOBS Act, the rules of the game changed to account for advances in technology and the Internet. Previously, we needed the SEC and the exchanges to act as the sole gatekeepers to people's pocketbooks so that investors had all the information they needed to make informed decisions. Today, the Internet can serve part of that function by providing increased transparency and making it more difficult for a business to take advantage of investors.

But even with the sunlight of the Internet, we can't just open the doors to generally soliciting the public for money. (You still can't post an ad to raise money for your startup idea on the radio, in a newspaper, in a magazine, or on television.) Instead, the intent of Title III of the JOBS Act is that if you want to raise money to start or grow a business, you can do so by soliciting funds from people who know you. Specifically, you're limited to soliciting from the funding portal (discussed later) and your social networks. You can't step outside these bounds and directly solicit capital from someone who doesn't know you (although the people in your social networks may extend your solicitation to people they know, which offers you more layers of possible investors; see Chapter 9).

The SEC has laid out very specific rules for how you can direct people to your funding pitch/portal using Facebook, LinkedIn, Twitter, e-mail, and other online networks. See this book's website, www.dummies.com/go/crowd fundinvesting, for the details.

Using only SEC-registered websites

To prevent people from soliciting random folks for money, the JOBS Act mandates that anyone seeking crowdfund investments must do so via an

SEC-registered website or, in some cases, through a broker-dealer (a topic we discuss in Chapter 7). The websites, known as *funding portals,* help the SEC make sure that a company has disclosed as much information as possible so investors can make informed decisions. They also prevent a company from getting any of the funds unless it hits its stated campaign goal (see the earlier section "Realizing why an all-or-nothing funding provision exists").

In addition, the SEC-registered websites prevent investors from investing more than their annual limits (see Chapter 16).

If you're going to seek crowdfund investment support, you must use one of these SEC-registered websites (or a broker-dealer). Doing otherwise will land you in trouble. For a representative list of crowdfunding platforms, visit www. crowdfundingprofessional.org or www.crowdsourcing.org/caps. And for specifics about what crowdfunding portals can do for you, be sure to read Chapter 7.

Distinguishing Crowdfund Investing from Other Types of Financing

Before you dig deeper into what crowdfund investing is and how you can tap into it for supporting a new venture or a small business, you should have some sense of how it differs from the types of funding that have previously been available to businesses. In this section, we briefly describe what traditional financing has looked like and offer some insights into how crowdfund investing may be a game changer.

Self-funding

Do we really need to explain how self-funding your business differs from getting crowdfund investing support? One involves your own wallet, and the other involves a whole bunch of other wallets. (How many wallets? Check out Chapter 6 for help estimating the size of your crowd.)

With that technical explanation out of the way, here's how crowdfund investing changes your need to self-fund your business: It doesn't. The first dollars invested in your business should be your own money, and crowdfund investing doesn't alter that fact. If you're going to launch a business, you need to believe in its success all the way down to your core. To show this belief, you need to invest in your own company. If a potential crowdfund investor were to look at your campaign and see that you're starting off with $0, this fact would be a big red flag. By investing your own money, you demonstrate that you believe in yourself and your business model.

How much of your own money should you risk? It's important to understand how you work under stress with your money on the line. Aim to invest an amount that will give you just enough stress to drive you to work hard, but not so much stress that you'll be a worried mess and distracted from productivity.

Credit card financing

You start your business with your savings, but maybe your budget doesn't reflect every item you need. Or maybe you have opportunities to invest faster than you had planned. Either way, after your savings is tapped, the easiest source of funds is your credit cards. Unfortunately, credit cards are usually the most expensive form of debt that a business can utilize.

We know you've heard it before, but this advice bears repeating: If you use credit cards to fund your business, pay them off each and every month. If you can't do so, use them only when absolutely required. Otherwise, when you seek funding from a bank or another resource, your outstanding credit card debt will be a strike against you.

Can crowdfund investing reduce the necessity of relying on plastic? Very possibly — *if* you can plan far enough ahead to anticipate your upcoming expenses and spot future opportunities for growth before they're in your face and begging for cash. Whereas credit cards are quick fixes that often wreak long-term financial havoc, crowdfund investment campaigns demand longer-term planning and commitment.

Bank loans

Bank loans have traditionally been a source of capital for small businesses, but one of the reasons that Title III of the JOBS Act passed is that banks are not lending like they used to. Capital is not flowing from the people who have it to the people who can use it to grow businesses and create jobs.

To qualify for a bank loan these days, you likely need a lot of collateral to secure your loan, three years of business financials to support your case, and an ongoing relationship with your bank. If you're an entrepreneur or a new small business owner, chances are, you don't meet these qualifications.

Furthermore, with the financial collapse in 2008, banks started charging a much higher interest rate on the money they lend to businesses. Even if you do meet the loan qualifications, you need to seriously study the interest rate that a bank is going to charge you and make sure that your revenues can meet your debt obligations. If the loan repayment is going to put too much financial (and personal) stress on you and your business, it will distract your attention from focusing on growing your business.

Crowdfund investments can be structured in various ways to suit the specific needs of your business. In many cases, a crowdfund investment campaign will offer investors an equity stake in the operation (meaning, they own stock in your company and earn dividends if you make a profit). However, your campaign could be structured so that your crowd is actually giving you loans, and you're repaying those loans with interest over a set amount of time. Clearly, the way in which you choose to structure your campaign determines whether your crowdfund investments closely mirror the services that banks provide through small business loans (in the case of debt-based crowdfund investing) or are quite distinct from bank loans (in the case of equity-based investments).

Should you look to crowdfund investing to completely replace your need for bank loans? Probably not, even if you opt for a debt-based crowdfund investment structure. Instead, your goal may be to seek a combination of both types of financing (in addition to self-funding and any other financial resources you can muster). But if the banks slam their doors in your face, spend some quality time with Parts II and III of this book, and take heart in the knowledge that this new funding avenue is available to you.

Private money: Angel investors, venture capitalists, and private equity investors

What exactly is *private money?* It's money that comes from companies or very wealthy individuals — people called *accredited investors* by the SEC — who, just like regular investors, want to maximize the returns of their investment portfolios. The concept of an *accredited investor* came into being with the creation of the SEC in the early 1930s. The idea was that, as the 1929 stock market crash illustrated, marketing stock investments to the public at large could be dangerous for the entire economy, and only certain investors should have the greatest freedoms to risk their money on certain types of investments.

To be qualified as an accredited investor today, you must have a liquid net worth of at least $1 million (excluding the value of your home), or you must have earned more than $200,000 for each of the last two calendar years ($300,000 if you're married). The SEC deems that investors with this much capital can fully and freely make investment decisions in both public and private companies.

Private money organizations aggregate capital from a mix of accredited investors (including companies and financial institutions) for the purpose of making investments primarily in private companies or nonpublic offerings. The goal of these organizations is to pool large amounts of investment capital and employ investment experts who can find and invest in great deals that will deliver higher rates of return than more traditional investments in public companies. (Of course, these deals also carry a lot of risk.)

There are three types of private money investors, which differ based on the size of the investment made and when during the company's lifecycle the investment is made. At each stage, these private investment firms provide not only capital, but also advice, connections, merger/acquisition targets, and external accountability and expertise to help companies succeed. The goal of these private money organizations is to create an exit for themselves (as well as the entrepreneur) that will deliver at least a tenfold (or *10x*) multiple on invested capital.

Here's a brief overview of the three types of private money entities:

- ✔ **Angel investors:** These people usually make bets on companies at their earliest stages (sometimes called *seed-stage* investments) and can play the role of a guardian angel. Angel investors usually form groups to allow them to jointly review investment opportunities, share information, and provide a potential pool of dollars that will attract good company founders who want both expertise and cash. Typically, these types of investors have some experience in entrepreneurial ventures and want the excitement of being part of something and helping it succeed. Individual angel investors typically make investments in the $25,000 to $100,000 range, which are small compared to later-stage investments.

- ✔ **Venture capitalists:** These investors (which are usually firms, not individuals) often invest between $1 million and $10 million in companies that have begun to grow out of the seed stage and are showing traction and results in their market space. The companies may or may not have revenue but likely are not profitable because they're spending all they make, in addition to the money that's invested in them, in order to grow as quickly and effectively as possible. Venture capitalists invest in companies that are believed to have very high growth potential and need capital to be able to scale quickly to take advantage of the market.

- ✔ **Private equity investors:** These firms tend to invest even larger amounts than the venture capitalists and look for more established companies with profits and successes that are looking for growth-stage capital.

Today, the lines between venture capital and private equity are fairly blurry. Many times, the way the firm wants to position itself from a marketing and strategy perspective makes the distinction (as opposed to what the firm invests in).

Obviously, getting your hands on private investor money could be a life changer when you're starting or growing your business. But the vast majority of businesses never touch the money supplied by accredited investors. And prior to the JOBS Act, *unaccredited investors* (people whose liquid net worth or annual income doesn't meet the accredited investor thresholds) were severely restricted from directly investing in many private businesses.

The JOBS Act opened up private company investment, in limited and regulated ways, to everyone. This significant regulatory change occurred in part because lots of people today (as opposed to in the 1930s, when so many of our financial regulations were crafted) have some level of investment savvy thanks to their retirement plans, which are invested in stocks, bonds, and mutual funds. In addition, the Internet and social networks have democratized access to information in real time that was unimaginable even a decade ago. Everyone with an Internet connection (more than 80 percent of the U.S. population) has access to information directly, as well as via their social networks, that can be used to make investment decisions.

Obviously, crowdfund investing doesn't compete with or replace the need for professional private money. As we explain earlier in this chapter, crowdfund investment campaigns have funding caps that are significantly lower than most venture capital and private equity investments. Instead, crowdfund investing runs parallel to private money, funneling funds to types of businesses that previously didn't stand a chance of receiving private support.

Putting Your Baby Online for the World to See

We devote a significant portion of this book — Parts II and III, to be exact — to detailed explanations of how to plan, launch, and run a crowdfund investing campaign, and how to interact with investors when it succeeds. Here, we whet your appetite by explaining just the basics about how a crowdfund investing campaign works and what to expect when you take your brilliant idea and business plan online.

Mapping out your goals and plans

The starting point of any crowdfund investing campaign is getting your brand advocates — your existing customers, your family members and friends, and anyone else who knows and trusts you — onboard with your business and financial goals. To do so, you first have to know what your goals are, and you have to get specific. A great idea is helpful, but a business plan that spells out the financial needs you'll face as you start or grow your company is even more crucial (see Chapter 5).

Keeping in mind the financial caps for a crowdfund investing campaign, and especially keeping in the mind the all-or-nothing funding provision that we outline earlier in the chapter, you want to set a realistic campaign goal.

If your business is very small and you can achieve a significant amount of growth with just $20,000, don't try to raise $200,000 just because the government says you're allowed. Stick with what you really need, and work every step of your campaign with energy, enthusiasm, and professionalism so your crowd knows they can trust you.

At the same time you're deciding on an amount of money you need to raise, you need to consider the form those funds will take. As we explain in Chapter 5, you can structure your crowdfund investment campaign in order to offer investors equity ownership of your company, or you can opt to treat their investments as debt to be repaid over a set amount of time (with interest). Consider the other types of financing available to you, and make a decision that fits your company's overall needs.

Engaging existing advocates of your brand

Communicating your specific goals to your customers, friends, family members, and other advocates, as well as explaining the specific ways in which funds will be used, is the next major step of your campaign. This step takes place either through a broker-dealer or online, via an SEC-approved website that serves as your funding portal. (Chapter 7 explains what broker-dealers and funding portals can do for you.) Here, we briefly explain how this online solicitation works.

You *cannot* discuss the terms of your campaign offering outside the funding portal. Doing so is a violation of the legislation. No matter how jazzed you are about getting your idea off the ground, you can share only your concept and goals with people in person, on the phone, via e-mail, and so on. If those people are interested in knowing what investment in your idea would entail, you must direct them to your online funding portal or your broker-dealer for the specifics.

Tapping into your online network

Crowdfund investing is where financing meets online social networks. Through your online funding portal, you communicate your campaign pitch to every contact in your Facebook, LinkedIn, Twitter, and other social network accounts. Those people, who are your first-tier contacts, have the opportunity (again, via the broker-dealer or SEC-approved funding portal) to share the campaign pitch with their own social network contacts. Therefore, your pitch can spread to larger concentric circles of contacts and social networks over time — from the people who know you personally to the friends of friends who may prove to be your best investors because they share your passion for your business and want to make an investment.

Turning to your established customer base

If you already run a business and you're looking to grow, you need to bring your existing customer base into your campaign. These are the people who know your business, your product, and you. As long as you've been treating them right and providing a good product or service, they're very likely to want to support your efforts by becoming equity or debt investors.

Although you can't directly solicit campaign funds in your existing store, on the phone, or in any way other than via the online funding portal, you can certainly inform your customers about your campaign. Ask them to join your social network(s) and to visit your campaign page on the funding portal website.

Promoting interest throughout the campaign

When your campaign goes live, you (and possibly a staff person you use/hire to serve as your community manager throughout the campaign; see Chapter 6) must be prepared to respond to questions, concerns, and criticisms posted on the funding portal site by people who review your pitch. From start to finish, your online campaign may last up to three months, and you should be prepared to stay engaged consistently so your pledges start strong and stay vibrant throughout.

You want to start strong right out of the gate so your campaign gets immediate traction. If a potential investor sees that response to your pitch is anemic in the weeks immediately following your launch, you'll be fighting harder to get that person onboard. If she sees, instead, that your pitch has garnered immediate interest and resulted in robust pledges, she'll be more likely to join your crowd and to share her enthusiasm with her own networks. Your best chance at success is to get your committed supporters to pledge their funds early on and let them spread the word on your behalf. The ripples of their enthusiasm can spread far and wide, and you may find that you get investments from people you've never met who are taking a chance on you because a friend of a friend says you're trustworthy, hardworking, and worth the risk.

Managing (lots of) investor knowledge

Assuming that you successfully complete your crowdfund investing campaign (by gathering online pledges that meet or exceed your stated goal), you collect the money you need and gain access to a pool of investor knowledge. Handled correctly, the crowd knowledge that you gain may be even more valuable than the money.

Some of the people who invest in your company may bring to bear direct knowledge of your business. People like to be useful, and when they have money involved, they *really* like to be useful. After you get a sense of the size of your crowd, who your biggest investors are, and the background that these people bring to the table, you can start thinking about how to communicate with investors and ask for their help. You may find that some investors can offer technical expertise, others can provide excellent word-of-mouth promotion, and others may be pains in the neck who question and criticize every move you make.

You and your community manager (described in Chapter 6) need to have a plan for how to process, evaluate, respond to, and incorporate all the knowledge that will be offered to you. Your funding portal may provide the structure to handle this step; ideally, it should have online groups or virtual rooms dedicated to subjects such as sales, marketing, and branding. There should be discussion threads in each location, and you and your team should monitor them.

Be open to criticism, but know your business model and know what you want to accomplish. Don't let outside advice steer you away from what you know is correct.

Rewarding your investors or paying back your debt

The financing structure you choose during your campaign determines how you reward your investors:

- **Repaying debt:** If you choose to finance your venture with debt, you determine a repayment schedule upfront that includes principal and interest payments. You must be confident about generating revenue immediately so that you can cover these payments. (A startup without revenue should think twice before choosing this model.)

- **Paying dividends on equity:** If you choose to offer your crowdfund investors equity, the type of equity you choose determines when investors get paid. Investors with *common stock* usually are in the investment for the long haul, and their exit will match yours. A *preferred stock* offering means that investors expect a dividend, which is paid out of the cash your business generates.

In the section "Sharing the wealth" later in this chapter, we explain some of the first-stage thinking that must occur before you determine whether offering equity to your investors is the right move. You always want to be certain that you aren't giving away control of your business. Plan to keep your lawyer and accountant on standby to help with the specifics of rewarding your investors.

Understanding Your Risks

No decision to raise outside money should be taken lightly. Having outside investors means that you have to answer to people (and you may have to share your equity). Poor investor management can distract you from growing your business. Even worse, failure to reach your campaign goal and raise the money you set out to raise can be a red flag to your existing customer base.

Before you set out on your crowdfund investing campaign, you should clearly understand some risks that may differ from those you face when raising money through other means. We cover these risks in this section.

Protecting your business's intellectual property

If you've seen the movie *The Social Network,* you understand the need to protect your intellectual property. You can do so in several ways:

- ✔ **Don't tell anyone about it.** This strategy is foolproof, but it means that you can't run a crowdfund investing campaign. People need to hear and see what you're talking about, or they'll never trust you enough to invest in you.

- ✔ **Hire an intellectual property lawyer.** You can — and may need to — go down the road of filing a patent and/or securing trademark and copyright protection for your ideas and materials. This route takes time and money, which may seem like a deterrent. After all, if your idea turns out to be a flop, that money was spent for no reason.

  However, as we explain in Chapter 13, failing to secure your intellectual property rights can lead to disaster, including a crowd revolt. We walk you through the basics of patents, trademarks, and copyright protection in Chapter 10. At a minimum, you should consult an attorney if you have any inkling that you've created intellectual property that needs to be secured.

- ✔ **Rely on your funding portal for help.** In addition to taking the steps suggested in the previous bullet, look for a crowdfund investing platform that requires investors to sign nondisclosure agreements and has data rooms where you can upload private information (so it isn't available to the general public). These data rooms should be password protected. Portals that have data rooms allow you to see who looked at your files and for how long. When many companies are in the process of selling or merging a business, this is how they manage their sensitive intellectual property and let prospective buyers view what they've got. If anyone walks off and duplicates it, with a data room and log you can hold people accountable.

Nondisclosure agreements will not prevent signers from passing on information to their friends or associates. If you have a great idea, the best way to protect it is through patent, copyright, or trademark registration.

✔ **Roll the dice.** You can simply choose to put your intellectual property out in the open for everyone to see. Chances are, what you think is sensitive isn't of interest to anyone else. But be prepared for the worst-case scenario so you aren't devastated if a theft occurs.

Facing community opposition

Successfully managing criticism of your project could be the difference between your success and failure. Your business is your baby, and your first reaction when someone criticizes it and your business model may be to want to strike back in defense. When you first see opposition, you need to act right away (in a way that's more professional than striking back). Have a plan in place for how you're going to deal with criticism.

The first thing you need to do is to figure out if the opposition is real or if someone is trying to sabotage your project. One of your competitors could find out about your campaign and set out to undermine it. The best thing to do in this case is to identify the troublemaker and post the identification for everyone to see. Handled responsibly and correctly, this situation could actually end up benefiting you. It could show your investors that you're level headed and you aren't going to get distracted from your goals.

If you're facing true community opposition, you need to listen to what's being said and respond accordingly. Some concerns will be legitimate, and others won't. In some cases, you'll get negative comments from people who simply don't understand your business. Instead of getting frustrated, take the opportunity to better explain what you do.

If the concerns are legitimate and someone has found a hole in your business model, respond in a respectful manner for all to see. As an entrepreneur, you can't think of everything yourself. You're busy building a business, which requires big-picture thinking from about 30,000 feet in the air. If you're able to take the critique and absorb it thoughtfully, you can win even greater respect from your crowd.

The most important thing when facing opposition is to respond calmly, fairly, and quickly. Make it your goal to turn the opposition into your funders.

Your biggest risk in crowdfund investing is having your company image or brand tarnished. This can happen when people make negative comments about you, your business, or your product or service. Don't take such comments as personal attacks. Your job is to address the frustration and protect your brand.

Sharing the wealth

One of the biggest risks in crowdfund investing is failing to understand the value of equity. Sharing the wealth is important, but you need to be judicious in how you do it. First and foremost, *never* give up control of your business. Simply put, *never* give up more than 50 percent of your equity when raising capital through crowdfund investing.

Most entrepreneurs go through multiple rounds of financing. You need to think strategically and ask yourself, "How many times do I think I need to go out and raise money? In each of those rounds, how much equity will I have to give up?"

As a general rule, the earlier you are in the development of a project, the greater the equity you need to give up. Someone with an idea who needs to build a proof of concept may give up 20 percent to 25 percent of a business for the necessary money. Someone with an existing proof of concept may give up only 10 percent to 15 percent of the business for some growth capital. And someone who's already generating revenue may be able to give up a smaller amount.

Of course, the equity percentages are dependent upon how much money you need as well. Raising smaller dollar amounts means you can give away less equity. Unfortunately, the larger the dollar amount you need, the greater the likelihood that you'll have to relinquish a larger amount of equity.

Think of equity as an apple pie. You always want at least half the pie for yourself. If you're going to give away pieces of it, the first slice may be half of the remaining half. The next piece may be a quarter of the remaining half, and the next may be an eighth. Figure 3-1 can help you visualize what we're talking about.

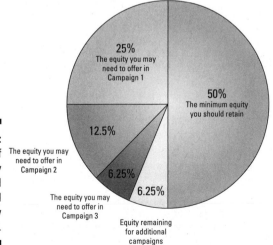

Figure 3-1:
Your slice of the equity pie should never fall below 50 percent.

Be fair and don't be overly miserly, though. Using equity is a great way to get people to work with you. You may even be able to trade equity for services (such as legal, accounting, design, or computer services).

Keeping it legal

You must conduct all your business activities — and especially any fundraising — in a fully legal and transparent fashion. You're required to disclose all relevant information that might affect your business in a *material* (which is accountant-ese for "significant") way. When in doubt about whether something is material, disclose it! Do not cut corners, do not intentionally omit important information, do not mislead people with false statements, and do not commit fraud of any kind. You don't want to end up losing your funding, losing your reputation, or even — in a serious case of fraud — losing your freedom.

Your actions during a crowdfund investing campaign affect not only you but also other entrepreneurs attempting to finance ventures through this new investment vehicle. The ability for companies to raise capital via crowdfund investing was a hard-fought battle. We personally spent thousands of hours and thousands of our own dollars to deliver this opportunity to you and every other small business and startup in America. Give us a hand! Demonstrate to the SEC, state regulators, the news media, and your friends and neighbors that you want to be an example of how businesses use crowdfund investing in ways that benefit everyone, including your customers, shareholders, and community.

Staying Legal: From the Lawyer's Experience

The following section is provided in conjunction with Doug Ellenoff of Ellenoff, Grossman & Schole (EGS). Consider EGS the leading crowdfunding law firm. They have over 30 years of experience working with startups, small businesses, and capital raising. They're sponsors of the Crowdfunding Professional Association (CfPA), speakers at most events on crowdfunding, and representatives of the industry in front of the SEC, as well as at Financial Industry Regulatory Authority (FINRA) meetings. The following is a general guideline and should not be considered legal advice about crowdfunding. We encourage you to consult with your own lawyer.

Proceeding with caution

Although crowdfund investing is trendy and happening, and it may facilitate your raising much-needed capital, make no mistake about it: You're engaging in a securities transaction subject to many federal and state anti-fraud laws. Even though you aren't staging an IPO, you're engaging in a private placement of securities. Crowdfund investing requires a commitment on your part that is similar to your commitment to an IPO; you must fully, fairly, and accurately share all meaningful information about your business opportunity with the crowd — the good, the bad, and the potentially ugly.

Aiming for full disclosure

A balanced presentation of what you're offering to the crowd must be your primary objective. People in the securities bar refer to this effort as *full disclosure,* which obligates you to share all details of your business opportunity as it actually exists at the time you're raising money. You can't portray the opportunity as it may exist in the future assuming that you have already raised and used the requested funding. Don't misunderstand this important point. You should certainly make clear what your intentions and hopes are for the use of the proposed funding and where you'll be in your projected business model if all goes well, but be very careful about any promises that you make.

You're required to clearly distinguish where you are versus where you hope to be. You must include all relevant and meaningful information and associated risks about the opportunity and not intentionally or unintentionally forget to include something that the crowd should know about in order to make an informed investment decision. Achieving full disclosure requires a lot of thought and possible research on your part. And you should consult other experienced entrepreneurs who have been through the process previously, as well as securities professionals such as lawyers, accountants, and bankers.

All this effort will not only reduce your concerns about potential liability but also cause you to better think through your business and how to describe it in a manner that will increase your likelihood of successfully raising your funds. Your concerns for the crowd to truly appreciate both the risks and benefits of participating with you should be equal to your need for obtaining the funds for your business.

Whether you choose to do it yourself or with professionals, you need to fully acquaint yourself with the type of information that is normally associated with raising debt or equity securities. This information includes the risks involved with investing in any crowdfund investing campaign generally, along with the particular risks of your business and the type of securities you're offering. Don't be afraid to be loud and clear that this is not only high-risk investing but that the investor may very well lose all or a portion of what he invests. This necessary disclosure will better safeguard you later if your business opportunity fails and the investors claim that they didn't know the risks of investing in your opportunity. You owe the same, if not more, duty of forthrightness to the crowd than you do to your relatives; everyone who invests in you worked hard for his savings. You have a real burden in taking and spending their money on your crowdfund investing opportunity.

Finding your way to an SEC-registered portal

After you assemble your offering materials, including your business plan, terms of your offering, risk factors, subscription documents, and a purchaser questionnaire, you need to identify the appropriate funding portal to determine where your particular offering will most likely raise the required capital. Chapter 7 is devoted to this topic.

 We strongly encourage you to visit the FINRA website (`www.finra.com`) to confirm which websites are actually registered with the SEC and licensed to operate as funding portals or broker-dealers by FINRA. Do not invest with any other website.

You want to locate the portal that has the most visibility and online recognition. More likely than not, the better-known portals will have the most registered investors. Because neither you nor the portal will be able to market your financing external to the portal, the more active a portal community, the more fertile ecosystem it will be for you to accomplish your funding.

You should also inquire about their own commitment to marketing themselves. Recognize that there are going to be all kinds of industry- and geographic-specific portals and you want your proposed opportunity to be in the portal most closely aligned with your opportunity. (It would do you limited, if any good to have a consumer products company in a biotechnology portal.) The fit may end up having imperfect compatibility, but there should be a wide choice.

Taking your responsibility seriously

Between you and the funding portal/broker dealer, you have a responsibility to educate possible investors about crowdfund investing, generally, and your opportunity specifically. For example, you need to advise investors that, per the legislation (see Chapter 2), they're limited in how much they may invest in all crowdfund investing campaigns in each 12-month period. This, in turn, creates limits within that 12-month period of how much an investor can invest in each offering. Share with them that the limits exist for their protection and that the rules have been written this way because although each investor may think each opportunity in which she invests is a good investment and that the acquired securities will appreciate, statistically speaking that won't hold true. Investors are actually more likely to lose their money or not have access to it for an extended period of time.

You also want the crowd to appreciate that the securities you're offering in exchange for their investment are unable to be sold or transferred anytime soon, if ever, except in specific circumstances that may or may not present themselves.

The rules as currently written provide for a one-year holding period, but that presupposes that a market for such securities develops and that someone else wants to purchase them, which in reality may not be so easy to accomplish. This reality and the other characteristics of your offering are your obligation to make clear. You must educate your potential investors about the type of securities you're offering (notes, preferred stock, common) and the other relevant terms associated with those securities and any other contractual rights, privileges, or obligations that they may be subject to — good or bad. It's your responsibility to know what you're offering to the crowd and to explain everything in a simple and easily understandable way. (Consider using a glossary of terms and hot links.)

When your campaign is live on the funding portal, avoid reacting privately to communications from and with the crowd. Your responses, if any, must be publicly available to the crowd and become part of your offering materials, so be thoughtful and measured.

All investors and potential investors are entitled to all your shared ideas and responses. You need a current and future communications strategy for developing and fostering your image and relationship with the crowd. Don't just react; you may very well regret a quick emotional and reckless posting. You may also compromise your funding. One posting is just that: one. Hopefully, there will be many other positive shared views. If not, you may learn the hard way, no differently from guests on reality shows, that your opportunity isn't as attractive as you may have believed.

Remembering that communication is key

Keep in mind that communication skills are also necessary to comply with your post-funding obligations, both under the laws (annual report requirement) and per your duty to create ongoing transparency. You must update your actual investors (who, per the legislation, you have a legal responsibility to) about all the worthwhile milestones that you reach as you execute your plan. Again, don't forget to share bad news and developments as well (see Chapters 12 and 13 for guidance).

Imagine a holiday party in the future when all your friends and family are joined by the crowd at a gathering at your house, after this crowdfund investing opportunity has failed. Be comforted that no one is mad at you because not only were they all fully and fairly advised of what you were attempting to do, but also they lost only a small portion of their savings thanks to the investment limitations mandated under the rules. You did all that you said you were going to do, and the crowd was apprised of all the risks that may have been the reason the venture didn't work out as had been hoped.

We hope that following these steps will not only keep you out of legal trouble but also make you a better entrepreneur!

Chapter 4

Becoming Part of the Crowd: Investing with Caution

. . . .

. . . .

*T*his chapter offers both entrepreneurs and investors some insight into how and why someone would make a crowdfund investment and the risks associated with it. And make no mistake: Investing in startups and small enterprises is risky business. No matter how well you may know the person seeking funds, or how rock solid the business proposal seems, you must proceed with caution and prepare for worst-case scenarios (all of which will lighten your wallet).

If you're an entrepreneur, this chapter helps you better understand what's going through the minds of investors who are considering whether to fund your campaign. You can take this information into consideration when crafting your business model and maximizing the investment opportunity it presents.

If you're a potential investor, this chapter helps you begin to figure out whether crowdfund investing may be right for you, how much you can invest, and the role you'd play during and after a crowdfund-investing campaign. All these topics receive more detailed attention in Part V of this book.

By the way, becoming part of an investment crowd doesn't mean following the actions of the crowd. Successful investing of any kind requires that you make your own decisions. The wisdom of the crowd can emerge only if each investor uses his or her best judgment to decide whether an investment opportunity is a good one. Sharing these thoughts in an open dialogue guides the crowd toward reasonable decisions. Pooling these thoughts together is what creates crowd wisdom.

Avoiding herd mentality

Ever watch a herd of cattle on a farm? If one member of the herd moves in one direction, the rest of the herd usually follows. The leader may not always be making the right decision, particularly if it's heading for a cliff. (Okay, not many farms are likely to have dangerous cliffs, but bear with us — we're working toward an analogy here!) The momentum of the rest of the pack may push some of the herd off the cliff because, when they start moving forward en masse, it's tough to stop.

The same can be said for groups of individuals. If you succumb to herd mentality, you let other people influence your behavior, your purchases, your style, and so on. A crowd can be smart due to the combined brain waves it contains, but it can just as easily be stupid. If your biggest concern is fashion, following the crowd may lead only to some future embarrassment (when you realize that even Lady Gaga looks a bit silly in shoulder spikes and meat couture). But when it comes to making investment decisions, the stakes are much higher. Greed drives

people — including whole crowds of people — to do crazy things. This fact was one of the reasons that Bernie Madoff was so successful. He told his clients that he was making 10 percent a year on their investments (even though the markets at large weren't performing nearly as well), and people believed him. When his investors' financial statements showed earnings of 10 percent, they believed those statements were true, and they told others about the pot of gold they had found. In the end, the house of cards came tumbling down, and so did all their investments.

If you choose to become a crowdfund investor, your goal should be to contribute to the wisdom of the crowd: to ask pertinent questions, shine a light on dubious statements, push for clarity and transparency from the entrepreneur or business owner, and make your own decisions based on the collective wisdom of the crowd. You can't afford simply to follow the herd. If you yield control to the herd, instead of listening, contributing, and deciding with the crowd, your investment may go over a cliff.

Considering How This Investment Fits (Or Doesn't Fit) into Your Portfolio

If you've ever taken an investment course, the first thing you learned is that you don't protect yourself from loss by picking winning companies — you do it by diversifying your portfolio. In business, life happens, and sometimes bad things happen to good businesses. When those bad things happen, your investment can disappear. To hedge against this risk, your best bet is to invest broadly.

If you invest in the public markets, you diversify by investing in a combination of stocks (large and small, both domestic and international) and bonds. This means that you invest in risky stocks that have the potential to grow rapidly (and also drop rapidly) and bonds that are relatively low risk and, hence, offer a lower return. In addition, if you have a good financial planner, you've probably been counseled to keep six months' worth of cash on hand so you don't have to worry about market fluctuations either. The goal is to spread out your risk among all your investments. That way, if one goes belly up, it won't wipe out your entire savings.

You need to approach your crowdfund investments with the intention of using them to diversify your portfolio. Making a decision to invest in a crowdfund offering should take into account your investment psychology: If you're completely risk averse, you have no business investing in small, private companies. If, however, you can tolerate volatility and risk in a small portion of your portfolio for the sake of potentially receiving some significant financial returns, a crowdfund investment may make sense.

In any case, a crowdfund investment should be a small part of your portfolio. (Less than 10 percent of your portfolio should be in high-risk investments, and crowdfunding may be a portion of that 10 percent if you have other high-risk investments.) Whether you're investing in a campaign that offers you equity in the company or that's selling debt (which will be repaid to you in steady increments over a set period of time), you should treat a crowdfund investment as the riskiest part of your portfolio. (We explain the equity and debt options available through crowdfund investment in detail in Chapter 5.) That's because statistics show that, on average, 50 percent of new companies fail within their first year.

You have to be very smart when considering your crowdfund investment options (for example, investing only in products or services you'd buy yourself, revenue models you understand, and entrepreneurs you know and trust). But no matter how smart you think your decision may be, you also have to be prepared for failure (see the upcoming section "Preparing for the worst-case scenario"). Therefore, if you choose to put money into a crowdfund investment, you likely want to scale back on the funds you put into other high-risk investments, such as emerging-market stocks, so that you don't exceed 10 percent of your portfolio in high-risk investments.

In the upcoming section "Calculating your maximum investment (with the SEC's help)," we explain that you can't invest your entire income and savings in crowdfund investment campaigns; the Securities and Exchange Commission (SEC) won't let you. But working within the SEC parameters, if you decide what amount between 0 percent and 10 percent of your portfolio is the right amount for you to put into crowdfund investments, don't exceed that percentage. In addition, within the allotted amount, spread your risk over several investments. If you want to play it safe, as venture capitalists do (see Chapter 3 for an explanation of what they actually do), spread your risk over 20 crowdfund investments. (For every 20 investments they make, venture capitalists believe the odds are that 2 will be winners.)

Weighing the risks and potential rewards of crowdfund investing

This statistic bears repeating: On average, 50 percent of investments in early-stage companies fail. So, the risks of crowdfund investment seem pretty clear: You can lose some or all of your money.

Among the failures, 50 percent of early-stage companies run out of cash before they can succeed. The other 50 percent of failures suffer from poor management decisions, poor hiring decisions, poor use of funds, and so on. Therefore, as a potential crowdfund investor, you have to make the effort to figure out a couple key things about the business you're considering:

- ✔ If its campaign is successful, will it have enough cash to meet its stated milestones?
- ✔ Have the owners and managers thought through crucial decisions such as who to hire and how to use the money being raised?

Luckily, you don't have to be a super sleuth to find answers. As we explain in Chapter 15, the business or entrepreneur seeking funds is required to provide a lot of information in its campaign pitch. Your job is to read (and watch and listen to) all that information and to participate in online crowd conversations when you find certain answers to be lacking. You can't be a passive investor; you must commit to taking an active role in finding out as much information as possible.

Becoming an active investor can be a reward unto itself; doing so offers you a sense of participation and control that more traditional investments can't provide. It also teaches you how to be savvy in all your investment decisions.

In addition, of course, you hope to make investment choices that may pan out in the long run with rewards you can't get anywhere else. If you're able to identify even one company whose idea is brilliant, whose business model is flawless, and whose management is rock solid, you just may find yourself in a position to reap serious financial benefits down the line.

Calculating your maximum investment (with the SEC's help)

If you're an unaccredited investor (meaning your net worth is less than $1 million excluding your primary residence, and you haven't earned more than $200,000 for each of the past two years), you can't invest every dime you've got in crowdfund investment campaigns. Doing so would be a nightmare for your portfolio (you'd be doing the opposite of diversifying), and it also wouldn't be legal. That's because, per the JOBS Act, the SEC sets specific limits on how much any individual can invest. The limits are based on how much you make (your annual income) or have in your savings (your net worth).

If you can't quote your annual income off the top of your head, look at your tax return from last year. The adjusted gross income (AGI) on line 37 of Form 1040 is what you're looking for. If you don't have your tax forms handy, just grab one of your paychecks and look for the gross income amount. That amount is what you make before taxes. Multiply the number by how many pay periods you have in a year. (If you're paid every two weeks, multiply by 26. If you're paid monthly, multiply by 12. If you're paid twice a month, multiply by 24.)

Net worth is the value of all your stocks, bonds, and savings outside the equity that you have in your house. This figure includes what you have in your retirement account. To calculate your net worth, log on to your online investment account, dig up your investment statements, determine how much you have in the bank, and start adding.

Table 4-1 offers the breakdown of how much the SEC allows you to risk on crowdfund investments based on your annual income or net worth. Note that the SEC allows you to use the greater of these two figures when calculating your limit.

Table 4-1	SEC Investment Limits Based on Annual Income or Net Worth	
If Your Annual Income or Net Worth Is . . .	**You Can Invest Up To . . .**	**Which Caps Out At . . .**
Less than $40,000	$2,000	$2,000
$40,000 to $99,999.99	5% of your annual income or net worth	$5,000
$100,000 or more	10% of your annual income or net worth up to $100,000	$100,000

To clarify what these limits look like, consider these examples:

- If you make $28,000 per year and your net worth is lower than that amount, you can invest up to $2,000 per year.

- If you have $45,000 in net worth and earn less than that amount in annual income, you can invest up to $2,250 per year (which is 5 percent of your net worth).

- ✔ If you make $99,999 per year, and your net worth is lower than that amount, you can invest up to $4,999.95 (which is 5 percent of your annual income).

- ✔ If you have $325,000 in net worth and earn less than that amount each year, you can invest up to $32,500 (which is 10 percent of your net worth).

Keep in mind that each example reflects an *aggregate amount* (the total amount that this individual can put into all his or her crowdfund investments each year). For example, if you earn $28,000 per year and your net worth is less than that amount, your cap is $2,000 for all your crowdfund investments for the entire year. Earlier in this chapter, we encourage diversity in crowdfund investing (because the failure rate for these types of ventures is so high). Therefore, if your annual cap is $2,000, you shouldn't invest most of that amount in a single campaign. Doing so impedes your ability to invest in other crowdfund investment projects for the rest of the calendar year. It also breaks the rules that venture capitalists use for their investments, which is to make small investments in several companies to diversify your risk.

What are the rules for accredited investors? The SEC has determined that accredited investors are individuals with income above $200,000 per year if single ($300,000 per year if married) or with a net worth over $1 million (excluding the value of your home). If your income/net worth qualifies you as an accredited investor, with the proper legal disclosures, the SEC allows you to make investments of any amount you choose in any private company. Although having this flexibility to make investments at any level may sound like a great thing, it also means there are no guardrails to help limit potential losses from investments in companies that fail.

If you are an accredited investor, we strongly urge you to use caution when investing in private companies. Use the same principles of portfolio investing that an unaccredited investor uses. High-risk investments (including crowdfund investments) should not comprise more than 10 percent of your investment portfolio. No matter how much of a sure thing the investment may seem to you, do not put all your eggs in one high-risk basket. Venture capitalists make ten investments in startups to try to get one large winner. Following their example, aim to make a larger number of small-dollar investments in crowdfund investing, and remember that no investment comes with a guarantee. There is no substitute for doing your homework on the companies you are considering and then using your own best judgment to make prudent investment decisions.

If you're an accredited investor, you have two options when it comes to funneling dollars into crowdfund-investing campaigns:

- ✔ If you're investing through an online crowdfunding portal (see Chapter 7), you're limited to caps that are provided by the legislation. So, although normally you could invest whatever you like because accredited investors can invest as they see fit, the legislation restricts your cap to $100,000 (even if your net worth is, say, $1.2 million).

> ✔ If you are investing directly into a company (outside of a funding portal or broker-dealer) that is running a crowdfunding offering online, you can invest as much as you want, provided that the *company* doesn't exceed its yearly cap of $1 million of crowdfunded investments per the legislation. From the SEC's point of view, you're investing parallel to the crowdfund investments collected on the portal, and your investment counts in the tally of how much the company has generated via crowdfund investing. If the company doesn't hit its campaign funding target online, depending on what you agree to with the entrepreneur, you may or may not have the option to withdraw or to keep your funds in. Therefore, if you're making an investment outside of a funding portal or broker-dealer, make sure you have a lawyer involved.

Preparing for the worst-case scenario

Although you certainly hope for the best-case scenario when making an investment decision, you must plan for the worst. The worst-case scenario in crowdfund investing:

YOU COULD LOSE YOUR ENTIRE INVESTMENT.

Is that clear enough?

Obviously, we aren't trying to say that all investments in small companies or startups are bad. If we believed that were true, we wouldn't have worked so hard to open up investment in small businesses and startups to people of all income levels. And most of the time, small businesses and startups aren't engaging in fraudulent or other illegal activities. Instead, the vast majority of the time, when a business fails, a variety of legitimate, above-board factors contribute to the failure, including having false market expectations and failing to execute the business plan.

As an investor, you have to set your expectations low when you think about what your returns may be from a crowdfund investment. You can't invest money that you need to tap into within the next year (because you're tied to the initial investment for at least that length of time; see the upcoming section "Staying put for at least a year"). And you can't invest money assuming that you'll earn a certain percentage of return within a certain amount of time; new and small businesses simply aren't that predictable. As we say earlier in the chapter, risk only a very small percentage of your total investment portfolio on crowdfund investments. That way, if you make a good investment, you can be excited, and if you make a poor investment, it doesn't prevent your retirement or otherwise devastate your long-term financial situation.

Studying the Candidates

If you decide that you want to put a small portion of your investment portfolio into one or several small businesses and startups, a number of crowdfund investing platforms (websites) are available to help you make the best decisions possible. You want to take a lesson from angel investors and venture capitalists (see Chapter 3) and invest small amounts in a number of companies. If you were to invest in ten companies, for example, you could assume that, over time, some of them would lose money, some would break even, and a few would make money. If you're lucky, maybe one would have the chance to generate a very positive outcome.

To pave the way for a possible positive outcome, you have to do your homework. Nothing replaces a thorough review of all information available on the investment in question. One of the biggest benefits of crowdfund investing is that lots of individuals are doing the same research at the same time, and you can use online forums to discuss tactics and information. That said, collaborative efforts should never take the place of your own primary research so that you fully understand what you're investing in and what the risks are. What follows are some of the steps you can take to help in your study of the companies attempting to raise capital via crowdfund investing.

Knowing how your money will be used

A company wants to grow, so it runs a campaign to raise the necessary capital via crowdfund investing. What exactly will it do with the money being raised? The question is obvious, but you have to make sure you get a concrete answer.

Look at the campaign proposal and how much the company wants to raise. Carefully review its plans for using the funding. Ask yourself these questions:

✔ **Do you think the amount of money being raised is enough to enact the company's plans? Do you think the company is asking for too much?** For example, say the business plan is to start a cable television channel and the company is attempting to raise $200,000. If the plan states that the company can be operational with that money alone, that's a red flag. The legal bill alone for working with cable companies and the Federal Communications Commission (FCC) would likely cost more than $200,000.

On the flip side, if a business plan suggests that it will cost $200,000 to start a small landscaping business, you should find out a great deal more information before deciding to invest because that number seems high. (Maybe it isn't, but you need to study the plan to find out.)

✔ **Do the company's assumptions and timelines feel credible?** Does the plan suggest that the company can open a restaurant in three weeks? On the other hand, does it suggest that three years of research are required before the company can decide on a restaurant location? Both timelines seem unreasonable and should raise red flags. Working quickly is very important, but opening a restaurant in three weeks would require cutting so many corners that it would likely result in problems downstream. Conversely, three years of location research sounds like analysis paralysis.

✔ **Has this company used investor money wisely in the past?** If this isn't the first time this company has raised money from debt or equity, ask questions about its financial history. If the business has used debt in the past, did it repay the debt on time? If the company offered equity in the past, does it still have good relationships with those earlier investors, and did the company use the money to grow?

If you can't glean these answers from the information the company itself has provided, use the online crowdfund investing forums to ask very specific questions. If you don't get satisfactory answers from the company in a timely manner, don't invest.

Reviewing available financial information

When you make investments in the public stock markets, you can review quarterly and annual reports to see a company's revenues, expenses, profits, and losses, as well as the typical ratios that investors review prior to making investment decisions. The SEC mandates that public companies provide all this information. After all, by the time a company becomes public, it has well-organized financial functions and long track records of experience to create this data in a timely manner.

Companies seeking crowdfund investments will likely be newly formed or very young companies, many of which are creating externally visible financial reports for the first time. This fact doesn't mean that you should expect any less accuracy or completeness from them. To promote transparency of financial information, the SEC requires companies using crowdfund investments to supply certain information to potential investors (such as prior years' tax returns or reviewed or audited financial statements depending on the amount of money being sought, if the company is already operating). You should take full advantage of any financial information supplied by the company during your decision-making process, and if you don't see the kind of detail that allows you to make a decision you feel confident in, walk away. See Chapter 15 for more detailed suggestions for analyzing the financial data supplied in an investment proposal.

Reading online opinions and questions about a proposal

All pitches on crowdfund investing websites (called *funding portals;* see Chapter 7) offer potential investors the ability to post questions and read comments and answers from other potential and current investors and company representatives. Keep a few things in mind when you enter these conversations:

- ✔ **Perform due diligence before asking.** When asking questions of the company, remember that these are small companies that are very time constrained. Review what has already been asked and answered. That way, if your question has already been answered, you save time for yourself, as well as for the business owner or representative.

- ✔ **Be a constructive part of the dialogue.** Posting random or unrelated comments or making inflammatory statements is not appropriate. Be respectful of everyone in the conversation.

- ✔ **Leverage other investors' experience.** Let others in the online community help you build your investment skills. Try to find a few trusted individuals you can chat with online about the merits and weaknesses of investments you're considering.

Talking with people you trust before committing your money

With all the research and collaboration you do online as you make the best decisions possible about crowdfund investing, don't forget to talk to people in the three-dimensional world as well. Ask for feedback from people you know whose judgment and knowledge you respect when it comes to investing. Although you may find some great information and insight online, we recommend finding one or more people you can talk with on a regular basis about any crowdfund investing you do.

Consider forming an informal discussion group to talk about crowdfund investing opportunities. You and a few trusted friends could meet once or twice a month over coffee to talk about a handful of companies that each of you has found online; you can present and discuss the pros and cons of each. You may be amazed at how hearing different perspectives opens up new lines of thinking or uncovers potential challenges or opportunities for your crowdfund investments. This kind of sounding board is one way to add a layer of protection against fraud. Few investments come with guarantees, but having multiple brains targeted on the same situation usually yields better results for everyone involved.

Staying Alert to Potential Problems

One of the big differences between crowdfund investing and regular stock investing is that if you're part of a crowd, you have actual contact with the business owner. If a crowdfund investment campaign is successful and the owner receives the full funding, he likely will set up a forum for communication with investors. (As we explain in Chapter 3, crowdfund investing works on an all-or-nothing basis; if the campaign doesn't garner full support for the stated financial goal, the business receives nothing.)

If you choose to be part of a company's crowd, we encourage you to take part in whatever communication forum it creates and follow the rules that the business owner sets up with regard to how you communicate with the business. Even if you don't take part in the discussion, be sure to monitor the forum to stay abreast of the company's progress and keep your eyes open for any potential problems that may arise. In this section, we note some specific situations that may raise a red flag.

Requesting communication when things get too quiet

During the crowdfund investment pitch, an entrepreneur should tell her supporters how often she plans to relay information to them. If the entrepreneur goes radio silent for a longer period of time, you can interpret the quiet as a good or bad thing. The silence could mean that the company is very busy making you money. However, it could also mean that problems have emerged. Communication is extremely important in a business investment relationship.

As an investor, you want the entrepreneur spending 98 percent of her time building the business to give you a return. You don't want to overburden the entrepreneur with constant questions about how things are going. However, a certain amount of communication from the entrepreneur is absolutely required. If more than 90 days go by with no communication, you should post a question on the company's online crowdfund investing forum to ask what's going on. Doing so reminds the entrepreneur to update her investors. It also holds her accountable and reminds her that she isn't the only owner of her company anymore.

 If you post a question online and don't receive a response within a few days, send a follow-up e-mail to the entrepreneur. Let her know that you posted a question on the forum, and tell her the day and date of the question. Then repeat the question in the body of the e-mail.

Gauging product or service quality early in the venture

Chances are, if you invest in a company, you know either the entrepreneur or the product or service he's building. If you're familiar with the product or service, you may be able to offer valuable insight to the entrepreneur. Early on in the venture, try to gauge the quality of what's being created (assuming that the entrepreneur shares adequate information with you regarding the product or service). If you see major red flags, be sure to let the entrepreneur know. Some examples of red flags might be

- ✔ Material that won't hold up in the heat or the cold when those are conditions that will be regularly experienced
- ✔ Ingredients that can cause dangerous allergic reactions
- ✔ Products that require Food and Drug Administration (FDA) approval, which will take a long time to secure
- ✔ A lack of planning for how to distribute an e-commerce product that's difficult and expensive to ship
- ✔ A product or service that could run into copyright issues

Keep in mind that the business is the entrepreneur's baby. He is living, eating, and breathing this business day and night. When you reach out with a critique, try very hard not to be offensive. Let the entrepreneur know why you're qualified to give your advice. Also, read through the forums to see if someone else has already brought up your points. Part of your job as an investor is to help the entrepreneur stay focused. If he has ten investors giving him the same advice, he has to spend ten times as much time responding to the posts.

Your ultimate goal in your investment is to make a return on your dollars. Communicate with the business owner in a way that helps him build the best possible product or service that will make you the most amount of money. For specific ideas about how to provide feedback to the entrepreneur and to make yourself a truly valuable investor, be sure to check out Chapter 17.

Responding to (or ignoring) discontented investors

Every member of a crowd isn't going to be happy with everything the entrepreneur does, and at some point you're bound to read complaints on the online forum. (Complaints can range from "Why did you go with that color?"

to "Einstein's theory of relativity totally discounts your hypothesis.") When you do, consider whether the complaints represent a serious concern or whether they can be easily addressed — or even written off as silly and baseless. If a complaint represents a serious concern, start paying closer attention to the forum discussion and the company's communication. If you think the complaints may be easily addressed, consider whether you can help the entrepreneur by offering your own response. (If you can't do so in an educated way, stand back and let the entrepreneur respond.)

Some people like to complain; doing so makes them feel powerful. Responding to baseless complaints gives them undue credence and can distract the entire group. Gauge comments carefully and respond (or don't) accordingly.

Offering advice and support when it's warranted

In a traditional investment situation involving venture capital or private equity (which we explain in Chapter 3), the investors often assign someone to the company to mentor and give advice. In a crowdfund investment situation, every investor has something of value to add to the company. For the investor, the hard part is figuring out what's truly valuable to the entrepreneur and how to present it in an encouraging way. For instance, if you run a shipping storefront and the entrepreneur is planning on shipping a lot of products, offering advice on shipping materials would be very helpful. On the flip side, here are a couple examples that would *not* be helpful:

- ✔ If the entrepreneur is starting a Laundromat and you say, "I love OxiClean. It helps me to get stains out of my clothes. I think you should create a similar product and sell it out of your store." (In this case, the business owner probably isn't a chemist.)

- ✔ If the entrepreneur is starting a beauty salon in Oklahoma and you say, "On my trips to Southeast Asia, I love getting pedicures and they cost only $4. You need to make sure that you're price-competitive with this market." (Exactly zero of this salon's target customers are going to travel to Thailand to save a few bucks on a mani-pedi.)

If you bring knowledge from personal experience that could be useful to the entrepreneur, and if you have the bandwidth in your day to give it, monitor the discussion forums to find the right time and place to offer your advice. Also, note how the entrepreneur responds to advice. Try to shape your golden nuggets in a way that will be welcomed by the entrepreneur and easy for her to implement.

Also, realize that even if you have great knowledge to offer, you don't always have to give it. If an entrepreneur is dealing with a large crowd (dozens or even hundreds of people), too much advice is a major distraction. Carefully pick the times to offer your wisdom.

Preparing an Investment Exit Strategy

When buying stocks or bonds of publically traded companies, you have what's referred to as a *liquid market* for these investments because of the stock markets like NASDAQ and the New York Stock Exchange — places where willing buyers and sellers meet. The market is *liquid* because you likely won't have a tough time selling your holdings. In the private market, securities (either debt or equity) tend to be more *illiquid* (meaning harder to sell) because there may not be an established market for those securities. As a result, when you commit to crowdfund investing, you must think differently about how and when you hope to get your money back and/or see a return on your investments.

In this section, we encourage you to spend time early on (ideally, before you invest) considering the best way for you to exit your investments. (This topic receives a lot more attention in Chapter 18.)

Staying put for at least a year

One of the most important things to know about crowdfund investment is that you must hold such an equity investment for at least 12 months from the time of purchase. By law, the equity investment is illiquid for the first 12 months. (And in almost all cases, debt-based crowdfund investments will have repayment terms that last more than one year.) This one-year hold period is an important part of the JOBS Act because it reduces the chances of *pump-and-dump schemes,* which use hype and misinformation to pump up a private company's stock price (above its true value) so the instigators of the scheme can then dump their shares and receive large profits (to the detriment of other investors). This provision disallows anything that looks like day trading and promotes a buy-and-hold investment philosophy.

Even after the 12-month holding period is over, you may find selling your shares or your debt to be a challenge. The SEC sets rules about how your sale can take place and what kinds of private-shares stock markets can be used for this purpose. We believe that great new innovations will take place to benefit private companies and crowdfund investors who require secondary markets for such sales. These secondary markets already exist for other shares of commonly known, hyper-growth private companies (like Twitter or Socialcam), which is good news. What we still need to find out is how shares of crowdfund-investing companies will trade on these exchanges.

Looking for signs that it's time to jump ship

After your 12-month holding period has expired, you'll be wise to watch for signs that indicate whether it's time to sell your crowdfund securities or whether the company is growing as expected. The biggest sign of trouble would be if the entrepreneur hasn't met any of the stated benchmarks for the previous 12 months and is still a long way from making a return on your dollar. If that's the case, you have to decide if it's best for you to sell your shares, recover whatever you can, and move on, or if you'd be better off staying put. The type and amount of communication that you've received from the entrepreneur is important as well. If he's a long way from reaching his goals but he's given you solid reasons why all throughout the 12-month period, it may be wise to stick around a little longer.

Keep in mind that turning a profit almost always takes longer than originally planned; unexpected costs and problems almost always arise. How the entrepreneur deals with these unexpected situations may be the most important indicator of how you should act. If you've been constantly disappointed with the entrepreneur for 12 months, the time to jump ship is now. If the entrepreneur has communicated effectively with investors, explained the unexpected issues and how they're being resolved, and done some reforecasting so you know when profits may be arriving, you may have enough faith in him to stick with the investment.

Achieving the greatest profits from a success story

To really benefit from a crowdfund investment, you need to get in and stay in. You won't make a quick buck with this type of investment, but if you keep your eyes on the long-term prize and ride the waves of volatility, you may reap some major rewards. For example, a major individual investor or a larger business may purchase the company, the company may take its stock public, or you may simply collect very healthy dividends for years to come. Of course, not every investment you make will carry the "major rewards" potential. After a year or more of being involved as an investor, you'll have a strong sense of which investments are poised for greatness and which are going to stink up your portfolio.

Your best bet when it comes to achieving the greatest long-term profits is to consider yourself part of the business. Consider your cash investment as only one part; the other part is the active role you play in marketing the business, the idea, and the entrepreneur. Your marketing efforts help build value in the business that the business may not otherwise achieve. When it eventually comes time for you to exit, a buyer (of the company's stock or of the entire company) will look at the strategic value this purchase brings. For example, if you and the other investors can show an acquirer where the company's strategic value exists outside of its profit and loss, your payoff will increase.

Part II
Planning Your Crowdfund Investing Campaign

The 5th Wave   By Rich Tennant

"Here's my pitch for investors in our jazz club. I think we should just freestyle our financial needs, improvise ideas for growth, and make up our long-range goals as we go along."

In this part . . .

The chapters in this part were written with the entrepreneur and small business owner in mind. They provide the foundational information required to begin developing a crowdfund investing campaign.

Before you can request business funding of any kind, of course, you have to craft a sound business plan and define your financial needs. Chapter 5 is a quick overview of how to accomplish these crucial first steps.

With a business plan in hand, you can then turn your attention to some tasks specific to crowdfund investing: envisioning how large your crowd needs to be and what types of people may populate it (Chapter 6) and selecting an online funding platform to host your campaign (Chapter 7). Do you have a great social network? Well, if not, Chapter 8 provides you with expert advice on how to build and maintain one.

Chapter 5

Defining Your Goals and Financial Needs

*W*hat's the difference between writing a full business plan and doing a crowdfund investment offering? If you're serious about starting a business, the answer is nothing. When putting together a crowdfund investment offering, in essence, you're whittling down your business idea to an executive summary. The executive summary traditionally gets people either to open the door to the rest of your idea or to toss it in the trash. (If you've ever tried to raise venture capital — a topic we cover in Chapter 3 — you realize that your idea hits the trash can about 97.5 percent of the time.)

The key to making people want to learn more about your idea is to be salient and concise in your executive summary. You need to get across why you need to raise money, what problem you solve, how your problem makes money, how you'll use the money, and why you're the right person to do the job. You must define your goals and financial needs, and we show you how in this chapter. If you can do this step well, and potential investors open the door just a crack, then you can get to work convincing your crowd to invest in you (a process we discuss in Chapter 9).

The topics covered in this chapter largely overlap with what you would do to construct a traditional business plan. This foundational info is just as crucial to a business funded via crowdfund investing as a business funded via any other means; you'll never raise even $1 if you fail to understand the principles in this chapter. We cover the steps in broad strokes here, and you can follow up with more detailed resources if needed (such as *Business Plans For Dummies,* 2nd Edition, by Paul Tiffany, PhD, and Steven D. Peterson, PhD [Wiley]).

The first half of this chapter focuses on subjects that are relevant for startup businesses. If you're already running a small business — you know your target market and have a solid organizational model in place — you may find the financial discussions in the second half of the chapter most useful (starting with "Crunching Numbers: Figuring Out How Much Money You Need").

Conducting Market Research

So, you've got an idea to start an organic farm in your community to sell vegetables to your local restaurants and spur the farm-to-table movement. What's next? *Don't* go out and start planting! First, find out if this idea is a smart one. In this section, we show you how.

Asking key questions

To determine if you've got a solid business idea, you need to understand the market dynamics. Start by asking questions like these:

- Why is an organic farm better than what's currently available?
- Do people in my community care about organic foods?
- How much do they currently pay for produce, and how price sensitive are they?
- Can I make a living off of being an organic farmer?

Essentially, you're asking the *who, what, when, where, how,* and *why* of starting a business. You could try to answer these questions yourself, but that won't do you much good. Instead, you need to conduct research by asking people who could someday be your customers. For the organic farmer, this means walking in the doors of your local restaurants (your potential customers) and asking the owners, "Do you buy organic produce? Do you have problems with supply? Would you prefer to source it locally? How much do you currently pay for potatoes? Would you buy from a local farmer who's passionate about farming organically?"

You have to spill the beans (bad pun, sorry) and tell people about your idea. Then — and this is critical — you must listen to their answers! If you hear over and over that they don't care about what you're proposing, you should think twice about starting this particular business. You don't need to build something that no one wants. On the other hand, you may hear responses like, "I'm fine with my potatoes, but what I'd really like to source locally are tomatoes and cheese." In this case, you may want to consider altering your plan, expanding your questions, and approaching the next person this way: "Which of the following items are most important to you when it comes to sourcing locally: potatoes, tomatoes, or cheese?"

The *who, what, when, where, how,* and *why* of a business idea can be phrased this way:

- ✔ Who is your target market?
- ✔ What is the problem you're solving?
- ✔ When do you want to start?
- ✔ Where do you want to do it?
- ✔ How are you going to fund it?
- ✔ Why are you the right person to solve the problem?

Studying the competitive landscape online

Before you use the Internet to raise capital for your idea, use it to conduct a little competitive analysis. Research similar businesses — such as local organic farms, to continue our example — online. Check out their websites. See what kinds of products (in this case, produce) they offer. Ideally, you want to find pricing information, too, but you may need to call these businesses directly to try to get it.

Also, check out the websites of similar businesses in other regions so you can find out how various entities approach their mission. For our farmer, the goal is to figure out how other farmers grow their vegetables. Do they operate year-round? How many people do they employ? What's their motto?

Check to see if an appropriate industry organization (an organic farmers association, in this case) exists. If so, see if its website has any useful information on starting a business. Google expressions like "top mistakes organic farmers make." Keep track of all this information in a computer file, along with links to where you found the information.

Clearly, a wealth of information about every type of business imaginable is available to you on the Internet. This information can clarify your business opportunity and save you from wasting a lot of time and other people's money later on. Do the research you need to make sure you understand the market. Later, when potential investors ask you *why* questions (and trust us, they're going to ask), you'll have instant answers thanks to this research, which will make you look smart and boost investors' trust in you.

Socializing your idea

After you do some research on the market opportunity and adjust your plans accordingly, you want to socialize the idea with some of the people you'll later be asking to become your investors. In Chapter 6, we explain who potential members of your crowd may be. For the moment, you want to keep it simple and keep your idea close to home. Begin with the people closest to you and tell them why you want to start this business. Explain what you learned in your research. Ask them for their thoughts.

Find out whether these people might consider helping to fund your dream if you ran a crowdfund investing campaign. If they seem at all interested, be prepared to explain how they might benefit. Toss out a couple scenarios for crowdfund investments to get their feedback. (For example, you want to raise $100,000 and you'll sell 20 percent equity in the business with the goal of selling to a larger regional organic farm in five years. Or you want to raise $100,000 of debt from the crowd, and you'll pay 8 percent interest on it over five years.) Pay close attention to how they respond to these possibilities. If someone is really turned off by one investment opportunity and strongly favors another, make a mental note. You want to find out what your best financing options may be, in addition to whether this business idea as a whole has legs.

Whenever you share your business ideas, check your ego at the door. There's nothing more upsetting than someone telling you that your baby is a bad idea, but get ready to hear that over and over. Try not to get discouraged because not everyone is your potential customer, and not everyone understands the market you've researched. Don't be defensive; listen carefully to the critiques as well as the kudos, and glean what you can from them.

Getting Specific about the Problems You Can Solve

If you're starting a business, you're seeking to solve some sort of problem. Either the solution doesn't exist yet, or you believe you can solve it better than the current options on the market. Dig deep, and get specific about what your business will offer.

To raise money via crowdfund investing, you need to get serious in your planning. Potential investors will dig deep into your plan, pick it apart, and try to find holes. They'll second-guess every claim you make, so make sure your claims are well founded. In this section, we start you on the right path.

Increasing product or service quality

No matter how good any product or service is, it can always be done better. Think of the razor wars. (You *did* realize this war was going on, right?) First, we had the single blade, and then came the double blade. Now we've got nothing less than a rotating quadruple blade.

If your business angle is to do something better than your competitors (as opposed to creating something new), you need to show your investors why you're qualified to do it better. Spend the time to lay out in your plan the faults of your future competitors. Spell out their weaknesses point by point, and show how you can do things better. Make a simple chart like the one shown in Table 5-1, and rank each quality on a scale of 1 to 5. At the bottom, average the sum of the totals for each company.

Table 5-1	Competitive Analysis Chart		
Business Quality	*Company 1*	*Company 2*	*Us*
Product quality	2	5	5
Service quality	3	4	5
On-time delivery	4	1	5
Knowledge	2	2	5
Reputation	2	4	1
Customer focus	2	4	3
Customer service	2	4	5
Responsiveness	3	4	5
Average	**2.5**	**3.5**	**4.3**

This exercise helps you as well. You can't expect perfection with your own product or service, no matter how hard you try. By spelling out each crucial business quality, you can determine which ones you can improve the most and which ones are likely to return the most money to your pocket.

Developing new products or services

One of the greatest business models involves creating a brand-new product or service. In this case, you're addressing a problem with no existing solution. The key to raising money in this situation is proving three things to your investors:

✔ The problem truly does exist.

✔ The problem is big enough that it needs a solution.

✔ You have the solution your customers will want.

Spend time upfront detailing the problem and giving solid examples of the issues it creates. Then launch into a detailed description of your solution. For instance, no one likes getting an oil change every 3,000 miles. In fact, most people wait much longer to do so because they don't want to take the time out of their busy schedules to go to the mechanic. This is a problem that everyone can understand. For some new cars, this oil change problem has been addressed, but there is still no good solution for the majority of cars on the road today. If you were able to develop a substance to add to your car that made oil changes a thing of the past, you'd be a millionaire a hundred times over. (No one has come up with this solution yet. Start thinking!)

After you show your investors what the problem is, make sure that your solution is an actual solution. You need hard data proving that you're able to do something no one before you has been able to do. That data may center on you (your education, experience, and unique skills), a product prototype, market research that conclusively illustrates demand for this new product or service, or anything else that can persuade the investor to trust you. The closer you can get to demonstrating the actual solution (a prototype or the full solution is best), the more impressed your potential investors will be.

Lowering consumer costs

When Michael Dell set out to start a computer company, he saw a problem: The logistics of existing computer companies drove costs too high, and he believed he could deliver a product of similar quality with lower costs by improving the logistics of the industry. He was wildly successful.

Traditionally, however, starting a company based primarily on lowering costs of existing products is very dangerous. As a startup, you'll be much more sensitive to variations in price than your established competitors. They could very easily slash their costs (even to the point of incurring loss) to put you out of business before you get up and running.

If you're going to make lowering customer costs one of your business cornerstones, you'd better have a sound plan in place for how to do so. Do you have an in with a low-cost supplier? Have you developed a technology that allows you to produce the product much less expensively? You need something in your arsenal stronger than your own belief that you can deliver a product to your customers at a lower price than your competitors.

Attracting an untapped segment of the market

There are two ways to get business: attracting new customers and turning existing customers into more avid users of your product or service. If you've found an untapped segment of the market for your business, and if you know how to attract these potential customers, you stand to make a lot of money. From your potential investors' point of view, the key is defining exactly how you're going to accomplish what no one else before you has been able to do. Potential investors want details, facts, and data — not wishes and dreams. Make sure you have solid market research showing that you can do what you plan.

Identifying Your Target Market

The next step in your business planning process is to get specific about your target market. Defining who your customers will be is critical.

Have you ever heard the phrase "It's impossible to boil the ocean"? It's a great metaphor for why finding and focusing on your target market is important. When you start a business, the funds available to use for marketing your company to drive sales are limited (always, no matter how much you raise through crowdfund investing or any other means). You never have an infinite pool of dollars. Therefore, you cannot market your business to every person everywhere.

Say that you have $75,000 for marketing your new organic farm to your community. How will you spend it? You could spend your entire budget on shotgun-style direct mail advertising to everyone in the state or city you're located in . . . and likely you won't find your market and your business will fail.

Many great books are available that focus on finding your target market (you may want to check out *Small Business Marketing For Dummies,* 2nd Edition, by Barbara Findlay Schenck [Wiley]). For our purposes here, we want to make a couple quick points about how to find your target market and use it to build your business. You can't boil the ocean, but you can take a gallon of water from the ocean and boil it quite effectively. Here's how:

> ✔ **Determine whose pain you can ease.** Human beings buy things either to stop pain they're experiencing now or to reduce the chances of pain they'll experience in the future. Think about that for a moment to see if it rings true in your own life. You can wrap lots of other reasons around a decision to buy a product or service, but if you really dig, it comes down to stopping current or future pain. Why do you buy food? To stop current or future hunger pangs (or boredom or stress . . . that's a topic

for another book). Purchasing a car, purchasing a plane ticket versus a train ticket, purchasing clothing, going to see a movie, visiting the doctor, buying organic versus conventional foods . . . it all comes back to stopping pain.

Your target market is the potential customer who has the greatest need for your product — the person whose pain you have the best chance of easing. That person (often called a *marketing persona*) is most likely to spend money immediately to get what you're offering.

Going back to our organic farm example, maybe after conducting market research, you determine that the two target marketing personas to focus on are small, individually owned restaurants that support local/sustainable produce and moms who shop in the farmers' markets in your area because they're willing to spend more money and time to use organic products. Focusing on these personas will give you the greatest chance for success so you can build your core customer.

✔ **Let your core customers spread the word.** Humans are herd creatures. Your passionate core customers will market for you and build your business. Have you ever used an online review site, like Yelp? These sites are one tool that core customers (or detractors) use to spread the word. You can turn your target market customers into your greatest marketing assets by delivering exactly what they need and expect.

When you know who your target market is, you can analyze how large that market is. Are there enough restaurants and moms focused on organic food in your selected geography to build a profitable business? How many customers buying how much per week (or month or year) do you need? These numbers are crucial in determining your financial needs, including how much you need in crowdfund investments. (See the upcoming section "Crunching Numbers: Figuring Out How Much Money You Need.")

Noting the Phase Your Business Is In

Before you seek crowdfund investing or any other financial support, you must carefully consider what stage of development your business is in. Your business phase significantly alters how much money you need to raise and how you'll spend it. At each stage of development, you have different challenges to overcome and opportunities to take advantage of.

As you read this section, be honest with yourself in your assessment of where you are. At the same time, try to identify a reasonable next milestone that you can reach with the money you're trying to raise. All investors want to know what their capital will be used for and what it will achieve. Crowdfund investors, for example, will want to know that you're using their money to reach a destination — not as a bridge to nowhere. Always keeping in mind the stage your business is in helps you stay on track with what you can achieve and how much capital you need to get there.

Keep in mind that our focus in this section is squarely on startups. If you're already running a small business, you still need to consider how to describe your phase to potential crowdfund investors and how to spell out your expansion goals. You're able to approach the investor with hard data about your past successes and current operations, which builds trust quickly. Your real challenge is keeping your growth expectations realistic and explaining them clearly to people who don't know anything about your business.

Starting with a new idea

You've just had a great conversation at Starbucks with a close friend about organic produce, and now the two of you have decided to go into business together. You envision starting in your backyards and then moving to a community garden and finally out to the burbs. You're in the "new idea" phase.

Can you start applying for loans and looking for investors as soon as you leave Starbucks? Uh, no. When your idea is this fresh, you need to take some time to shape it and figure out its strengths and weaknesses. You also need to work out some of the details about how this idea can come to fruition. For example, think about the types of activities you'll need to conduct to make the idea become reality (such as preparing your backyard for planting). Then list the equipment required (rake, hoe, seeds, water, soil) and the costs of these activities and items. With these basics in hand, get to work constructing a full business plan; doing so not only forces you to think through everything it will take to launch your business but also shows potential investors that you're serious about this idea.

Not sure how to write a business plan? You're in luck: A whole world of resources is available to you. You can pay for an online program such as Business Plan Pro (www.businessplanpro.com) or Funding Roadmap (www.fundingroadmap.com), which walks you through a series of simple questions and then offers a business plan outline appropriate for your idea. Or you can look for guidance from any number of books, including *Business Plans For Dummies,* 2nd Edition, by Paul Tiffany, PhD, and Steven D. Peterson, PhD (Wiley). You can also check out the website of the Small Business Administration (www.sba.gov), which is an excellent resource for preparing a business plan.

With your idea fully baked, you'll be ready to look for funding to take you to the next phase: creating your proof of concept.

Preparing a proof of concept

You may have the world's coolest idea, but until you try it out in the real world, you don't know for certain what will happen. *Proof of concept* is the business phase in which you bring your idea into reality on a small scale so you can prove to potential investors that it can work. You test it on a few potential customers and learn where your assumptions were right and where they were wrong. Doing so allows you to tweak (or even pivot) your plans so they're on target for success. (In some cases, you learn that the idea is not what you thought it was going to be, and you go back to square one on a new idea.) For example, our friend Alix had an idea to start a mac-and-cheese food truck. To prepare her proof of concept, she went into the kitchen to make her recipes and test them on her friends to find out which ones were the best.

Don't assume that this phase is a breeze. Very few ideas are perfect right out of the gate, and you don't want to underestimate the time and money you'll need to get your proof of concept right. Most of the time, entrepreneurs discover that part (or even all) of their plans are wrong, and they must pivot to a new plan. Try to anticipate the time and capital that would be required to pivot your plan so that you can more accurately state your needs when seeking investors' support for this phase.

After you've successfully proven your concept, your new business is ready to meet your target market.

Getting ready to grow

At this stage, you know what works in the real world, and you're ready to start operations for real. If you're the organic farmer, you've proven that you can grow a mean green pepper in your backyard, and you're ready to grow a few hundred (or thousand) pepper plants. If you're the mac-and-cheese whiz, you're ready to share your creations with taste buds outside your own kitchen.

You should budget for how you scale your operations to rapidly and effectively grow to take full advantage of your target market (your core customers). Think carefully about how to do this. If you want to raise capital to grow, and your plan is to use the money specifically for marketing, then prior to launching a campaign you need to test out on a small scale the marketing campaign you want to launch and see the impact it has financially. Use the data from your tests to corroborate your story.

Crunching Numbers: Figuring Out How Much Money You Need

So, you know you want to start or grow your business, and you know you don't have enough money. Now comes the hard part: figuring out exactly how much you need and for what. We promise you, no matter what number you come up with during this exercise, it won't be enough. There are *always* unexpected costs and expenses when starting a business. Some of them can be avoided, and some can't. One of your authors, Zak, runs a successful Main Street business called Pure Mountain Olive Oil. It's a chain of olive oil and balsamic vinegar tasting emporiums in the Northeast. With every new shop Zak opens, it gets easier to estimate the needed expenses, but costs always pop up that he hoped he could avoid.

The hardest time in any business is between when you decide to start the business and when you start making revenue. When you seriously decide to start your own business, money starts flowing out of your pocket. Until you can reverse the cash flow and start generating revenue, you need to be extremely careful about what you spend money on. (Actually, you *always* need to be careful how you're spending your money, but that's especially true when you're in the pre-revenue stage.)

In this section, we try to ease the pain of the pre-revenue stage just a bit by helping you predict your most likely expenses, determine how much funding you need to seek, and estimate how long your initial funding will last. How long will your pre-revenue stage last? That depends entirely on the specifics of your business, including your industry, your product or service, and the phase you're currently in. Only some serious research can help you estimate your answer.

Anticipating how funds will be used

You have your business idea and perhaps a vague concept of how much money you need to get things up and going. Getting specific about how you'll use money can help you pin down the total number of dollars you're going to need to get off the ground. Anticipating how funds will be used is something you can't take lightly. To do this step effectively, you need to understand your industry well.

Talk to as many people as possible who have similar businesses to find out their costs. Try to find businesses as similar to yours as possible, but ones that you won't be in direct competition with. Reach out to these companies' managers and ask them to shed some light on the types of costs you're in for. If you don't have connections with any of these companies, just start smiling and dialing and see if you can find someone who will give you 20 minutes to answer some questions. You'll be surprised by the response; people like being helpful. And the worst thing someone can tell you is no. In the best-case scenario, you could meet a potential mentor to help you with your business. As with all things, try to phrase your questions or pitch in a way that shows the benefit to the person you're talking to ("If I can get some solid advice at this stage, I'll do a better job of bringing great quality, organic local produce to our community").

Business expenses

This expense category includes labor, product and/or service costs, consultant fees, rent, utilities, and other general and administrative costs. When you're figuring out your business expenses, you need to think things through clearly. For instance, if you want to pay a manager $50,000 in yearly salary, it's going to cost you a lot more than $50,000. Here are some labor-related questions you need to answer in order to get as close to this true cost as possible:

✔ Are you going to use a payroll company? If so, how much does it charge?

✔ How much is workers' compensation per employee in your state and industry?

✔ How much does disability insurance cost?

✔ What other benefits will you offer? Health insurance? If so, how much will you offer: the full premium, 50 percent of the premium, or some other percentage? What company will you use for health insurance? How much does that company charge to manage your plan?

You'll be surprised how fast these hidden costs add up. Many businesses get discouraged and take shortcuts (paying people under the table) to save money. If you're tempted to do so, take a step back. Cutting corners this way will be disastrous to your business. It sets a horrible precedent and will come back to bite you. Follow the laws of the land, pay what you need to pay, or don't start your business at all!

Of course, labor isn't the only business expense to consider carefully. Each of the items we list at the start of the section deserves scrutiny. For example, if you're opening a Main Street business, you must ask a lawyer to closely review your lease to make sure you aren't being hit with hidden costs. Be aware that some leases require you to have insurance, and some require you to pay for utilities. (Not sure what to expect in utility costs? You can find out what the previous tenant was paying — and then add 10 percent to be safe.)

If you have a lawyer in your network who can help you with a task like reviewing a real estate lease, that's great. If not, you need to budget for an attorney's fee as well. Call three real estate attorneys (three is a good number when getting quotes of any kind) and ask them how much they would charge to review your lease. Some lawyers charge by the hour (which can add up incredibly fast!), and some charge by the job. For a task like this, it's best to find someone who will quote you for the job.

With so many variables at play in the category of business expenses, how can you ever be certain that you're budgeting accurately? You can't. But you can try to get close and then prepare for more. For example, when Zak figures out labor expenses for a new Pure Mountain Olive Oil location, he adds in 10 percent extra to cover unexpected costs that pop up. He also adds about 20 percent to other budgeted cash expenses when opening a new location. If things go well, he has a couple percentage points left over that give him a little extra wiggle room to get sales up and running.

Research costs

You can never, ever do enough research before opening your business. Depending on your industry and your level of experience in it, research costs will vary greatly. You want to do as much industry research yourself as possible. But you have a limited number of hours in the day and an endless list of things calling for your attention. Figure out what needs to be figured out, and delegate research tasks if you must. If you need to outsource some research work, budget accordingly and don't skimp. Quality upfront research can be the difference between success and failure.

Marketing and advertising costs

In Zak's experience, the day that local marketers and advertisers find out his company is opening a new location in their region, the incessant sales calls begin. Newspapers, the chamber of commerce, radio stations, local blogs, hotels that print guest books . . . the list of solicitors goes on and on. Some of these opportunities sound great and are hard to pass up. But if you go into a sales meeting with an ad rep without a solid understanding of how much you can spend, you'll feel like you're in a wind tunnel. Everything will sound great, but you'll have no idea what you can afford.

Before you can figure out your marketing and advertising budget, you need to figure out *how* you want to market your product. How do you want to get in front of your customers? Do you want to be a word-of-mouth business, or do you want to get in front of every customer in your area? When you have these answers, you should set aside a monthly budget and *stick to it.* There will always be more opportunities for you to spend money on advertising than there is money in your budget. Spend your money smartly, place your ad dollars correctly, and don't overspend.

Legal fees

Did you know that prior to the legalization of crowdfund investing in 2012, it would have cost you easily $15,000 in legal fees to sell stock in your business to raise cash? So, if you went out and raised $20,000 by selling stocks, you'd be left with only $5,000 to start your business. Luckily, those initial legal fees have now been spread out among all offerings because we've streamlined the process of raising capital by narrowing the scope and using standard documents. However, that doesn't mean you won't need a lawyer.

Depending on the industry you enter and/or how sensitive your information is, you may need to hire lawyers immediately for things outside of raising capital. For instance, if you're building that organic farm, you may need a lawyer who can make sure you're following all the Food and Drug Administration rules surrounding farming produce. Or if you have some special intellectual property and you don't want to give out your secret sauce, you'll very likely (in some cases, even prior to funding) hire an intellectual property lawyer to do some patent, copyright, and trademark work for you.

The only way to figure out your legal costs is to research lawyers who focus on the work you need done. Keep in mind that lawyers outside of big cities can be just as good as lawyers within those cities — for a fraction of the cost. Don't discount your local lawyer; just make sure she has the experience you need.

If you skip calculating legal expenses for your business, you'll end up looking silly. Investors want to know that you're budgeting for lawyers in case you ever need them. Leaving lawyers out of the equation makes you look like you don't understand the important role they play in business and in protecting your investors' assets.

Bookkeeping, accounting, and auditing fees

If you seek crowdfund investments, working with an accountant is pretty much mandated by the JOBS Act. If you're doing an offering under $100,000, you're off the hook at first. But a year after your company launches, you have to file your financials with both the Securities and Exchange Commission (SEC) and the Internal Revenue Service (IRS). Unless you have a degree in accounting and/or feel comfortable using accounting programs like QuickBooks (http://quickbooks.intuit.com) or Sage 50 (http://na.sage.com/sage-50-accounting-us), you should consider first hiring a part-time bookkeeper and then an accountant.

Bookkeeping

At the very beginning stages of your business (if you aren't going to do all the accounting yourself), a bookkeeper can keep track of all your expenses.

As soon as you get funding, buy an accordion folder; label the tabs by month; and whenever you buy anything business related, note what you bought on the receipt and stuff it in the folder. You'll be able to give this folder to your bookkeeper and make his life easier.

To find a bookkeeper, you can search craigslist (www.craigslist.org), online job boards like Monster (www.monster.com), or even your local newspaper. Banks are also great references for bookkeepers. To be on the safe side, budget $10 to $20 per hour for a bookkeeper depending on where you're operating. If you don't budget anything for bookkeeping, be prepared to tell your investors that you plan on doing the bookkeeping and you have the knowledge or experience to do it.

Accounting and auditing

Unless you or your bookkeeper plans to prepare your company's taxes, you should budget to hire a tax accountant and get quotes for how much the preparation will cost. (If you're going to do it yourself, budget for the cost of tax software.)

As we note earlier in this section, anyone raising funds via crowdfund investing must submit financial reports to the SEC and the IRS. An accountant can be quite valuable in ensuring the accuracy of these reports. And if you raise more than $500,000 via crowdfund investing, you need audited financials.

An auditor goes through the records in your accounting program and tests them for accuracy. You have to match up what's in the system with documentation outside the system. If you want to raise more than $500,000 in crowdfund investments, you actually have to have an audit done before you seek financing so you should have a decent idea of what auditing costs. If you haven't had an audit done before, be aware that audit costs increase as the size of your business increases. If you're a startup, audits can start around $10,000 (depending on where you're operating) and go up dramatically from there.

Compliance costs

To be compliant with local and industry regulations, you have to be prepared to spend some money. You may need a business license or a permit to do what you want; a lawyer or trade association can help you figure out what's required. Make note of each cost on a spreadsheet. You'll most likely sum them up in one line on the financials you present to potential investors, but you look smarter to your investors when you can give the breakdown to someone who asks, "What's this expense related to compliance?"

Fees to participate in crowdfund investing

You should also budget for costs related to doing a crowdfund investment offering. These costs include a *success fee* that goes to the funding portal website (see Chapter 7) that hosts your funding pitch, handles the backend, and transfers the money (from investors to you) and respective shares (from you to investors). This fee should be easily found in a funding portal's terms and conditions. With guidance from us in Chapter 7, take a close look at the platforms where you may list your pitch and compare their fees and what you get for the cost.

As we note in Chapter 6, you may also need to hire a community manager to guide you through the crowdfund investing process. If you do, you need to budget for this person's time.

Also, you need to keep in touch with your investors post-funding (as we explain in Chapter 12). If your funding portal doesn't feature a communication tool that you can use after you've raised your money, you need to find such a tool and budget for it. Fees for these tools vary based on the size of your business and the number of investors.

You can use free tools such as Google Groups (`http://groups.google.com`) or investor relation tools that are part of broker-dealers like Gate Impact (`www.gateimpact.com`). Another option is to visit sites like SeedInvest (`www.seedinvest.com`), crowdfunder (`www.crowdfunder.com`), or Wefunder (`www.wefunder.com`) to learn more about their fees and interact with others who are researching services to understand the cost benefit. The lowest fees may or may not be the best option for you. Make sure you compare the services provided so you understand what services are available and at what cost, so you can make those cost-benefit decisions, based on good information.

Predicting how long the money will last

Money never seems to last as long as you expect. The game of business is to never run out of cash. When you spell out all the expenses you anticipate incurring to start your business, you have to figure out when (month by month) you'll likely incur each of them. Take a look at all those expenses and your available funding, and calculate when your cash is going to run out. Before that date, you'd better be able to start earning cash from your business activity.

The report in which you calculate your cash balance is called the *statement of cash flows*. Some free tools can help you generate this report. If you have Microsoft Excel, open it up and choose File⇨New from Template. In the search feature that pops up, enter "Cash Flow." You should find a template that allows you to enter your beginning cash, your expenses by month (paid in cash), and your cash balance at the end of the month. You can also find these templates on Google.

Figure 5-1 shows an example of what a statement of cash flows for a given month may look like. It starts with the money that you raised less the costs of raising the money. Then you enter your anticipated expenses for the first month of business (including recurring expenses, such as salaries, and occasional expenses that will likely hit in that month). You can generate this report for each month, summing up the total expenses and subtracting them from the cash on hand at the beginning of the month.

	Beginning	January 2014
Cash summary		
Cash on hand (beginning of month)	$55,000	$55,000
Cash available (on hand and receipts, before cash out)		
Cash position (end of month)	$51,150	$47,840
Cash receipts		
Cash sales		
Collections from CR accounts		
Loan/other cash		
Total cash receipts		
Cash paid out		
Purchases (specify)		$500
Gross wages (exact withdrawal)		$3,000
Supplies (office and operations)		$250
Repairs and maintenance		
Advertising		$500
Rent		$1,250
Utilities		$285
Crowdfund investing platform fees	$3,850	$200
Legal and accounting		$400
Trade/compliance (aggregate figure)		$75
Other startup costs		$400
Reserve and/or escrow		$300
TOTAL CASH PAID OUT	**$3,850**	**$7,160**

Figure 5-1:
A sample statement of cash flows for the first month of business.

Getting Real about Whether Crowdfund Investing Is Right for Your Business

Regardless of what stage your business is in, you need to target your fundraising efforts to sources that are the best fit. Think about what your business is offering from a product, service, and investment perspective. Think about where you are now and what type of financing option would have the most appeal to the type of investors you're seeking.

Also, as you think about your growth trajectory, consider how many rounds of funding you think you'll need over the next few years to reach your growth goals. Consider which sources make the most sense for repeat financing and which are most likely one-time sources of support only. Check out Chapter 3 for an overview of the primary funding sources available to businesses.

In this section, we don't cover bank loans, venture capital, and other traditional sources of business financing. Instead, we focus on helping you determine whether crowdfund investing (or donation-based crowdfunding) is realistic for your business.

Opting for crowdfund investment

Throughout this book, we spell out how crowdfund investment works and how it differs from other funding sources. We feel it's essential to note here that crowdfund investment, by law, is all-or-nothing fundraising. This means that if you set your fundraising goal at $100,000 and you raise $99,800, you don't get a dime. You must set a realistic goal in order to succeed, and you must be willing to work hard on your pitch (a topic we cover in Chapter 9) and your follow-up communication with potential investors.

What tells you whether crowdfund investment makes sense for your business? For starters, these things must be true:

- You're comfortable in the social media world and have existing social networks via Facebook, Twitter, LinkedIn, or other sites.

- You're looking to raise $1 million or less from this source. See Chapter 3 for an overview of this and other rules that apply to crowdfund investing.

- You have an idea that you can clearly communicate to your friends, family members, and other potential supporters.

✔ Your idea solves a problem and, therefore, has a target market that you can define in your pitch.

✔ You're willing to be transparent with potential investors about who you are, why you're passionate about this idea, and why you know you can succeed. (In Chapter 6, we discuss the necessity of achieving this kind of transparency.)

If you can say with confidence that all these things are true for you, then crowdfund investing may prove to be a vital resource for your company. If that's the case, you need to determine early on whether you prefer to raise money via crowdfund investing by taking on debt or by selling equity.

Taking on debt

If you borrow money to buy a new car, you sign a piece of paper that says you'll pay back that loan over a certain number of years at a specific interest rate. You're signing a personal loan or note — a *debt instrument.* You're agreeing to make payments every month on your obligation until that loan is paid off.

Businesses can borrow money, too, by taking on debt. As with personal loans, it's critically important that your business has money to pay its loan obligation each month. Hence, debt isn't something that startups or early-stage businesses use often because they generally haven't started to generate revenue and don't have money to pay their loan. However, if you do have a steady flow of cash, and if borrowing some money will allow you to expand or grow faster (hence, leading to more income), borrowing money from investors may be the right thing for you. Doing so not only allows you to use other people's money to grow but keeps you in control. (In the next section, we talk about how equity gives up bits of control every time you issue it.)

Because a debt-based crowdfund investment allows you to raise funds without giving up equity in your business, certain types of businesses (such as Main Street retail shops and restaurants) may prefer to offer debt instead of equity. That's because they are quick to generate cash but most likely won't have a splashy initial public offering (IPO).

Businesses can deduct the interest they pay on their business loans. The interest is deducted from the sales they make when calculating their profits. (That's a big plus to borrowing money.)

If your business borrows money from crowdfund investors, you may be on the hook for a set amount of interest and principal each month, or you may offer *revenue-based financing.* In the revenue-based financing model, you agree to pay investors a percent of your revenue each month for a set period of time (for example, five years). A restaurant or a dry cleaner may prefer revenue-based financing because it allows them to pay less during months when sales are slower. (When business is great, the payback bumps up.)

Either way, the repercussions of not being able to pay off debt can be severe, so you absolutely don't want to borrow more than you can afford to repay.

Offering equity participation

If you have potential investors who want (and will likely demand) a share in your business, and if you're willing to exchange equity in your business in order to grow it, this method of crowdfund investment can be a great way to go. Keep in mind that selling equity means taking on long-term partners. Bringing on investors is a bit like jumping into bed with someone, so make sure you're ready to get intimate before you decide to sell equity. You don't want to wake up and regret the decision! We discuss the risks associated with offering equity participation in Chapter 3.

Equity can come in many different forms like common stock, preferred stock, warrants, and options. These topics are outside the scope of this book, but we encourage you to become familiar with them with help from a lawyer, financial advisor, and accountant so you can understand their differences before making any decisions.

Equity comes with certain rights and benefits for the investors; these benefits differ depending on the type of equity offered, but certainly a biggie is that the investors benefit from an increase in company value. The benefit of equity to a business is that it doesn't have to be paid back to investors immediately.

The biggest disadvantage for a business that offers equity is this: As owners, the investors have a say in the business and can vote on major business decisions. We strongly encourage you never to hand investors more than 50 percent ownership of your company for this reason. On the flip side, giving them some skin in the game will make investors more likely to become evangelists for your business.

Considering crowdfunding

At the risk of muddying the waters, we should mention that crowdfunding — which is donation-based (instead of debt- or equity-based) — may also be worth considering as a funding source. It can be a good option if you have a consumer product you're selling at a price point that's less than $500 and you're essentially pre-selling your inventory. This strategy could work if you're looking for working capital to take your proof of concept and put it into production.

Consider the example of the Pebble watch. A group of entrepreneurs over the course of 18 months created three revisions of their idea for a Bluetooth watch to pair with your iPhone or Android phone. No venture capital firm (see Chapter 3) would fund them, so they took their third-round prototype that was ready for production to a crowdfunding website called Kickstarter (www.kickstarter.com). Their goal was to raise $300,000 in order to create an initial production run of the watches. Anyone who donated to the crowdfunding campaign was essentially pre-purchasing a watch.

Convertible debt, anyone?

If you (and your investors) are really sophisticated, you may opt for convertible debt. This is an instrument that some potential high-growth businesses in Silicon Valley use to raise capital. Early-stage companies raise cash by selling debt today; then, at a future date, this debt can be converted to equity at favorable terms to the investor. For many businesses and investors, this approach may be overly complicated and create challenges downstream when and if you convert the debt into equity and have to agree on a valuation.

This type of instrument should be used very carefully. We suggest you have a financial advisor involved to help you understand the risks and potential rewards of convertible debt.

Determining Your Company's Valuation

Valuation is a topic covered in depth in many academic books and college courses. Our goal here isn't to teach you all about valuation but to indicate how you should approach it. Why is valuation important? Without knowing how much your business is worth, you can't know how much its equity is worth. So, if you plan to offer an equity offering via crowdfund investing, you have to calculate your valuation.

You don't want to inflate your valuation in an effort to impress potential investors. Crowdfund investing is built on trust; people who know you (or know about you) are putting their money into your business because they believe in you, your idea, and the business opportunity. If you want their support, you have to be reasonable, honest, and transparent.

If you run an existing small business and don't want to hire someone to help you calculate the value, then back to Excel with you! If you choose File⇨New from Template and enter "Valuation" in the search box, you should see a template called "Small Business Valuation." Using this template, you simply look at your company's profit and loss statement for the year and enter those values in the cells. A valuation will be calculated at the bottom based on industry standards. (***Note:*** You can change the valuation, but be prepared to defend why you do.) The beauty about using this Excel function is that you can tell anyone who asks exactly where you got it and share the form with her.

Calculating a startup's value may seem a lot trickier, but you can (and should) try to keep it simple. Think of the key components it takes to launch a business: funds to cover the hard costs of getting the business up and running, and people to do the job. Investors say all the time, "I'm investing in the team." For this reason, human resources are worth more than cash or goods. When you approach the valuation of your business, don't undersell the value of your ability to execute your plan.

Start your valuation process by summing up all the business expenses you spelled out with the help of the earlier section "Anticipating how funds will be used." This money represents one portion of the total value of your startup. The other portion is your time and your ability to execute your plan. (If you're working with a team, the entire team's time and ability factor in.)

Here's how you may present your valuation estimate to your investors: "I'm trying to raise $100,000 to cover startup expenses. I think that money is 20 percent of the key to success. My passion, commitment, dedication, and ability to execute the plan make up the other 80 percent. Hence, the value of my business is $500,000." Figure 5-2 illustrates what this valuation looks like.

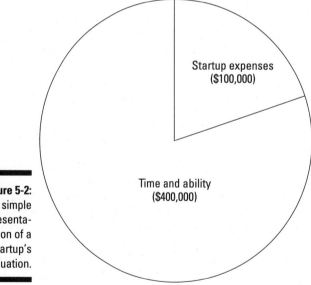

Figure 5-2:
A simple representation of a startup's valuation.

Startup expenses
($100,000)

Time and ability
($400,000)

The beauty of doing a startup valuation this way is that it's subjective, easy to understand, and easy to negotiate. When you socialize your idea with your friends (and eventual backers), they may say, "Are you kidding? That

$100,000 is worth more than 20 percent." You can talk it out and adjust your figures based on crowd feedback. But remember not to set too high a valuation or you may inflate your funding target. And *never* set such a low valuation that the amount of equity funds you raise is equal to or more than 50 percent of your business! If you do so, you lose control of the business you've worked so hard to create.

Is it possible to get more sophisticated about valuation? Sure. Doing so requires hiring someone who can created detailed financials and understands valuation methodologies that are based on multiples of sales, multiples of earnings, discounted cash flows, assets, and so on. But as long as you're realistic and willing to discuss your valuation estimate with your crowd, you shouldn't need to spend the money to go this route.

Imagining Your Ideal Exit Strategy

You need to begin your business venture with the end in mind. Imagine a time after you've raised the capital, reached your milestones, and achieved success in your business. What do you want to happen next? Different types of businesses have different possible exit strategies. Be sure you understand where your possible exits exist so your expectations are realistic:

- ✔ **None:** Expecting not to exit can be an excellent end goal. You build a successful business that supports you and your family, and you want to run it until you retire or pass it on to your children. Don't sell this plan short. Millions of Main Street and community businesses successfully execute this plan.

- ✔ **Sale:** In this situation, you have a business that another entrepreneur can purchase and effectively run, or you have a business that a larger company wants to buy as part of its growth strategy. Many businesses are started with this exit strategy in mind. If this is your plan, make sure that no matter what time horizon you're considering for your sale, you run the company for long-term success. Whoever looks at your business as a possible acquisition will examine all aspects to ensure it can succeed in the future. Most businesses are purchased based on a multiple of revenue and future growth potential. By running your business for long-term success, you give yourself the best chance for a successful sale.

- ✔ **Merger:** You and the leader of another company (maybe a competitor or a complementary business) believe that you can have greater success together than separately. You must determine who will run the joint operation and how revenues and equity will be shared.

✔ **Private secondary market trading:** As a startup, you offered equity in your business to raise crowdfund investment capital, and the individuals who hold those shares — including you! — may want to try to find buyers for their shares. If you want to exit by selling your own equity this way, you can use what are called *secondary* or *private* markets that enable individuals who own stock in private companies to meet in an online stock exchange that specializes in private company shares.

✔ **Initial public offering:** An IPO is the exit event of all exit events for you and for anyone who ever bought a share in your business. But if this is the payday you're holding out for, don't hold your breath; the chance of IPO'ing is extremely slim. Based on the regulatory filings and ongoing compliance needs for publically traded companies, many experts suggest that you need over $1 billion in annual revenues to think about filing for an IPO. If it motivates you to keep this goal as your ideal exit strategy, we won't argue. However, don't shut the door to an acquisition if the opportunity arises; even for rising-star companies, an acquisition usually makes more sense than an IPO.

Chapter 6

Focusing on Your People: Building Your Crowd and Your Team

In This Chapter

▶ Coaxing the right crowd into your corner

▶ Preparing to give the crowd what it needs

▶ Searching for the right talent to join your team

*M*uch of this book focuses on figuring out what you want to accomplish through a crowdfund investing venture and how to accomplish it. This chapter is all about the who.

Two whos (forgive us, Dr. Seuss) are especially important to your success: your crowd of investors and your talent team. In this chapter, we help you envision the members of your crowd and prepare yourself for winning their support. We then turn our attention toward attracting talent to your team — volunteers, paid staff members, or both — so you know your ideas are being expertly executed even when you're otherwise occupied.

Picturing Your Crowd

In Chapter 5, you find out how to construct a business model that incorporates crowdfund investing. Outside of crafting your business model (which must be rock solid if you want to succeed), assembling your crowd is your number-one priority.

The people who choose to join your crowd will validate that your idea is good enough to support, your revenue model makes sense, and you're a trustworthy entrepreneur deserving of their money. (People who think that your idea stinks, your revenue model is patched together with chewing gum and bandages, and you're likely to run away to South America with their money aren't going to join your crowd.) Your crowd will be not only your initial investors but also your consultants, your future customers, and your word-of-mouth advertisers. (Some members of your crowd may even become future employees.)

You can see why getting the right crowd on your side is crucial. In this section, we show you how to begin figuring out what your crowd looks like.

Estimating how many investors you need

Before you envision specific faces in your crowd, you want to get a sense of how many faces (and wallets) you need. If the subject of this book were raising venture capital, you might envision just one angel investor with a very large wallet who could make your every wish come true. But with crowdfund investing, you have to make some rough calculations to determine the number of investors you're likely to need.

You need to consider a couple pieces of information en route to estimating the size of your crowd:

- ✔ **How much money you're trying to raise through crowdfund investing:** If you haven't already done so, check out the financial discussion in Chapter 5 and try to determine at least an estimate of your crowdfund investing goal.

  Crowdfund investing is an all-or-nothing method of funding (see Chapter 3). Be realistic in your expectations, or else you risk getting zero for your efforts. Don't aim for $1 million in crowdfund investments unless you're extremely confident that you need that much money right away, plus you have a great idea, an existing social network, and a marketing pitch that can convince a whole lot of people to believe in you. Your first time out of the gate, you may be better off setting your funding goal much lower so your chances of achieving it are greater.

- ✔ **The maximum investment level allowed from an individual crowdfund investor:** We explain in Chapter 4 that, per regulations established by the Securities and Exchange Commission (SEC), the maximum amount differs from person to person based on the individual's annual income or net worth.

  The statute states that each year, someone can invest "(i) the greater of $2,000 or 5 percent of the annual income or net worth of such investor, as applicable, if either the annual income or the net worth of the investor is less than $100,000; and (ii) 10% of the annual income or net worth of such investor, as applicable, not to exceed a maximum aggregate amount sold of $100,000, if either the annual income or net worth of the investor is equal to or more than $100,000."

  The maximum amount for any one person to contribute to a crowdfund investment project is $100,000, but the cap is much lower for people with modest incomes. For example, someone who earns $40,000 a year could contribute a maximum of $2,000 (which is 5 percent of his income); someone who earns $75,000 a year could contribute a maximum of $3,750 (which is also 5 percent); and someone who earns $150,000 a year could contribute a maximum of $15,000 (10 percent of his income).

If you're an accredited investor, keep in mind that these rules don't necessarily apply to you unless you're making an investment through a crowdfunding portal. In that case the maximum you can invest is $100,000.

An individual's maximum participation amount is the total amount he can contribute among *all* crowdfund investment opportunities each year (see Chapter 4).

With these two pieces of information in mind, you need to get real. Unless you have a specific reason to believe that your friends, family members, existing customers, or other close contacts are frothing at the mouth to put money into your venture, you shouldn't plan on many people maxing out their crowdfund investing capacity with you. Instead, you need to estimate how much money an average investor in your crowd is likely to risk on your project. (And yes, no matter how great your idea is, this type of investment is a risk; we discuss that subject in depth in Chapter 4.)

What's a reasonable expectation from each investor? Although crowdfund investing is new, the concept of crowdfunding isn't, and history may offer some helpful clues. (See Chapter 1 if you aren't sure how crowdfunding and crowdfund investing differ.)

Consider a specific type of crowdfunding event, such as a fundraising run or a political campaign. For donation-based platforms such as these, the average donation in recent years has been $80. The average contribution to a local AIDS walk in recent years has been $80. The average amount donated to the last presidential campaign was $80. The average amount raised on the crowdfunding website RocketHub for an indie band was $80.

Does that mean you should just divide your total funding goal by $80 to determine your crowd size? Maybe. Say your crowdfund investing goal is $25,000; divide it by 80 to determine you need 312.5 supporters. (Good luck finding that half a person.) That number can serve as a good starting point for your crowd size, which you may refine based on further considerations that we discuss in the upcoming section "Identifying potential investors."

Should you then ask your potential investors to each contribute exactly $80? Absolutely not! A concept called *Pareto's principle,* which derives from crowdfunding, tells us that 80 percent of your financing will come from 20 percent of the crowd, who will make donations of $1,000 and higher.

Using the example of aiming for $25,000, you can estimate that 80 percent of that amount ($20,000) will be given to you in the form of donations of $1,000 and up. In other words, you can expect 20 or fewer investors to provide that $20,000. If the remaining $5,000 comes to you in average investments of $80, you need about 62 people to provide that amount. (Actually, the number is 62.5, but we're going to leave that poor half-person alone.) You're then estimating that you need 82 total investors:

Pareto	Dollar Amount	Number of Investors
80%	$20,000	20
20%	$5,000	62
100%	**$25,000**	**82**

We aren't claiming that the Pareto principle is firm science, but it does provide a general framework for estimating your crowd size.

Setting the minimum investment level

When you establish the parameters for investment in your business or project, you may determine that you don't want to bother with tiny investments. You don't want people buying into your venture for $1 or $5, for example, because you could run yourself ragged trying to meet the needs and answer the questions of hundreds or thousands of equity investors.

Some SEC-compliant online platforms (see Chapter 7) may set minimum amounts you can raise; others will enable you to have the option of setting a minimum investment level for each crowd investor, and you probably should exercise that option. But in setting a minimum investment, you don't want to shut the door on people eager to participate but unable to supply major dollars. So, how do you strike a balance?

Start with the assumption that an average investment in your crowdfund investing venture may somewhat resemble an average donation to a crowdfunded project. As we note in the preceding section, the average such donation has, of late, been $80. You probably don't want your minimum to be higher than that amount.

Depending on the amount of money you're trying to raise and the estimated size of your crowd, you may even decide that a $25 or $40 or $50 minimum investment is appropriate.

Identifying potential investors

The principle of crowdfund investing is based on a community of interrelated people coming together to support someone they know and trust with their money to help launch an initiative. These investors are rewarded with equity in the initiative or earned interest on a loan.

In this section, we point out some fairly obvious and not-so-obvious considerations when you start envisioning the faces in your crowd.

Starting with friends and family

The legislation that supports crowdfund investing (see Chapter 2) states that an entrepreneur (also known as an *issuer*), via her pitch on the funding portal, will use her online social networks as the first tier of contact for seeking investments. In Chapter 9, we discuss how to make your marketing pitch for your crowdfund investing project to your social networks in order to drive people to your funding portal page to evaluate your offering. Here, we simply want to note that given this stipulation, you're undoubtedly going to be reaching out first to the people who know you best: your friends and family members.

Even with people you know extremely well, you're only allowed to explain your business concept and goals and to notify them that your investment pitch is on the funding portal. You aren't allowed to disclose details of the pitch via any means except the online portal. In other words, you can't call or e-mail your cousin or your former roommate and explain your investment offering ("If you invest X amount of money, you get X amount of equity"). Doing so violates the JOBS Act and can get you in serious trouble with the SEC. Always, always send people to the funding portal to find out what the investment looks like!

Don't be shy about letting these people have a vested interest in your business or project. You may find that they provide the most honest and constructive criticism that can help you hone your ideas. You may even be able to glean certain skills from this particular crowd that can help you achieve your goals. (Do you count any graphic designers among your friends? Computer programmers? Amateur bakers willing to taste-test version 11 of your best new cupcake recipe?)

Stretching through your social network

If your intention were simply to fund your business with help from friends and family, you wouldn't require a crowdfund investing platform. You could probably achieve that goal with some persuasive phone calls and some old-fashioned IOUs.

A key function of crowdfund investing is to enable you to reach further into your social network contacts and drive your second- and third-degree connections to view your pitch online. Your second-degree connections are friends of friends, people you know through your friends. Third-degree connections are people your friends know who you haven't met yet.

To get a sense of your first-, second-, and third-degree connections, log onto your LinkedIn account. (If you don't yet have a LinkedIn account, you need to stop reading this book immediately and build your LinkedIn profile before doing anything else. Go!) Under Contact, go to your Network Statistics section. What you find is a visual representation of your connections that demonstrates the power of online social networks. If you have 100 first-degree connections, for example, you likely have 20 times that number of second-degree connections. When you look at third-degree connections, you may be amazed at the number.

Although you certainly can't predict which of your social network contacts (especially the second- and third-degree contacts) may come onboard with you, spending just a little time getting a sense of the scope of your social networks can help you gain a better picture of the crowd you're trying to assemble.

Figuring out if your network features any industry players

In the earlier section "Estimating how many investors you need," we mention that you may be able to adjust the estimated size of your crowd based on specific information you can glean from your social networks. Here's what we mean: As you peruse your first-, second-, and even third-tier contacts on a site like LinkedIn, note how many of these people are familiar with your industry. Search your social networks for terms related to your business (such as *baker* or *biotech engineer*). The goal is to locate people who share similar interests as you, friend them, and introduce them to your idea (being certain to send them to your funding portal page for any specifics about your investment offering). Doing so can build your credibility, and these people may then introduce you to other contacts who can help you.

If you're starting a tech company, for example, and your social networks are teeming with techies, you may reasonably assume that a well-constructed business model is going to attract positive attention from the industry insiders. More than even your mom and dad, your industry peers may recognize the value of what you're proposing and be willing to risk investment. Keep in mind the collective power of the crowd: The more industry players you have as investors, the more solid input you'll receive for your business.

If you're starting a company in the biomedical field and your social networks are populated mostly by people with zero background in that field, your pitch may be tougher. You may also make a reasonable assumption that you need a larger crowd. Why? Your contacts may still be willing to roll the dice and invest, but without industry knowledge, they may not recognize the true potential of your plans and may opt to risk a bit less than the industry insiders.

Determining if you've got experienced investors in your crowd

This step may be a bit tougher because it requires knowing more than just a contact's profession. But if you can take some time upfront to peruse postings on your social networks, you may discover that certain people have a track record of investing in startups or supporting entrepreneurs in other ways. Don't underestimate the value of locating even a handful of such people; anyone who has successfully navigated these waters before may be a prime candidate for investing in you.

Reach out to these people online. If they aren't your first-degree connections, LinkedIn makes it easy for you to ask for introductions from your shared connections. In doing so, you're not only socializing your idea to drive people to your online pitch but also moving that idea down the chain until you get in touch with the desired contacts.

If you're lucky enough to spot quite a few experienced investors in your crowd, you may be looking at some great candidates for higher-level investments (which could potentially reduce your overall crowd size).

Building a database

If you take the time to get more familiar with the people in your social networks — including the second- and third-tier contacts — be sure to keep track of the industry insiders, experienced investors, and other folks who seem like the likeliest candidates for investment in your venture. As you move toward executing your crowdfunding investing campaign, this list can help you refine your marketing efforts and ensure that you're spending your resources (including your precious time) wisely.

Respecting What Crowd Investors Need from You

By seeking funding for a project or new business, you're embarking on a process that may last for many years. Over those years, you'll be building and maintaining relationships not only with your customers but also with your investors. Your customers may expect nothing more than a good product or service in exchange for their money, but investors are different. Anyone who gives you money upfront to support your vision is bound to have *expectations* about what will come from that investment. We put the word *expectations* in italics because it's the most important part of managing investors: You must carefully manage their expectations from the first minute you contact them about the investment opportunity, and this section gets you started.

Consider an example: You want to expand your greenhouse and landscaping business, and you're seeking $20,000 to do so. You have a solid business that has grown 7 percent to 8 percent each year for the last three years, has earned 15 percent profits each year, and boasts happy, repeat customers. When seeking investors, you must set their expectations to the realities of the landscaping business and prepare them for the possible upside and downside of your industry. You must accurately inform them of what you think the most likely outcome will be, based on data, facts, and your best judgments and planning.

Stating a clear vision

Managing investor expectations starts with stating a clear vision for your business. We talk a lot about being clear in this chapter — being clear with your investors, your team, and yourself. To state a clear vision for your business, first ask yourself these questions:

- What problem is my business trying to solve?
- How is my product or service going to solve that problem better than the existing options?
- How am I going to use the money I raise to help me build my business?
- How am I going to make a return for my investors?

Your vision should be able to clearly answer all these questions. Entrepreneurs often make the mistake of trying to have their businesses be the answer for everything. What can happen is that an entrepreneur tries to have her business do everything, but it ends up not doing anything well. Having a clear and realistic vision is the first step in avoiding this pitfall.

Be very succinct in your vision, and communicate it to your investors and your team. But don't overestimate what you're going to achieve. The best approach is to under-promise and over-deliver.

Any experienced entrepreneur or investor will ask you, "What's your elevator pitch?" Imagine that you and an investor get into an elevator at the ground floor. You hit the button for the top floor. In the length of time it takes to get to the top, you need to explain your business proposition to your investor. She needs to understand the problem, your solution, and how you make money. (She does *not,* however, hear about a specific investment opportunity; you encourage her to visit the funding portal for that information.) In most cases, you have about 30 seconds to accomplish this. Turn to Chapter 9 for help reducing your idea down to powerful, digestible sound bites. Think you can't? The founders of Facebook knew how to do so, and now they're running a $100 billion business. If they can craft a winning elevator pitch, so can you. Give it a shot, and test out your pitch on a few of your friends who will likely be investing in you.

Aiming for honesty and financial transparency

Making wild claims or selling people your best-case scenario is a recipe for disaster. People deal with expectations in interesting ways. If they expect to make 5 percent per year on an investment and they make 6 percent, they're usually thrilled. If you set the expectation that they'll make 10 percent and they actually make 8 percent, they may think investing with you was a mistake. And just as you don't want an angry customer talking about how bad your product or service is, you don't want an angry investor talking about how she lost money in your venture.

As you work to establish realistic expectations, you need also to control investor assumptions about you or your venture. The more you can disclose about yourself, your project, or your business, the better. Investors make decisions based on these disclosures, and you want them making informed, responsible decisions so they can become happy investors. You definitely don't want to be caught down the line doing something that your investors didn't expect.

Good or bad, risk or reward, investors want to know they have all the information at their fingertips to make sound decisions. Here, we walk you through some of the fundamental information that investors need from you before they join your crowd.

Sharing your personal background and experience

Any business planning book you read or class you take will tell you that the people leading the company are more important than the company itself. No matter how great your idea may be, investors need to feel confident in the leadership of the company before they invest.

Spend the time upfront to clearly lay out your personal background for your campaign. You have to show off your strengths so people will be confident giving you their money, but you must understand your weaknesses as well. Many online products are available that can provide insights into your personality (see the sidebar "Testing your personality" in this chapter). The book *Personal Branding For Dummies,* by Susan Chritton (Wiley), is a good resource for exercises that can help you get to know yourself better so you can construct a personal brand to represent to the world.

Testing your personality

Think you have what it takes to be a successful entrepreneur? Take this quick, unscientific test and see how you do. Answer each question with 1 to 5 points: 1 means *not really* and 5 means *ooooh yeah!*

✔ Do you thrive on chaos?

✔ Do you think sending a ship to Mars is an achievable task?

✔ Are you incredibly outgoing?

✔ Does the phrase *few words and lots of action* describe your personality?

✔ When someone else may say "no," do you prefer to say "not now"?

✔ Does changing priorities midstream and still meeting your deadline sound workable?

✔ Would you say that people like you and love working with you?

✔ Do you like people and love working with them?

Add up your score. This test isn't scientific, but it does give you a sense of whether you're up for the job of being an entrepreneur. If you scored under 20, you can stop reading this chapter and jump instead to the chapters about investing in other people's projects. If you scored between 20 and 30, you may be able to do it, but you're going to need some serious collaborators. If you scored between 30 and 35, welcome to the entrepreneurial club. And if your score is over 35, "We've got a winner!"

Being an entrepreneur means you must have a vision, the ability to communicate clearly, passion to succeed, a deep sense of commitment to your goal, an understanding that things change, and a unique ability to act both as a leader and as a team player. You have to be willing to clean the toilet and be fine with doing so, even for the long term. If you can say that's true for you, then you'll do just fine.

Become comfortable talking about both your strengths and weaknesses so that when people ask you about them you're prepared to answer. Before you throw yourself to the wolves, start in your comfort zone: Talk to your friends and family members and ask them why they think you'll be successful. Listen carefully to their answers so you can better determine your best qualities to present to potential investors.

Touting your creativity, passion, and motivation

You don't need to be a seasoned entrepreneur who has created multiple successful companies in order for people to be confident in investing in you. People want to see the creativity, passion, and motivation that you bring to this venture. They want to feel certain that you're 100 percent behind your business and believe in its success.

Talk about why you love your business, what excites you about it, and why you started it (or are attempting to start it). Make your investors feel your passion, and they'll be much more likely to invest in you. Investors need to know that you're authentic, and they're going to ask questions about what drives you. ("Is he really that passionate about chocolate-covered gummy bears, or is he just trying to make a quick buck?") Obviously, your financials, strategies, and tactics must make sense for an investor to jump onboard, but passion and drive are key elements of what you're selling.

Knowing your limits

Investors want to know your passion, but they also want to know that you're realistic. Say you want to raise $20,000 for your landscaping business that has $100,000 in yearly revenues. If you claim that this extra $20,000 will allow you to grow the business to $500,000 in yearly revenues, investors will know that plan is flawed.

Be honest with both yourself and your potential investors about what you're capable of doing. People like to see that you understand your limitations. The best way to accomplish this step is to show investors how the money will be used and the impact you expect it to have on your business based on history and facts. If you've done a similar project before, say so and explain the results. If you've never done anything like this before, say so and explain the research you've conducted to arrive at your conclusions. You may not be able to claim complete certainty about the outcomes, but the more hard facts you can present, the more your investors will believe that you're a realist.

Posting financial information

The amount of money you're raising will determine the amount of financial information you need to disclose to potential investors (see this book's website, www.dummies.com/go/crowdfundinvesting, for a breakdown). The thought of posting your company's financial data (such as a balance sheet, income statement, and statement of cash flows) may be enough to throw you into a panic attack. You may be thinking, "What if my competitors see this?" or "Why should I post all my sensitive data for the whole world to see?" Especially for small businesses, financial reports can feel like very personal information. But if you want to participate in crowdfund investing, you need to get over your disclosure fears. The reality is that you have to make financial disclosures to attract potential investors.

Here's something to keep in mind as you select an online platform to host your crowdfund investment listing (a subject we focus on in Chapter 7): If you choose a platform that enables you to put sensitive data into a private data room, you have better control over what gets shared. In this situation, you can make limited disclosures in the public part of your listing. Then, your more sensitive financial data can be housed in this data room so it's available only to people who provide their real names and contact information and meet some threshold of credibility as potential investors. You should also have the opportunity to track who has logged into this section of your listing, see how much time they spent in the data room, and identify which documents they reviewed.

What types of financial information are potential investors most likely to care about?

- ✔ **If you already run a business,** potential investors want to know the financial status of your company. Be transparent about your company's revenue, profit margins, and debt obligations. Per the JOBS Act, at a minimum you need to provide the following financial information:

  - Your prior-year tax returns and financial statements

  - A description of the stated purpose and intended use of the proceeds

  - The target offering amount, the deadline to reach the target offering amount, and regular updates regarding the progress of the issuer in meeting the target offering amount

  - The share price for equity participation and the methodology used for determining the price, as well as a reasonable opportunity to rescind the commitment to purchase the securities

  - A description of the ownership and capital structure of the issuer, including a lot of detail about the terms of the securities being sold

  - The terms of any other outstanding securities of the company, including a summary of the differences between them

- ✔ **If this is your first business, or the first business you've owned yourself,** be prepared to provide all the components mentioned above minus any prior-year financial statements. You'll need to supply personal tax returns to the online crowdfund investing portal, but those returns won't be revealed to investors. Instead, your tax records simply confirm to the portal (and, therefore, to the SEC) that you're a real person contributing to society (or at least to the government's coffers). Requiring your tax records is one of many ways the SEC aims to prevent crowdfund investing fraud.

If you feel uncomfortable sharing this information, put yourself in the shoes of a potential investor. Funding a small business of any kind is a risk; that's a known fact. Funding a small business without having a thorough understanding of its fiscal health is financial suicide. If financial disclosure of any kind is uncomfortable for you, crowdfund investing may not be the best way for you to raise capital.

When you ask investors for money, they become (in a sense) your business partners. They have the right to ask questions about the financial health of their investments. Investors need concrete, honest numbers, and you want to be the one to share those numbers. In the absence of information, an investor may search you or your company online and make assumptions based on what he finds. Be proactive; give your contacts the financial background they need to become informed investors. And trust us, if you don't disclose something about your numbers that someone other than you knows, chances are pretty good that it will be disclosed on your behalf, in a manner you didn't want. Take the initiative and be transparent.

Preparing for ongoing communication

After you launch your crowdfund investing campaign (a process we walk you through in Part III of this book), be prepared for ongoing communication with your investors and/or lenders. When you launch your campaign to raise capital, you won't simply make a one-time marketing pitch and then wait for the money to roll in. Potential investors are going to have questions and expect answers in a timely fashion. Anyone truly interested in you and your idea will monitor your campaign page to see how well you communicate before deciding whether to commit dollars to your efforts.

Set up a schedule for yourself so you can answer all the questions that are asked about you and about your business. Don't feel compelled to sit in front of your computer day and night so each question receives an immediate answer. But do feel compelled to demonstrate responsibility, honesty, and transparency with your answers. Keep in mind that for every question someone asks, that person likely has more questions that he hasn't asked; do your best to spot gaps in the information you've provided and to fill them even before someone makes that request.

Be aware that potential investors may begin communicating with each other openly on your campaign page as well. In most cases, this step is positive for the campaign because it indicates that interest and engagement in what you're trying to achieve are rising. (If you find that some comments and questions become harassing or unprofessional, consult with your online platform about its policies and procedures for dealing with these situations.) Monitor these discussions to make sure that no quality question is left unanswered. By being proactive about your campaign communication, you'll show potential investors that you want and value their feedback. After all, the collective knowledge of the crowd is much greater than the knowledge of any one person. Show your contacts that you value their knowledge — not just their dollars — and they'll be more likely to commit.

Finding Talent to Support Your Goals

There's no such thing as a one-man show in business. A great business isn't built on the back of a single individual. (Even Steve Jobs and Mark

Zuckerberg needed help.) Luckily, your crowd won't expect you to know everything or to have all the answers. Actually, the contrary is true: If you try to come across as a know-it-all, you'll most likely fail because people generally don't trust someone who can't admit that he doesn't know everything. (Hey, even Socrates had his bad days!)

Your best bet when approaching your endeavor is to take a good look at yourself and figure out what your strengths and weaknesses are. (See the earlier section "Sharing your personal background and experience" for some thoughts.) Then go out and find people to help you address your weaknesses.

 Building a business isn't just about identifying a problem and addressing it with a solution. It's about finding the right team to help you build that solution. Trying to do everything on your own is most likely a recipe for disaster. Locating the right people is crucial, as is figuring out which roles they can play. (You may want to check out *Human Resources Kit For Dummies,* 3rd Edition, by Max Messmer [Wiley], for guidance.) We discuss some hiring basics here, as well as some staffing issues specific to crowdfund investing.

Identifying a community manager to run your investment campaign

As we discuss earlier in this chapter (see "Preparing for ongoing communication"), communication is critically important in crowdfund investing. If you don't have the time or the skills to offer consistent, valuable communication to your potential investors (and, later in the process, to your investment crowd) on your online funding portal, you may be able to find someone to engage the crowd in an active, ongoing dialogue. That person would be your community manager.

The role of a community manager would be similar to that of an investor relations representative at a public company. This person would serve as a key contact for investors to learn more about the company and its management and to conduct due diligence. The community manager may not be able (per SEC regulations, which are still developing) to solicit potential investors on your behalf, but he could post additional information about your company on the funding portal's discussion board or comments section. Keep in mind that if you need to bring someone onboard, you must be willing to pay that person. You either need to have the money upfront to hire this person or budget this expense and disclose it to your potential investors. Let your community manager know that her commitment won't exceed the length of time it takes to get funding (as determined by the SEC) — most likely no longer than three months. So, if you need to hire a community manager, budget for three months of her time.

If you aren't going to play the role of community manager yourself, you should plan to have a single designated person be the spokesperson and answer *all questions*. Why? Because you are liable for everything this person says. The more people you have responding to questions, the greater your liability for misstatements, errors, or omissions. Any *material* (significant) misstatement or failure to disclose material facts about your investment campaign could get *you* in hot water with the SEC, so you have to proactively coach and consistently monitor what this person is saying and typing.

To be clear, the extent to which a community manager may communicate with your crowd and use social media on your behalf is still to be determined by the SEC. Before you hire anyone to step into this role, you need to make 100 percent certain that you're up to date on the SEC regulations that are evolving surrounding crowdfund investing. As of this writing, those rules are still being considered by the SEC. Essentially, your community manager is your public relations department before you have a public relations department. This individual must have excellent writing skills; be able to answer questions clearly and concisely; and be dedicated to creating credibility and authenticity for you, your company, and your brand. She must be able to respond quickly. In an ideal scenario, this person:

✔ Knows you very well and believes in both you and your idea

✔ Will come to work for you after you've successfully raised capital through crowdfund investing

✔ Will set the bar for what you represent as a company and create strong initial branding for your organization

Where do you find such an individual? The answer depends largely on your personal circumstances:

✔ **If you're already running a going concern with revenue, employees, and some success under your belt,** you may have someone on staff who would be great in this capacity. (Keep in mind that even if the person you have in mind has marketing or sales experience, you should set aside some time for training and role-play to walk through different scenarios of how to answer questions on the online funding portal.)

✔ **If you're trying to fund a startup,** consider whether you know anyone with experience starting and running a business. If not, consider whether you know anyone who studied finance, accounting, marketing, law, public relations, or entrepreneurship. If you can't identify candidates within your immediate network, bring your social network into play. Go to Facebook, LinkedIn, or Twitter and ask, "Who knows someone who can help me build or practice my investor pitch?" If you still come up short, find the Small Business Administration (SBA) office in your area or the local economic development organization. These organizations stand ready to help entrepreneurs and small businesses succeed. They may not be able to help you raise capital, but they can be rich sources of information about how to start and run a business.

Because you're promising a financial return on your investors' money, you have to be careful to coach your community manager on how to answer questions. Review the materials on your crowdfund investing platform's website regarding what types of claims and promises you can and cannot make. Also, you *must* talk with an attorney who can advise you clearly about what you can and cannot promise in your written or oral communication regarding returns on any investments made in your company. You and your community manager should never say or write things like "I guarantee 20 percent return on your investment in year one" or "There is no doubt this idea is a winner." Nothing in business or investing is guaranteed, and making any kind of claim like this can, at a minimum, get your crowdfund investing campaign removed from its platform or, much worse, land you in a lawsuit or in hot water with the SEC for making false claims.

In fact, your community manager should be coached to always answer investor questions about the campaign offering by directing people to the information posted on the funding portal that spells out the offering details. The community manager shouldn't answer individual questions about the offering itself (such as questions about the value of equity or the terms of debt repayment). Instead, if she determines that the information on your portal is lacking clarity, she can help you pinpoint the problems and update the written information.

Building the rest of your team

Your community manager may be the only person you hire specifically to support your crowdfund investing campaign. Of course, depending on the project you're trying to finance, you may or may not have plans to make additional hires after the investment campaign is complete. You may be raising money with the intention of utilizing your existing staff (if you have one) or doing the vast majority of the work yourself (if you run a small business).

But assuming that your campaign is a success, and assuming that some of the money you raise is earmarked for additional hires, you want to approach the hiring process with your new investors in mind. Does that mean that your crowd gets to choose your staff members? No. However, you may want to tap your crowd when soliciting résumés. Doing so helps them recognize that the hiring process is underway (a good sign that you're enacting your business plan) and reminds them that you value their contributions.

To control your crowd's expectations, you must state clearly in any job-related communication that you — and you alone — are responsible for making hiring decisions based on the talents of the candidate pool. If an investor starts asking questions or making statements that indicate he expects you to hire him (or his brother or his mechanic) for the job, be respectful but firm. Remind him that you have a large number of potential candidates and will make a decision that best supports the company's success so that every investor may be ultimately rewarded.

Defining your expectations from team members

When you have employees onboard — whether 2 or 20 — be sure to set accurate and measurable expectations for your staff. Time and again, potentially great employees fail or become frustrated and leave because they don't have accurate expectations about the job or how to succeed. (With employees, as with your investors, you must constantly strive to control expectations — both yours and theirs!)

Remember that human capital is the only thing more important than financial capital. Even when you're running a thousand miles per hour to keep up with the needs of your company or project, take the time to set, measure, and communicate your expectations. Doing so is especially important when you have a crowd of investors involved; the last thing you want is for an angry employee to reach out to that crowd with complaints or concerns about how you're running your business. (After all, you very likely won't be the only person with access to your investors' contact information.)

Staying in the loop at all times

Both during and after your crowdfund investing campaign, stay aware of what your community manager and other staff members are doing, especially in relation to your crowd. You don't want to micromanage (by dictating how to answer every investor question, for example), but don't take yourself out of the loop either. Your business is your baby. No one knows the business like you do, and no one cares as much about its success as you.

During your crowdfund investing campaign, set up a time each day for you and the community manager to review the communication that's happening. You want to ensure that your community manager is

✔ Responding to all pertinent issues

✔ Responding correctly and in the manner you want

✔ Complying with the law that limits what a company can say to a potential investor

✔ Continuing to leverage the online platform and other social media outlets to push your campaign forward

Also, make yourself available to your community manager throughout the day because he's very likely going to need information and action from you. Things are going to happen quickly, and if he can't get the information he needs in a timely manner, your campaign will suffer.

After the crowdfund investing campaign is complete, you may not need a daily meeting with your staff members, but you do want to meet on a regular basis. Especially if you don't work in the same office as your team (perhaps not even in the same city or state), you want to enforce the idea that you are actively involved in the business and care deeply about their job performance. The earlier you can put a process in place for regular communication and updates with your team, the better positioned you'll be to manage your project, your company, and your investors.

Chapter 7

Picking a Powerful Crowdfund Investing Platform

....

In This Chapter

▶ Figuring out what the law requires from funding platforms

▶ Researching the services a funding portal offers

▶ Getting specific in your portal shopping

....

*P*icking a powerful online crowdfund investing platform is just as important as pitching a winning idea to potential investors (a topic we cover in Chapter 9). That's because the JOBS Act legislation states that you can use this type of platform to seek crowdfund investment; you cannot — we repeat, *cannot* — set up your own website, call people on the phone, put a notice in your local paper about the terms and details of your offering, or use other means to raise funds this way. (As we explain in this chapter, crowdfund investing also can take place using a broker-dealer, but the online funding platforms are usually less expensive and more suitable for the relatively small amounts being raised.) This requirement ensures that the Securities and Exchange Commission (SEC) can keep tabs on all crowdfund investing activity to protect investors and verify that everyone's playing by the rules, which are spelled out on this book's website, www.dummies.com/go/crowdfundinvesting.

Crowdfund investment funding platforms of all shapes and sizes are popping up to meet demand. Your job is to find the one that best suits your needs. Generally speaking, the more products and services a platform offers, the more you'll pay for using it. Some platforms are bare bones, offering no advice and no means for you to communicate with your investors after you receive funding (see Chapter 12 to gauge why such communication is essential). Other platforms are more robust; they contain tools that help you both pre- and post-funding (such as business plan templates and data rooms that let you store sensitive information with restricted access). You want to find the right portal to fit your needs: one that helps you achieve transparency, helps your investors become more informed, and helps the entire funding process be completely compliant with SEC regulations.

With all the options, how do you know which online platform to choose? This chapter is your initial guide, and after you're done reading it your next stop is www.crowdfundingprofessional.org, the website of the Crowdfunding Professional Association, a crowdfunding industry trade association that we helped to launch when the JOBS Act was signed. It's a one-stop shop for entrepreneurs seeking to secure crowdfund investments, online platforms seeking to offer crowdfund investments, and investors looking for education on making such investments. On that site, you find a list of all the SEC-registered funding platforms; you can compare them and see which have passed a technology accreditation program known as the Crowdfunding Accreditation for Platform Standards (CAPS) meant to promote the adoption of best practices to build an efficient, confident crowdfunding market.

Understanding JOBS Act Provisions about Investment Platforms

To connect entrepreneurs with their social networks and help investors get the tools they need to make sound decisions, while at the same time protecting against fraud, the JOBS Act contains provisions that specify minimum activities that an online crowdfund investment platform must do. In this section, we describe these activities. But first, we explain the difference between an online funding portal (the type of platform we focus on in this chapter) and a broker-dealer that can also host a crowdfund investment campaign.

Distinguishing funding portals from broker-dealers

The JOBS Act distinguishes between two types of crowdfund investment platforms: online funding portals and broker-dealers. Here's why: Prior to the legalization of crowdfund investing, anyone seeking to raise capital needed to do so under the guidance of a broker-dealer — an individual or business registered with agencies including the Financial Industry Regulatory Authority (FINRA; www.finra.org) and North American Securities Administrators Association (NASAA; www.nasaa.org). Broker-dealers pay compliance and oversight costs that can exceed $100,000 each year, and they pass such costs on to consumers in every transaction. This situation isn't so bad when a broker-dealer is handling very large and complex offerings because prudent oversight does prevent fraud. However, these compliance and oversight costs are the same for a $10,000 offering as for a $100 million offering. For this reason, most broker-dealers won't bother with capital raises of less than $1 million; working with smaller amounts doesn't make financial sense based on their cost structures because they can't pass on all the associated costs in small deals.

That's where online funding portals come in. The JOBS Act allows such portals to support smaller capital raises without being able to perform all the duties that a broker-dealer performs. For example, a funding platform isn't allowed to analyze a business opportunity, conduct business valuation, or find investors — duties that cost a lot of money. Allowing funding portals to exist, and offering their use to small businesses and entrepreneurs that don't necessarily require the full-service package that a broker-dealer provides, creates a simpler cost structure with lower fees associated with an equity investment offering.

A funding portal doesn't have to register as a broker-dealer as long as it doesn't perform any of these duties:

✔ Offer investment advice or recommendations

✔ Find investors on behalf of the issuer

✔ Compensate employees, agents, or other persons for such solicitation or based on the sale of securities displayed or referenced on its website or portal

✔ Hold, manage, possess, or otherwise handle investor funds or securities

✔ Engage in any other activities that the SEC determines to be inappropriate

If the online platform just lists an entrepreneur's or company's pitch, uses a third party to manage the transfer of both cash and stock, and offers general support services that don't fall into these categories of activities, it can register as a crowdfund investment portal. If it conducts any of these activities, it must register as a full broker-dealer.

Meeting SEC requirements for registration

Whether you choose a funding portal or a broker-dealer to support your crowdfund investment campaign, that entity must be registered with FINRA. FINRA acts as the self-regulating organization that oversees the industry and makes sure the platforms are performing their specified roles. (If a platform goes astray, it faces punishment.) So, at a minimum, you need to make sure that the funding platform you select is registered with FINRA. The FINRA website has a broker check feature that easily allows a person to determine if a platform is registered with FINRA and whether that person has been subject to any discipline.

What else are you looking for from an online portal? Following are the services we recommend looking for as you decide which organization to work with to raise money via crowdfunding.

Containing key social media tools

As we explain in Part I of this book, crowdfund investing sits at the intersection of social networking and community capital. You use your Facebook, LinkedIn, Twitter, Google+, and other social media accounts to engage with your networks and request money for your business venture. Therefore, any online funding portal must feature tools that connect you to your social networks. When comparing platforms, look for one that has the most robust (and easy to use) social media connectivity tools — ways to direct your networks to your pitch.

Not sure what we're talking about? Think about the Facebook Connect button. It's that box that appears when you click the "connect to Facebook" icon on a site other than Facebook (for example, Twitter or YouTube). This is called a *plug-in*. The screen features a blue bar and requests your user login name and password. When you enter that information, the two sites are linked so that you can share what you're doing on one site (Twitter updates or videos you like on YouTube, for example) with your friends on Facebook. On your funding portal, you'll likely be asked to integrate your social media contacts using these plug-ins.

Integrating your social networks (Facebook, Google+, LinkedIn, Twitter, and so on) to your pitch page on the funding platform tells your friends that you have a pitch, and they can easily get to it via your shared social networks. From your online funding portal, you must log in to Facebook and grant access between the portal and your Facebook network. Then, once your connections arrive at the funding portal page, you can tell your crowd about your brilliant idea and the details of the offer.

Pretty cool, eh? The same process works for Twitter, allowing you to tweet that you're raising money and provide a link to your pitch. You can also notify your LinkedIn and Google+ networks that you have a pitch and where to go to get the details. Make sure that you work with an attorney and follow the letter of the law regarding what information you can include in your social media campaign.

Keep in mind that the SEC doesn't allow you to spam people you don't know, nor does it allow you to send pitches that contain much more than very basic information about your venture. It definitely doesn't want you using words like "Limited time — act now!" or "Amazing, definite success" or "Inability to lose, and guaranteed to win." The information must be focused on directing the user to the funding platform so she can review the complete equity or debt offering all in one place.

Integrating background checks

Think crowdfund investing is right for you? Think that it will be an easy way to access some untapped cash from your friends, family members, and existing customers? Unfortunately, fraudsters may think it's an easy way to access untapped cash as well. For this reason, anyone who wants to partake in crowdfund investing must submit to a background check, and the online funding portal (or the broker-dealer) you choose must perform a securities enforcement regulatory history check.

Per the JOBS Act, anyone who is a principal or who owns more than 20 percent of the equity in a business seeking crowdfund investments must submit to a background check. The check aims to prevent someone from fronting as another individual and running a fraudulent crowdfund investing campaign.

Be prepared to turn over your name, address, Social Security number, date of birth, e-mail address(es), cellphone number(s), and more. Before you can ask anyone for a dollar, the SEC wants to know that you exist; that you haven't been convicted of a crime (particularly fraud) in the past; and how you can be hunted down (by the SEC itself, by the Internal Revenue Service [IRS], by the police) if you try to pull the wool over their eyes. Although, at first, it may feel a bit strange to provide all this data, doing so is in your best interests and in the best interests of your company and your investors. This is the same type of information that is required from angel, venture capital, and private equity investors when they invest money in entrepreneurs.

Quizzing users on their investment knowledge

Investor education is imperative when it comes to crowdfund investing. Investors need to understand what it means to park their hard-earned dollars in a small business or a startup. As we note elsewhere in the book, the risks of this type of investment are significant; about 50 percent of business startups fail. When we crafted the framework for the crowdfund investment portion of the JOBS Act, we insisted — and Congress, the president, and the SEC agreed — that investors must broaden their scope of understanding before making a crowdfund investment decision.

After the background check: The crowd check

After someone passes the background check, he still needs to be vetted by the investment crowd. This step can be almost as important as the background check. In the world of social media, secrets are hard to keep. Type almost anyone's name into Google and you can find out a wealth of information about that person. Crowdfund investing is powerful precisely because it takes a process (raising capital for your business) that used to happen behind closed doors and puts it online for the world to see. Even if a fraudster manages to pass a background check, she'll be hard pressed to pass the crowd's check. If you have a checkered past, when you try to post your business online, people in your social network are going to warn everyone they know.

If someone tries to raise money on a crowdfund investing platform and doesn't have anyone in her social networks, that fact will raise a big red flag. Crowdfund investing is all about tapping into online networks to raise money. Someone who doesn't have *any* online networks is very possibly trying to hide what people will say about her.

For this reason, the legislation prescribes that crowdfund investment platforms (both funding portals and brokers-dealers) must do the following:

✔ Confirm that investors understand that they can lose their entire investment and can afford that loss.

✔ Warn investors of the speculative nature generally applicable to investments in startups, emerging businesses, and small issuers, including risks in the secondary market related to *illiquidity* (difficulty selling equity or debt shares to another buyer).

✔ Warn investors that, as minority share owners in a business, they have small voices, and investors with the majority of shares (and votes) can make decisions because they have control. This means, for example, that the company can vote to sell more equity, and, hence, each investor will own a smaller piece of a bigger pie. For example, if an investor owns 1 share out of 100 (1 percent) and the company votes to sell another 100 shares, she would then own only 0.5 percent of the company's equity. This process is called *dilution*.

✔ Warn investors that they are subject to restrictions on the sale of the security. The legislation requires that equity investors hold on to their crowdfund invested shares for at least one year. In Chapter 4, we discuss what you can do with them after that period ends.

As a business owner or entrepreneur, you want happy investors. An educated investor is more likely to make a good decision than one who doesn't know the facts (including all the risks that you know about at the time that the investment decision is being made) related to crowdfund investment. Therefore, you want to look for an online platform with robust investor education components.

Linking entrepreneurs and investors via social media

Crowdfund investing occurs online, via SEC-regulated and FINRA-registered crowdfund investing platforms (or via FINRA-registered broker-dealers). Although some crowdfund investors put money into people or companies they don't know well, most money that's raised from crowdfund investment comes from individuals the issuer (the entrepreneur or business owner) is already connected with. The online solicitation of potential crowdfund investors takes place primarily via social media to individuals who are known by the issuer. In the earlier section "Containing key social media tools," we explain how a funding portal links an investment pitch to the issuer's various networks, such as Facebook and Twitter.

Imagine you own a white-water rafting business and you're seeking to raise $100,000 to expand your operations by purchasing an additional boat. You've owned the business for five years, and you've been successful at growing the business by an average of 15 percent per year. You're active in your community; prior to owning your own business you had experience in outdoor tourism, and you're vice president of your local chamber of commerce. You sound like a great candidate for seeking investment from people who know you, right? Now imagine that you're terrified of social media and haven't even set up a Facebook account yet. What do you do? How can you communicate your skills, accomplishments, and previous results to potential crowdfund investors?

Here's the short answer: Get over your fears and get online. If you don't, you can stop reading this book right now. Crowdfund investment takes place online, and that's not going to change. Either you change, or you can't take advantage of the opportunities afforded by the JOBS Act.

The CEO and/or management team of a company seeking crowdfund investment *must* have at least one social media profile. Without this minimum level of online connectivity, the investment campaign can't launch. (Likewise, a potential investor can't tap into crowdfund investing without a social media presence. You can't mail a check to get in on this type of investment.)

Online funding platforms must enable effortless connectivity between their services and all leading social media platforms so that both issuers and potential investors can link their social media profiles on each platform.

Allowing contacts to bring other possible investors into the conversation

As an issuer's social media contacts begin to engage in a crowdfund investment offering, they may want to reach out to other people in their own social networks to share this opportunity with them. For this reason, per the JOBS Act, online funding platforms must provide ways to share links to an issuer's campaign.

The ability to easily share a link to a crowdfund investment campaign enables a pitch to go viral. What does that mean? Consider an example outside the crowdfund investing realm. A previously unknown gaming company built an Android game console called the OUYA, which allows people to create and play games using an open software system (so they aren't dependent on the Xbox or PlayStation platforms, for example). Under the old law, the company wasn't allowed to sell equity in the business, but consumers were allowed to preorder the software. The company raised $8,596,475, in less than 45 days on Kickstarter (http://kck.st/Mfvs9y) because the campaign went viral — friends shared the information with friends, who shared it with their friends, and the news spread like wildfire. Under the new law, the same viral spread can take place, but instead of only being able to preorder products, people can have a financial interest in the company.

Policing the SEC's rules

Online funding platforms must be vigilant regarding the SEC's rules on crowd-fund investing. Because this investment asset class is new (available as of 2013), the SEC regulations will inevitably evolve as experience with crowd-fund investing evolves. For example, maybe an issuer will be allowed to use new forms of social media for general solicitations, or perhaps the SEC's reporting requirements from issuers will be modified.

Anticipating such possibilities, a funding platform must monitor all SEC com-munications related to crowdfund investing, as well as regulation changes related to private capital markets or other related areas of the financial ser-vices industry.

A platform's ability to operate will depend on understanding and fully imple-menting all SEC regulations as they're enacted. You should select a crowd-fund investing platform that has a strong and productive relationship with the SEC so you don't have to change platforms midstream. How do you judge the platform's relationship with the SEC? For starters, check out its "About Us" page. See when the platform was founded and when it received accredi-tation from the Crowdfunding Accreditation for Platform Standards (CAPS). Find out when it was approved for registration by the SEC and FINRA at www.crowdfundingprofessional.org. And go to FINRA's website (www.finra.org) to make sure no compliance notices exist for the platform.

Spotting the Services a Good Platform Can Provide

As crowdfund investment matures, the strongest online funding portals will survive, and the rest will falter. But although this field is still young, you really want to take your time making a decision about which platform to use. Consider the services each platform provides, how many registered users (both entrepreneurs and investors) it has, its success rate to date (keeping in mind that crowdfund investing is an all-or-nothing type of funding, as we explain in Chapter 3), the reputation this platform has with other companies it has funded in the past, and its total combined social network. After all, picking the right platform could mean the difference between raising your target capital or not.

People love to talk about their successes. Go on to some of the top crowdfund investing portals and find a few successful campaigns. Reach out to the business owners and ask for 15 minutes of their time. Ask them to tell you what services they used that were the most useful, as well as what services the portal didn't offer that would've been useful.

It's one thing for the platform to give you the services to raise your money, but that's not the whole story. After you raise your money, you still need your platform to work for you. Make sure that the platform you choose gives you good services before, during, and after your campaign, such as the ones we describe in this section.

Keep in mind that the more useful services your funding portal offers, the less headaches you may have and the more time you should be able to spend on creating revenue. Your goal is to find one-stop business shopping via your funding portal.

Business plan templates

Okay, so you know you have to write a business plan, but unless you have an MBA — or a copy of *Business Plans For Dummies,* 2nd Edition, by Paul Tiffany and Steve D. Peterson (Wiley) — this could be a big black box for you. What information do you include? How long should each section be? How do you create the executive summary?

As we explain in Chapter 5, you must have a good business plan so your investors can get a concrete and concise understanding of what your business is and who you are. As you look through the myriad funding portals available, consider the business plan templates they offer.

If you choose a portal with a weak business plan template, be prepared to tap into another website that offers comprehensive business plan templates, such as `www.fundingroadmap.com`. Just be advised that using a separate site for your business plan template could incur additional costs. Alternatively, the Small Business Administration website (`www.sba.gov`) has an excellent section on writing business plans — and it's free.

Incorporation assistance

There are two main paths to incorporate your business:

- ✔ **You can consult with an attorney who is well versed in incorporation of businesses and understands the JOBS Act regulations.** Speaking with a legal professional when embarking on a new business is always a good idea. An attorney can help you complete the process of incorporation.

> ✔ **You can use one of the many online services (such as www.legal zoom.com and www.incorporate.com) to help you with the process.** You may want to search for a funding portal that has a relationship with such a service and can offer you a discount. (Every penny counts when you're starting up or trying to grow. Don't underestimate the importance of discounts on business services.) And keep in mind that you likely will still need an attorney to answer your questionvs and offer guidance.

Making sure you set up your company the right way is a very important step. You want to protect your company from the risk of regulatory or civil legal action. In addition, the tax and legal differences among various options can be significant, so spend time learning about them and figuring out which is best for you, your business, and your future shareholders.

If you create a plan and a list of questions you have about the process before you speak with an attorney, you can save time and money.

Intellectual property support

Depending on the type of business you're in, it could be very important that you protect your intellectual property by securing patents or securing copy-rights or trademarks (see Chapter 10). Hiring a lawyer to do so can be time consuming and expensive, so you may want to seek out a funding portal that can offer some help. But you must make sure the portal has a solid track record on this front; if it contracts with a cheap service and your paperwork isn't done correctly, you could stand to lose a great deal down the road.

Almost every day, we read news stories about businesses going to battle with each other over their intellectual property. Entire law firms are dedicated to intellectual property law. If your business model is based upon intellectual property that you created, you simply must safeguard it or else risk losing all your hard work.

Accounting and auditing help

Accounting and auditing are probably our least favorite parts of running a business. Most entrepreneurs want to spend their time making sales, building partnerships, and planning long-term strategies. But to run a business, you need to have a good handle on your money so you know where and how it's being spent, you pay the correct taxes, you file your expenses correctly, and so on.

A funding portal may offer some of these services, so be sure to explore how robust their services are and for what length of time they're available to you.

For instance, if the portal offers these services for only a short period of time (such as one month) after your campaign is complete, they won't be very useful to you. That short-term accounting support could help you get things set up initially, but you actually need the most help throughout the *entire* first fiscal year (for preparing both quarterly and year-end tax returns and financial reports).

Escrow agents

Escrow agents are folks who handle the cash that investors commit to a deal. They're like an intermediary bank, and every funding portal must work with an escrow agent. The JOBS Act states that a funding portal cannot be an escrow agent; it cannot hold the committed cash from investors until the all-or-nothing threshold has been met (see Chapter 3). This job must be out-sourced to an escrow agent who takes responsibility (and liability) for main-taining that cash. If a funding target is met, the escrow agent makes sure the cash gets to the entrepreneur. If a funding target is not met, the escrow agent makes sure the cash gets back to the investors.

Why can't a funding portal handle its own cash? Funding portals play a hands-off role in the crowdfund investment process, so they don't carry insurance to guard themselves against potential fraud or failure. Just imagine how awful it would be to commit some funds to an entrepreneur and to dis-cover that the person or entity holding the cash has disappeared or gone out of business. Using an insured escrow agent is a safeguard for investors' cash.

Stock transfer agents

Per the JOBS Act, an investor faces a 12-month holding period on any stock purchases (see Chapter 4). The main reason this provision exists is to pre-vent pump-and-dump schemes where people buy lots of stock in a company to boost up the price and then dump all of it, making a quick gain while everyone else suffers.

After the 12-month holding period passes, investors may want to sell their stock. As a business owner or entrepreneur, contracting with a funding portal that has a relationship with a stock transfer agent (who is monitored by the SEC and FINRA) means that you're giving your investors a valuable service. These agents make sure that the person selling the stock is the actual owner, so when it comes time to sell, the investor has complete confidence in his stock ownership. The benefit to the business owner is that the stock transfer agent helps protect you from people fraudulently selling stock in your com-pany that they don't own.

Filing and financial reporting tools

How you choose to incorporate your business dictates how you need to file your taxes and report your financials. To file and report on time (and accurately), you most likely need outside help, especially if you've never owned a business before. You may want a funding portal that connects you with tax- and financial-report-related tools that can ease your burden.

Don't procrastinate when thinking about issues such as taxes and financial reporting. Be proactive, and look for a platform that offers guidance and helpful tools, whether in the form of third-party recommendations or tools on the portal website that help you file taxes directly from your account.

Shopping for the Best Crowdfund Investing Platform

In this section, we discuss some additional considerations when shopping for a funding portal, including how much the online platform will cost and whether it has any limitations that will impede your efforts. We want you to be a savvy shopper, so we offer some specific questions to ask during your research.

Anticipating the cost

Expect that whatever funding portal you choose will, at a minimum, charge you a flat fee for registration and for conducting a background check on you. Beyond that flat fee, you'll likely be charged what's called a *success fee* if you hit your funding target. The success fee likely represents between 4 percent and 10 percent of the money your raise. (Broker-dealers charge much higher success fees because they have a higher cost structure.) Keep in mind that the more bells and whistles a funding platform has, the more it'll cost.

In all cases, you should be able to determine in advance the costs associated with your chosen funding portal; its terms and conditions should spell out its fees very clearly. You want to build these costs into the money you raise — assuming that you hit your all-or-nothing funding target. (If you don't hit your funding target, any time, energy, and money you put into your pitch will most likely be your loss.)

When you find out the costs associated with your chosen online platform, build those numbers into your financial projections. If you didn't account for these costs when budgeting (see Chapter 5), back up and do so before determining exactly how much you need to raise in your crowdfund investment campaign.

Asking the right questions

When choosing your funding portal, make sure that it offers good customer service. When you ask questions, expect good — and prompt! — answers. You shouldn't need to wait days for answers, and you shouldn't need to ask a question twice.

When you do find a responsive portal, make sure you're asking the right questions. Here are some suggestions:

- ✔ **What services do you offer?** After reading the preceding section, home in on the services you really need help with, and make sure the portal has what you need.

- ✔ **How can I create the best possible online pitch?** You benefit by getting advice from people who really understand crowdfund investing. A good portal wants to give you this type of advice because it wants you to succeed.

- ✔ **What percentage of projects you've hosted have been fully funded? What might make the difference between success and failure?** Again, you want a portal that's willing to share insights based on past experience.

- ✔ **How do you handle ongoing communication between companies and their investors when a campaign has succeeded?** You absolutely *need* an easy way to communicate with investors. You can't exchange e-mails with a few hundred people while trying to build a business! Chapter 12 is devoted to a discussion of communicating with your investment crowd.

- ✔ **Are you geared toward my type of business?** Some portals may be more suitable for Main Street businesses; some may be better for more tech-related businesses; and some work with a cross-section of industries and businesses.

- ✔ **Who owns the copyright?** A portal should make it clear that it holds no title or claim to your copyrights (if you have any). If a portal's contract is not crystal clear on this point, run in the other direction.

- ✔ **What are your limitations?** No portal can possibly offer every service an entrepreneur or business owner needs, but it should represent itself with accuracy and transparency. If you suspect that you're getting a half-baked answer to this question, keep shopping.

- ✔ **Can I get a refund?** Suppose that you try to raise money on a crowdfund investing platform, and you fail. Can you get a refund for the registration and background check fees you've paid to the funding portal? No platform can guarantee success in raising capital for your business; it can only provide a service to help you achieve your goals. Therefore, you should expect the answer here to be *no*. However, you want reassurance that if your failure relates in any way to significant technical issues caused by the platform itself, or to services that were promised but not delivered, you can seek a refund of these initial fees.

Any platform you choose should offer terms of service that a human being can read. Even after you select a funding portal, don't sign the paperwork if you can't understand it. Be sure to ask a lawyer for advice if you're unclear. Spending a small amount of money to know exactly what you're getting from your funding portal is worth it so you know your rights and responsibilities. You may want to ask for a generic contract to consider while you're shopping; any reputable portal should be willing to share its terms of service upfront so you can make an educated decision.

Why portals must abstain from curation (or any other investment advice)

Curation is a practice used by some donation-based crowdfunding platforms (see Chapter 2) that promotes some crowdfunding campaigns over others. An example would be Kickstarter's "Campaigns We Love" e-mails that draw attention to particular campaigns and increase their ability to raise capital. This practice is allowed on donation (or perks-based) crowdfunding platforms because individuals are giving money away and not expecting a financial return.

The SEC has determined that crowdfund investment portals cannot curate because the practice of promoting one investment opportunity over another would be deemed as "providing investment advice" to investors and picking "winners and losers." Only individuals and organizations that hold proper FINRA certifications can provide investment advice to individual investors. This

fact provides a very bright line to separate funding portals from broker-dealers. Portals must treat this distinction with extreme caution and not cross the line into curation or giving investment advice.

The SEC also has stated that funding portals may not make arbitrary decisions about which issuers to accept or reject from their platforms because doing so is a form of investment advice. Platforms may have set standards in their terms of service for activities or types of businesses they will not accept, and they may decline to provide services based on such predetermined standards. For example, a portal may have terms of service that state that it doesn't work with tobacco industry companies, and it may then legally decline to work with a company in that industry.

Chapter 8

Networking Your Way to Successful Funding

*T*his chapter was written in conjunction with Judy Robinett, one of the nation's leading super connectors. She has over 30 years of experience working with startups, small/medium enterprises, and Fortune 500 companies. Judy is a former CEO of a public company and an active angel investor who mentors entrepreneurs on funding strategies and investors on vetting deals. Most important, she understands that without a strong social network, it doesn't matter how good your idea is, you'll never get funded. This chapter is about helping you build that strong network.

Building Your Network before You Raise Money

Raising money is hard work. Your success depends on your network and funding strategy. You simply must build relationships and connections with contacts who will be interested in investing in your company.

Building a robust, deep, and wide network must start before your campaign on a crowdfund investing platform launches. Why? Your campaign will be over in fewer than 90 days. RocketHub statistics show that you must get

30 percent of your dollars from your social network before strangers will take your offer seriously and invest. Worse, people lose interest when they see that others haven't invested. Your deal becomes old news, or what investors call "shopped." If you've shopped your deal too long, people believe there must be a good reason others haven't already invested.

As we explain in Chapter 9, when you reach that magic 30 percent level of initial investment, strangers will consider investing. Strangers want to see that other people have vetted your offer and invested. Your initial funding provides crucial credibility (otherwise known as *social proof*) for those who don't personally know you or your company's team.

Interestingly, Kickstarter campaign statistics show an opposite trend: Very few friends and family invest, and it's up to you to develop a strong network and a robust PR strategy that will attract backers. Who helps out the most? Acquaintances and all those connected to them — strangers to you. Statistics from the Kickstarter website showed total pledges of $100 million in October 2011 with the typical ratio of outside referrals to the website community 8 to 1.

Matt Haughey has backed 84 projects on Kickstarter. How does he find them? Twitter. He knows that the more followers you have, the better your ability to cash in on good will. Check out Matt's blog (http://a.wholelottanothing.org) for more information.

Brian Probst founder of CruxCase (www.cruxcase.com) raised more than $248,000 from his Kickstarter campaign. His Utah-based company develops, designs, and manufactures keyboard cases for the iPad. Half of his backing came from outside strangers. (His PR firm, Max Borges Agency, pushed the story out to tech bloggers on sites like Yahoo! News, Mashable, and Wired.) The other half came from backers in the Kickstarter community.

Brian lists the following five factors that helped make his campaign a success:

- ✔ **Culture:** It's a product that appeals to innovators and early adopters.

- ✔ **Design:** The product features a highly designed aesthetic that mimics the design and finish of Apple products.

- ✔ **First mover:** The product was one of the first of its kind available.

- ✔ **Transparency:** Brian and his team were completely transparent about their flaws, challenges, and personalities, and they maintained constant communication with their backers. Because of this, the backers felt as though they truly knew Brian's team personally, so they trusted them.

- ✔ **Tell the story:** More than just offering your backers a product, you're also telling them a story. The backers are a huge part of this story. Brian and his team made their story compelling and made the backers want to join them and be a part of their success story.

Developing Trust

Angel investor Jean Hammond says, "No one writes a check the size that will buy a small house unless they know you, like you, and trust you." Jean has 20 active investments; one of her first was an early bet on Zipcar.

Establishing trust adds significant credibility to your deal, but how do you establish trust with strangers?

Investors will look hard at you as the company founder to determine if you're the right jockey to bet on. Equity investors focus heavily on character. When investors weigh their decisions, they want to make sure that you, your company, and your idea rate at least 90 percent in the following ways:

- ✔ Management is capable and motivated.
- ✔ Market demand is as expected.
- ✔ Production is scaled up as planned.
- ✔ Competition is held at bay and intellectual property is defendable.
- ✔ Liability and litigation are avoided.
- ✔ The company has sufficient capital.
- ✔ Existing customers are able and willing to pay.

Keep in mind that even if all these factors rate 90 percent or higher, your chances of success are still only 48 percent, so this is truly risky business for an investor!

Being Transparent

Investors always try to mitigate risk, and the best way to help them do so is to be transparent and honest in all your conversations and documents. This includes offering realistic and conservative revenue projections. Howard Stevenson has made more than 80 angel investments and headed the Entrepreneur Management Unit at Harvard Business School for more than 25 years. One of the red flags for him is when people running a company "say or do anything that is dishonest. If they do not have a strong moral code, your money is history."

Guy Kawasaki, author of the excellent book *The Art of the Start* (Portfolio Hardcover), includes these warnings to employees, investors, and entrepreneurs: Pontificating, theorizing, and terrorizing abounds these days in tech startups. Here is a simple test to help you figure out if the startup you work for is in trouble. All you have to do is listen to your CEO talk to people for a week and determine if she uses the following lines:

- ✔ "Let me tell you why the Sequoia memo really doesn't apply to us."
- ✔ "Our team is totally engaged and believes in the company."
- ✔ "Our market is so large that a 20 percent reduction won't matter to us."
- ✔ "We aren't changing our long-term strategy because this is a short-term problem."
- ✔ "It's still too early to tell if we'll be affected."
- ✔ "The sales pipeline that we've already booked is still strong."
- ✔ "The start of sales results is just around the corner."
- ✔ "We can accelerate revenue with a few tweaks to our product."
- ✔ "We can reduce expenses without affecting headcount."
- ✔ "Our investors are totally engaged and believe in the company."
- ✔ "We think we can raise another round right after the holidays."
- ✔ "We heard that our competitors are in trouble, but we've been more conservative with expenses."
- ✔ "We have 12 months of cash even with our most conservative sales forecast."
- ✔ "In these times, (Some Big Company) needs what we offer to increase sales."
- ✔ "In these times, (Some Big Company) needs what we offer to reduce costs."
- ✔ "We've built an extremely viral product so we can reduce our sales and marketing expenses."

By extension, if potential investors start reading or hearing these lines of thinking from you, they may want to run in the other direction.

State all assumptions and include source information in your go-to-market plan. Saying that you're going to be a billion-dollar company and do an IPO by capturing 2 percent of China's population as customers is a telltale sign of an amateur. Do your homework. Find several outsiders, including an investor, to review your plan for obvious red flags before you begin your campaign. And listen closely to what they share with you.

Acquiring Access to World-Class Connections

How do you show good judgment and savvy networking? If you're developing a video game and you have legal counsel from Judy's hometown of Franklin, Idaho (population 1,000), we're worried. Our first thought is that you haven't done your homework and may lack judgment.

If, instead, we read in your business plan that you've hired Silicon Legal Strategy, a boutique law firm in San Francisco with clients such as online game platform Zynga, that information is a clear signal that you understand powerful connections that come from advisors. This law firm has an extensive ecosystem of investors and strategic relationships with potential acquirers for your exit. Be smart in all of your relationships.

A significant way to acquire access to world-class connections is *not* to shop for the lowest cost. Find smart partners who bring more than expertise to the party.

The same is true with all your advisors, board of directors, and advisory board members. Prolific angel investor Dave Berkus wrote a blog post entitled "Use Your Board's 'Golden Contacts'" (`www.berkonomics.com/?p=1435`), in which he wrote the following:

> The CEO has every right to expect his or her board to help with issues when asked, particularly when board members have associates, friends, or contacts that they believe would be able to help solve a problem or provide a service requested or needed by the CEO. . . .

> Board members each have a collection of associates who, because of their relationship to the board member, usually would be willing to help provide a solution to a problem when called upon.

Looking for Angels or Venture Capitalists

Friends and family members invest from $30 billion to $100 billion in startups each year. Susan Preston, author of the excellent book *Angel Financing for Entrepreneurs: Early-stage Funding for Long-Term Success* (Jossey-Bass), calls this funding *love money*.

Aside from friends and family members, who coughs up the most cash for startup funding? Research from the Kauffman Foundation (www.kauffman.org), which supports and studies entrepreneurs and investors, shows that 90 percent of high-potential deals are funded by *angels*, sophisticated, wealthy investors. Chapter 3 introduces angel investors and other private equity investors such as venture capitalists. In this section, we suggest how you may work to overcome the odds by networking to get these private equity sources to notice your opportunity.

Considering why angels invest and how to meet them

Many angel investors are successful entrepreneurs who have built and sold a business. Others are professionals including doctors, dentists, managers, and others who have excess income they want to put to work in the venture asset class. Why do these people invest? This asset class (benchmarked by the Venture Capital Index) outperforms all others and has returned 25.1 percent on average over the past 20 years.

Angels often band together in groups to work together for greater success than lone-wolf investors achieve. More than 200 angel groups exist in the United States, and many have websites explaining how to apply. (A top-tier angel group is Tech Coast Angels [www.techcoastangels.com].) Be sure to network your way to a warm introduction if possible. Angels can be fickle, and it's good to have a champion for your deal on the inside.

Many angel investors will consider your company only if you receive a warm introduction from a mutual acquaintance. Literally thousands of deals are available, and investors prefer they come from someone they know. Referrals are the number-one way that investors find deals. Someone you know, like, and trust won't send a crook or a worthless deal your way. Social capital is too critical to burn.

If you're looking for angel groups, family offices, and private investors, contact the Angel Capital Association (www.angelcapitalasssociation.org). Also, your local chamber of commerce, university entrepreneur programs, incubators, and accountants and lawyers who work with startups will know where angels flock. Venture capitalist Jeffrey Bussgang notes that venture capitalists are heavy networkers, and you must have a warm introduction. Jeff's firm, Flybridge Capital (www.flybridge.com), has invested in 50 companies in its eight-year history and not one of them came in cold. One VC partner says that if you can't figure out how to get a warm introduction to him, then you can't figure out how to find customers.

The National Venture Capital Association (NVCA; www.nvca.org) provides outstanding information about venture capital funds. Also, many books contain listings of venture capital funds, as well as entrepreneur support organizations such as accelerators and incubators. It's also smart to watch the television show *Shark Tank* and Bloomberg's *Risk Takers* to learn the basics and trends.

Tapping resources for women

Women often find it very difficult to find funding and can contact Astia (www.astia.org) and Springboard (www.springboardenterprises.org) for assistance in preparing a pitch deck, go-to-market plan, and viable business model that will catch the attention of investors. Springboard has an outstanding success record, having startups receive $5.5 billion of funding, complete ten IPOs, and close 123 strategic sales — successful exits.

Kelly Hoey, founder of Women Innovate Mobile (WIM), has a superb accelerator in New York that focuses on women founders. WIM is the first early-stage startup accelerator launched for women-founded companies in mobile technology. WIM's goal is to provide women entrepreneurs with the guidance, feedback, and connections needed to make their startups best-in-class companies and formidable business concerns. WIM is a three-month, mentorship-driven accelerator. Startups selected for investment receive seed funding, office space, mobile-marketing promotions, and access to an incredible network of mentors, funders, and advisors. In exchange, WIM receives a 6 percent equity stake in each company.

Thinking small with micro VCs

An interesting trend is micro VCs, which may invest in early-stage niche markets. Micro VCs represent a relatively new style of firm — one that has emerged in parallel with the ability to leverage public cloud-computing technologies to launch companies with much less initial capital cost than in the past. It's a strategy that recognizes that it isn't smart for entrepreneurs to take too much outside capital before they know that they have a company that can grow exponentially.

Cindy Padnos, founder of Illuminate Ventures (www.illuminate.com), has an excellent track record as a micro VC investor. Of 14 investments made over eight years, four have exited profitably, only one has failed to return capital, and several are continuing toward home-run status. Check out the firm online and follow Cindy on Twitter at www.twitter.com/illuminatevc. Illuminate focuses on finding, funding, and accelerating great teams in the business-to-business cloud-computing space.

Micro VC firms do a relatively small number of early-stage investments each year and usually at a dollar level that can significantly impact fund performance. As a result, they're highly motivated to assist each portfolio company: They take board seats and work closely with the founders to accelerate progress to meet the milestones needed to secure the next round of financing and reserve funds to be able to invest through the life of the company. Micro VCs are often former entrepreneurs themselves with large networks. (Illuminate Ventures, for example, has an active 40-member business advisory council made up of world-class tech entrepreneurs and executives.) Because they typically invest in specific niches in which they have domain experience, micro VCs can provide access to a unique set of highly relevant contacts.

Focusing on family funds

Many wealthy families have family offices that are responsible for investments. There are an estimated 2,500 such offices in the United States. Candace Klein, founder of SoMoLend (www.somolend.com), has a family office as an investor, as well as angels. How did she find them? She participated in business plan competitions across the United States. Investors attend these competitions in hopes of beating other investors to a great deal. Candace has built a robust network of current and future investors that are watching her execute her business model. Candace actively tweets, blogs, and leverages PR efforts with articles, which have added more members to her social network.

Building a Powerful LinkedIn Profile

Facebook, Twitter, and LinkedIn plus public relations combine into a social media marketing effort designed to get the word out to potential investors. Author and social business stylist Jennifer Abernethy is one of the top 50 social media marketing leaders in the United States (according to *Social Media Marketing Magazine*) and understands how to build a social media marketing strategic plan.

To be a power networker offline, you also have to be one online. Most executives are on LinkedIn, so here are seven tips from Abernethy to build a powerful LinkedIn profile:

- ✔ **Get a powerful headshot.** Make sure it exudes the brand of you.

- ✔ **Make sure your LinkedIn Summary is filled out.** Use a conversational, social tone. Use first person.

- ✔ **Include a phone number and e-mail address in the summary.** This is the new social business. You must be social!

- ✔ **Invite people to call or e-mail you directly *or* direct them to where you want them to call.**

- ✔ **Post relevant updates/articles on LinkedIn that will begin to attract the type of business you want to attract.**

- ✔ **Post a slideshow presentation or video about your company using the SlideShare application on LinkedIn.**

- ✔ **Check to make sure your company has a dynamic page.** Add it under the Companies tab.

- ✔ **Make sure your top employees are representing your company well.** Give them wording to describe where they work. They're your top brand ambassadors, and they're digitally networking on behalf of your company, too.

Of course, LinkedIn isn't the only place where you should have a presence. Twitter is a powerful tool to attract funding as well. Naked Pizza founders Robbie Vitrano and Jeff Leach began tweeting fun one-liners, such as "Fast doesn't make you fat." Mark Cuban of *Shark Tank* fame and an early investor suggested spreading the world about their startup with Twitter. They received 8,000 investment inquiries, a quarter of which turned into investment dollars.

Creating Content

Social promotion involves quality content. Preston Andrew, Vice President of Business Development at Terillion, says:

> Often I get asked how businesses should attract more followers or likes. The answer isn't usually one they want to hear. The first thing I ask is who is in charge of their content creation? This usually draws a blank look, with the follow-up remark, "What department usually handles that?"

Simply put, businesses aren't adapting to the changes in marketing. If you don't have someone creating premium, thought-provoking, keyword-rich content for at least six hours every day, you are behind. (Normally I would say if you don't have a copywriter, graphic designer, and research analyst you are behind! Let's ease into this though.)

Content marketing does many things but a few things really well:

- It allows the organization or individual to establish expertise or to be looked upon as a thought leader.

- When focused content is created (usually through a blog), you're allowing the Google spiders to better understand what you do, therefore yielding better organic search rankings.

- It allows you to reach out to and promote others by including information about their organization in your content. (Hint, hint, this is how you get followers!) There are many different marketing philosophies, but if content marketing isn't at the foundation of your efforts, make the necessary adjustments and proper investment.

Building Your Circle of 50

You want to try to anticipate needs you'll have in the near and distant future. For example, at some point, you may need strategic help with your patent portfolio developing a family of patents. As your startup grows, you'll eventually need to have audited financials. And if you don't have a powerful board of directors, you'll need one. Not only do all these folks have tremendous skills, but if they're top tier in their field, they'll have their own established network that you can engage. The people who can fill your future needs should occupy your company's ecosystem, which is your *Circle of 50.*

Why 50? Research has shown that the majority of humans haven't changed their basic social groups over thousands of years. The numbers are generally the same in the various groups that surround us: 5-15-50-150. For in-depth information on this subject, read *Grouped,* by Paul Adams (New Riders). Here's a brief overview:

- **5:** Your friends and family members are your *strong links.* Generally speaking, your inner circle consists of about five individuals.

- **15:** The second circle of people who surround you are those you may turn to for emotional support even though they aren't your strongest links. This group generally comprises 15 people.

- **50:** This third circle is your Circle of 50! These are the *weak links,* the professional relationships that research indicates will actually be your most powerful resources.

To develop your Circle of 50, think about who you need to know and develop a plan to meet them. This is easier than it sounds. Be scrappy and resourceful. Let others know your intentions — educate them with a concise, clear, and compelling story. You'll be surprised to find out that most people will help you if you ask.

✔ **150:** You don't need this many close contacts. That's because at 150, groups tend to fall apart. (Fun fact: Roman armies comprised groups of 150 people.)

Heidi Roizen is a Venture Partner at Draper Fisher Jurvetson and offers this advice: "Funding for startups is often said to be more of a bet on the people than on the product or the market. Because of this, it is critical that the entrepreneur who seeks funding has built relationships with others in the entrepreneurial ecosystem that can then vouch for his or her knowledge, ideas, ethics, and passion."

Saying the Two Most Powerful Words: Help Me!

Dave Berkus, angel investor extraordinaire and author of books about entrepreneurs and investing, is clear that two of the most powerful words are *help me*. When looking for help, according to Berkus, you need to develop a strategy that includes six key actions:

✔ Attend top-tier industry conferences and talk to the speakers and leaders.

✔ Interview lawyers, accountants, and bankers to determine the quality of their services and the depth of their network.

✔ Target key opinion leaders (KOLs) in your industry who may be valuable advisors or board members.

✔ Locate tipping-point connectors that can immediately enlarge your network.

✔ Plan for luck, serendipity, and random encounters.

✔ Plan relationships needed through to your company's exit.

Dr. David Bearss and Dallin Anderson sold their life science company, Montigen, in less than five years for $45 million to strategic buyer SuperGen. How did they do this? They anticipated who the likely buyers would be and established strong relationships with them, keeping them aware of achieved milestones. The relationships developed, and a successful exit has made it possible for their second startup venture, Tolero Pharma, to quickly move forward.

As you strive to build relationships, two golden questions can accelerate the quality of people and information you can obtain:

- ✔ What other ideas might you have for me?
- ✔ Who else do you know that I should talk to?

We mention luck in the bulleted list at the beginning of this section. Why would you plan for luck? Richard Wiseman, author of *The Luck Factor* (Miramax), says lucky people generate their own good fortune via four basic principles:

- ✔ They're skilled at creating and noticing chance opportunities.
- ✔ They make lucky decisions by listening to their intuition.
- ✔ They create self-fulfilling prophesies and positive expectations.
- ✔ They adopt a resilient attitude that transforms bad luck into good.

Winners expect to win and aren't afraid to play a hunch. When bad luck comes, they see it as a bump in the road and keep going.

Organizations and groups are important to your overall success. Joining powerful groups is a great way to leverage your network to the next level. Imagine how long it would take to find and meet all the folks who attend a key conference or event.

Overcoming What's Holding You Back

We all have fears and insecurities. Dispel faulty assumptions and beliefs you may have about building relationships for your ecosystem. Keep these points in mind:

- ✔ **Many of the best connectors grew up shy.** To overcome shyness, pretend the other person is your best friend.
- ✔ **Don't fear being rejected.** If someone is rude, shame on him and move on. There are seven billion people on the planet, keep going.
- ✔ **Networking is about building win-win relationships, not passing out business cards.** Charlie Munger recommends that you pay attention to who you feel truly attracted to, which he says is about 5 out of 100 people. Let the others go. It's about quality, not quantity.

✔ **Build trust.** Kindness, listening, generosity, and follow-through will make you someone to know. This makes you attractive and puts you in the five-people-to-know category.

✔ **Unfortunately, there are bad actors.** This is true with bad angels (who are called *devils*) and bad venture capitalists (known as *vulture capitalists*). Often these people are bright, charming, and powerful, so keep your eyes open, do your homework, and be prepared to walk away. Be clear on the cost of the money — there is good money and bad money.

✔ **Your best connections are people you don't know.** Dispel the myth that all strangers are dangerous. Reach out to others. Follow Guy Kawasaki's advice: Go out there and get connected.

✔ **Don't let fear stop you.** Turn your anxiety into positive energy. Barbara Corcoran said that every day on her way to becoming a billion-dollar company, she worried about bankruptcy.

Developing an Infographic

One of the most valuable networking tools you can use is an *infographic*. Kelly Hoey of WIM says she wouldn't have been so successful without diverse relationships. Figure 8-1 shows her infographic indicating the relationship to organizations and people critical for the success of her organization.

You can use Post-it notes on the wall, a mind-mapping program, or a free infographic program, but get it down.

President Lyndon Johnson kept communication channels open with senators and representatives. He knew his success with Congress required good relationships and kept this as a priority. He kept big maps on his wall that had the following information:

✔ Where each bill was in committee

✔ What stage the bill was at

✔ What needed to happen for the bill to reach the next stage

He called individual congressmen, who could be obstacles at any stage, helped them understand how important this was to him, and promised whatever needed to get it through.

Doris Kearns Goodwin, who wrote *Lyndon Johnson and the American Dream* (St. Martin's Griffin), said that Johnson called one senator at 2 a.m. and said, "I hope I didn't wake you." LBJ said you had to court congressmen even more ardently than you courted your wife.

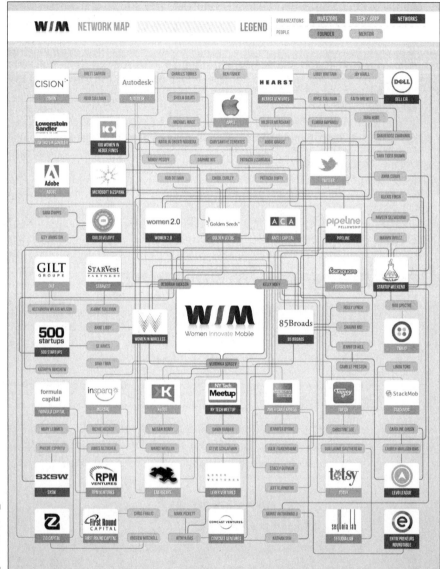

Figure 8-1:
WIM's
infographic.

Keep in mind these words by Sir Arthur Conan Doyle: "Skill is fine, and genius is splendid, but the right contacts are more valuable than either."

Part III
Managing Your Crowdfund Investing Campaign

The 5th Wave   By Rich Tennant

"It hasn't helped me sell more hot dogs, but I've had several inquiries for investment advice."

In this part . . .

If you're an entrepreneur or small business owner, the chapters in this part are your crash course in launching and running your online crowdfund investing campaign. Chapter 9 spells out how to market your pitch, how to tap into your social networks to greatest effect, and what to look for after your campaign goes live. In Chapter 10, we help you anticipate and prepare for potential campaign-related problems. And Chapter 11 talks you through what to do and expect after you run a successful campaign that achieves your funding goal.

Chapter 9

Making Your Pitch

*I*n this chapter, we help you build a winning pitch that will best position your business to potential investors to attract their investment. We discuss creating a hook to catch your investors and reel them in by using tools such as video, your website, and a good ol' fashioned elevator pitch. We also offer insights based on experiences with crowdfunding, and we walk you through how to manage your social networks.

Here's a quick tip to get you started: Building a winning pitch requires vetting each part of it with existing supporters, meaning any friends, family members, and others who have already shown interest in your idea. You may want to ask your earliest supporters to act as an informal advisory board. Doing so taps into the wisdom and power of the crowd from the start and prevents you from taking a pitch public before it's ready.

Putting Your Best Face Forward

If you're going on a job interview, even to an office where business casual reigns supreme, you should wear a suit. That's because first impressions matter so much. When you're pitching your business idea, you want that pitch to wear a suit as well; you should dress and polish it so it wows your potential investors.

To put your best face forward, you must first have a clear strategy regarding what you want to do, how you want to do it, how it's going to make money, and how you're going to pay back your investors. If you aren't completely confident in your strategy, spend some quality time with Chapter 5 and shore up your business plan. Then, take a step back and try to look at your plan from an outsider's perspective. What problem are you solving? Who is your customer? How will you make money? These are three very important parts of a pitch.

Let's say you want to start an organic farm that sells apples, potatoes, and artisanal cheese. Assume that you've already studied the competitive landscape, spoken to local restaurants, and gone to your regional farm convention so you understand new and innovative farming techniques and have built a network with other organic farmers. In this section, we walk you through the steps required to dress up your idea in its best professional clothing and make a potent impression that leads to the funding you need.

Writing a great headline

Your first step is to consolidate your business plan into an attention-grabbing one-sentence headline. Sound hard? It doesn't have to be.

Before you try to write the headline, sum up your aspirations and inspirations in a paragraph. You don't need to share this paragraph with anyone, so don't get frozen at this step. Just spend a few minutes writing directly from your heart about the *why,* and not just the *what* and the *how* of your business. Jot down the big-picture ideas that have motivated you to get this far in your planning.

For example, if you're an organic farmer, your paragraph could be something like this:

> Local food systems strengthen our local economies: When we buy local and choose to support local farm and food ventures, we reinforce our community, our environment, and our own health. Not only can we create local jobs, but we can provide a valuable service to the community, and our farm can enjoy 50 percent more of the profits by selling directly to purchasers rather than going through a massive wholesale produce corporation. Those corporations control the process to maximize profits at the expense of safety, force the use of nasty pesticides, and eat away at the margins of the farmers who produce the food.

From this paragraph, choose several keywords that represent what you're talking about. In this case, you might select *organic, farm, local, community, jobs,* and *profits.* (These are our choices; yours may be different). Take these keywords and write a few sentences around them that explain who you are, what you care about, and what you need. For example:

> "City boy turned organic farmer with three years of experience needs $100,000 to create community jobs."

"$100,000 needed to start local farm-to-table organic farm for the city of Anytown, USA."

"Profits from organic farming are greater, and the food is healthier. Let's create community jobs with $100,000."

Take your sentences to your informal advisory board or, at a minimum, to the friends and family members who are your greatest supporters. Ask them the following questions:

✔ Which headline resonates the most with you?

✔ Which headline would pique your interest enough to consider investing your money?

✔ What would you change in each headline to make it better?

✔ Which headlines turn you off and why?

✔ Is there another headline you like better?

✔ Who else would you recommend that I talk with about this headline?

Listen closely to the advice you get. The responses are key to determining if your one-liner is strong enough to pull other investors in.

Check your ego at the door. Asking your advisors what they think about your headline is akin to your feeling self-conscious about your weight and then asking someone you care about, and from whom you want an honest answer, if you look too fat in your jeans. You have to be prepared for the honest truth and be willing to listen, consider, and engage — not attack. Asking the hard questions requires listening to the tough answers. The responses may not be exactly what you want to hear, but they could save you agony later on and make your idea and business better at the same time!

Producing a quality video to sell your idea

Creating a video to pitch your idea to potential investors isn't optional; it's essential. Video is by far the fastest growing part of the web because it engages people more than flat text.

Before thinking about your own video, watch 10 to 20 videos that were part of a successful campaign on both perks-based and equity/debt-based crowd-fund investing sites. What do you like about them? What do you dislike? Next, do the same exercise but select projects or companies that seem likely to miss their funding targets or have missed their funding targets. Are there any common themes? Did these videos engage you, or did they bore you or turn you off?

A video won't be the *only* way you present your pitch, but it must be one of the ways you do so. The video will bring your passion to life for people you can't talk with in person. If this medium is new to you, don't panic. No one expects you to hire a production team and spend $10,000 on a video. (If you did, potential investors might frown on the expense as wasteful.) Follow the advice in this section, and ask for help from supporters with more experience. The outcome should be a video pitch that communicates your passion, your business strategy, and your financial need.

If you *really* don't think you have what it takes to make a quality video, many companies are waiting to help you solve this problem. They'll sit with you and learn about you, your idea, and how it will make money. Most likely, they come from a marketing and sales background and can use their knowledge and experience to help curate your entire crowdfund investing pitch. Keep in mind that in exchange for this service, they charge a fee or require you to fork over some equity (or both).

Scripting your message

A quality video starts with a script. A script doesn't need to spell out every word you're going to say; instead, it should act as a guide for all the points you need to hit on in your video. To reduce your stress, you don't even need to think of it as a script; think of it as answering a few questions that a friend is asking you about your business. In Chapter 5, we note that your business plan must cover the who, what, when, where, how, and why of your product or service. The questions you must touch on in your video include all these points:

- ✔ Who are you?
- ✔ What product or service do you need money to create, and what problem will it solve?
- ✔ Where will the business reside?
- ✔ What are the important milestones you'll reach with the money and when do you plan to reach them?
- ✔ How will you use the money to accomplish your goals?
- ✔ Why should your audience care?

In addition, following the foundational principles of crowdfund investing, you must strive to be honest, transparent, and authentic in your video pitch. Your goal with answering these questions (creating the script) is to explain your mission to a stranger in just a few succinct paragraphs and compel that person to invest in you. You don't necessarily have to write out exact answers. Instead, let the script feel more natural. Jot down brief bullet points that remind you of the key points you want to make, and then just speak from the heart.

Keep your pitch *under* five minutes so you can retain your audience's attention; two or three minutes is preferable. Make the beginning of your script the most powerful part because after one to two minutes, some people will tune out (even if they like what you're saying).

Rehearsing your presentation

With your script in hand, it's time to rehearse for the video shoot. Here are some pointers:

- Practice your script in front of the mirror.

- Get familiar enough with the script that you memorize the core concepts. You want to avoid reading the script when you're on camera.

  Don't panic: You don't have to memorize an exact script word for word. Instead, you just need to memorize the *content* of your presentation. Know your content completely. That way, you'll have the confidence and knowledge to answer questions about it in the video discussion.

- Work on acting naturally when the camera is rolling. Start by looking at yourself in the mirror, and then practice when looking at the camera itself. It may help to have someone look at you while you're rehearsing. (No one's around to watch? Put a wig on the camera!)

- Strive to engage with your audience. Doing so is absolutely crucial! You must show your passion, and by knowing your content completely, you can relax and let your passion shine.

- Prepare a stellar opening statement. The first 15 seconds of your video are the most important because you have to make sure to get people's attention.

- Be yourself. People care most about the human side of things, so keep in mind that you're really just trying to tell the story behind your project.

What if I don't own a video camera?

If you have a Mac, you're in luck. Most Macs have cameras built in that are fine for achieving what you need. Use the built-in program Photo Booth to record and iMovie to edit. Both programs come standard on your Mac.

If you have a PC, consider using an external digital camera. Use a digital single lens reflex (DSLR) camera because DSLR lenses generally give much better results.

If you have no camera at your disposal, reach out to your early supporters with a request for assistance. Chances are, someone you know can help out.

Ideally, you should tape one of your rehearsals and solicit feedback from your supporters. Very few people do their best work the very first time the camera is rolling.

Controlling your environment

Make sure your sound quality and the video's lighting are as good as you can make them. If you have a microphone that you can plug into your video camera (or into your computer, if you're using a built-in camera), use it! Pay attention to any background noises (traffic, music, an A/C unit, or the fridge, for example), which can ruin your video. Create a quiet space, and try to eliminate white noise and static by using your video editor. People can tolerate a video that isn't perfect, but they have a much lower tolerance for poor sound quality. Do whatever you can to have clear and crisp sound.

Cameras, like plants, function better with lots of light. Give your camera what it needs, and your video will look crisper and more polished. Set up a few extra lamps, and record during the daytime. Try to get some natural light, and bear in mind that mirrors can help by reflecting ambient light. Have some fun experimenting with what makes a good video. Try different types of lighting until you find what you like.

Shooting yourself (with the camera, please)

When it's time to record, here are some tips to keep in mind:

- ✔ Use the timer button to delay the start of recording so you have some time to situate yourself in front of the camera.

- ✔ When the camera starts recording, wait a few seconds before beginning your pitch; doing so will make the editing process easier.

- ✔ Expect that you'll record several videos to get what you want. This is normal.

- ✔ If you mess up, take a deep breath, look at the camera, and start again. If you get frustrated, take a break. (Frustration won't help your camera presence.)

- ✔ When you're done with the first take, review it carefully. Decide what you like and what you don't like. Then record your pitch again — and again — until it's perfect (or at least close). You're trying to raise money here, so "good enough" doesn't cut it.

Editing for maximum effect

When you're done recording, it's time to edit. The good news is that you can weave together bits and pieces from each take that you liked. Here are some pointers for editing:

✔ If you're working on a PC, use the program Windows Movie Maker. If you're on a Mac, use iMovie.

✔ Don't like how you look in a specific section? Weave in photos, video clips of your work, or testimonials from others. Make your video a visual showcase of what you're all about. (But don't overdo it! Your audience really wants to see your face.)

✔ Do *not* use material that belongs to others (illustrations, photos, music, logos, and so on) unless the owners explicitly authorize you to do so.

✔ Find and extract the clearest lines from each take. Also, try to keep in the fun and emotion — you don't want to strip out the elements that make you seem most human.

✔ Most important, put yourself in the shoes of a potential backer and make sure that your introduction makes viewers hope for more.

Uploading your pitch

When your video is complete, you need to show it to your supporters and solicit their feedback. If you need to re-record any parts of it or alter the editing, do so until your supporters feel great about the quality.

When you have a product you're proud of, upload it to an online video site such as YouTube, and then ask your funding portal (see Chapter 7) to link to it so potential investors can easily find it. *Note:* Regardless of which video website you choose, you must be certain that the video you upload is marked "private" so people browsing the web can't open it. Only potential investors who have visited the funding portal that supports your crowdfund investing campaign should have access to the video. Making the video available to the general public goes against SEC regulations.

Preparing your website

Headline, check! Video pitch, check! The next element to focus on is your website, which will also be linked to your funding portal. Your website should reflect all the things you emphasize in your video pitch and can offer more details about your product or service, your business strategy, the milestones you seek to achieve, and so on. You can use text, photos, additional videos, graphics, a blog, and more to get your points across. You want a clean, easy-to-navigate site that demonstrates to potential investors that you have answers to their questions, you've thought through the specifics of your venture, and you're professional.

If creating or updating your website to achieve all these goals seems overwhelming, keep these things in mind:

✔ Blogging platforms like WordPress (www.wordpress.com) make getting a website up and running relatively easy. *WordPress For Dummies,* 4th Edition, by Lisa Sabin-Wilson (Wiley), can get you started. Even easier than WordPress is Virb (www.virb.com). With Virb, for $10 per month, someone with absolutely no knowledge of web design can create his own professional-looking website, fully customized with just a few clicks of the mouse.

✔ Lots of people know how to create websites, and chances are that at least a couple of these people know you and support what you're trying to achieve. When in doubt, reach out to your early supporters for help.

✔ Likewise, your supporters can tell you whether what you're creating is truly useful and easy to navigate. They can offer tips for improving your site that may be crucial to sending the right message to potential investors.

Be very careful about how you use your website. You have to prepare for a situation in which someone visits your website for reasons *other* than finding out more about the investment opportunity. Per Securities and Exchange Commission (SEC) regulations, potential investors need to go to a crowdfunding portal or registered broker-dealer to learn about the crowdfund investment offering that you mention on your website. You can — and should — promote your business venture on your website so customers and potential investors understand what your business does. But the JOBS Act doesn't allow you to post a solicitation for capital on your own website; as we explain in Chapter 3, it allows you to reach out only to people who already populate your social networks.

So, use your website to explain your concept and strategy, to promote the vision of what you're trying to achieve, and to let investors find out more about who you are. But do *not* use it to request money. Let your funding portal handle those requests for you by tapping into your social networks (see Chapter 7). Otherwise, you could receive a very unpleasant letter from the SEC asking you to take down your pitch because you aren't following the rules, and at that point your fundraising opportunity is dead. Capiche?

Marketing offline: Your elevator pitch

To promote your business idea, you have to be prepared to talk to people, such as your current customers, to explain that they can learn about your crowdfunding campaign at the broker-dealer or crowdfunding platform website that you choose. However, the JOBS Act forbids you from requesting investments directly. Don't break the law! Here's what to avoid:

✔ Do *not* market your crowdfund investment offering to anyone who isn't part of your social network. Focus just on your concept instead.

✔ Do *not* state the terms of the offering, even if this person asks. If someone is interested in finding out more, encourage her to join your social network so you can then legally get her connected with your funding portal.

The vast majority of your investors will use your video pitch in making their decision, but preparing yourself to pitch your idea in person is very important. You should be ready to deliver your pitch in any situation and at any time (maybe even in an elevator!).

Using your data room to best effect

A *data room* is a virtual room on your funding portal (see Chapter 7) where you keep your more sensitive corporate documents so that only people who are known entities, and who have permission, can view them. Good data rooms provide a log of exactly who logged in, when these people logged in and logged out, and what documents they viewed and for how long. This information lets you assess which investors are more serious than others, as well as providing you information about what documents are most interesting to potential investors. How does a potential investor get permission to enter the data room? One goal of your video pitch should be to engage this person enough so that he's willing to give you his identity and request data room access.

Anyone who visits your funding portal should have access to your video pitch, a basic description of the business, your basic financial documents, FAQs, and any supplemental videos that you consider helpful to potential investors. Information confined to a data room may include the following:

✔ Full financials (*pro forma* documents, as well as financials from up to the past three years if you have that much financial history)

✔ An industry overview

✔ Definitions of any terms that are unique to your industry that a potential investor should understand so he can fully assess the investment opportunity

✔ A detailed product or service description

✔ Related press articles

✔ Competitive analysis

✔ Background information or CVs of the management team

✔ Your pricing strategy

✔ The structure of any prior securities agreements

✔ Information about intellectual property

✔ Tax information, if available

Answer these questions when drafting your spoken pitch:

✔ What is the problem you're solving, and why is it a relevant problem? (Include a sentence about market size.)

✔ Who are you?

✔ What is your solution?

✔ How will you earn money?

✔ What is the competitive landscape?

✔ Why are you and your team the best people to solve this problem?

✔ Where can interested parties go to learn more about the specifics of your offer?

Oh, and by the way, you need to answer all these questions in three minutes or less. In fact, the three-minute version is the *long* version; you should also create a one-minute version for social situations. Human beings have short attention spans, so you need to find the most compelling part of your story and really polish, sharpen, and shorten it down to the key points with the greatest impact. How can you say the same thing with higher-impact words? How can you say the same thing with fewer words? This is your advertisement for your company, and you may get only one shot, so don't be boring! Keep it brief and compelling so that people want to hear more.

Applying Lessons Learned from Perks-Based Crowdfunding

Perks-based crowdfunding (which we define in Chapter 2) has been active since 2007. We can look at how people make crowdfunding decisions and use that information as a framework for thinking about how people make decisions in crowdfund investing.

To be clear: Making a decision to contribute, such as to an arts-related project, is very different from making a decision to invest in an entrepreneur or a business that, based on your analysis, has an opportunity for a return. As you read this section, make sure you understand that perks-based ventures are not 100 percent correlated to what happens in equity- or debt-based crowdfunding. But we do believe that many of the social dynamics transfer because crowdfunding and crowdfund investing are, by their very nature, social activities.

Remembering why people participate

According to a report on global crowdfunding prepared by Massolution (www.massolution.com), in 2011 individuals contributed over $1.5 billion to crowdfunding efforts in support of over 1 million campaigns. This is a staggering amount of money. Massolution defines four basic types of crowdfunding efforts: donation based, reward based, equity based, and lending based. (We call the reward-based campaigns *perks based* because someone who donates to this type of effort gets a specific perk when the campaign succeeds.)

According to RocketHub (www.rockethub.com), one of the largest global perks-based crowdfunding platforms, the following are some common reasons that people participate in these campaigns:

✔ **Love:** People give money to support people or organizations they love. It sounds simple, and it is. Think about times when you've given to a cause simply because a friend asked you to.

✔ **Being part of something larger:** Human beings like being in packs and want to feel attachment, affiliation, and belonging. Why do so many membership clubs exist that align around causes, ideas, or ideals? People want to demonstrate their individuality, but usually they want to do so from within a group. Being part of a crowdfunding campaign is one way people can feel that they're making a difference in the larger community and that their lives and actions have meaning beyond what they can see and do in their daily routines.

✔ **Following and supporting passion:** Some salespeople are trying simply to earn a dollar. Others actually use the product they're selling, can speak about it with passion, and are clearly engaged with it. (Have you ever been to an Apple Store? Every person working there is clearly engaged with the brand and wants to share that enthusiasm with others.) Passion is intoxicating; we all want more of it in our lives. People who contribute to crowdfunding campaigns often do so because they're inspired by the passion of the campaign organizers.

✔ **Rewards and recognition:** Remember the gold stars you used to get in elementary school? (What? You never got any? Maybe you remember the gold stars that the annoying person sitting next to you always got.) Another basic human dynamic is the desire to be recognized in your peer group or in the community or world at large.

In the donation- or perks-based crowdfunding model, some people give so they can be recognized as the first ones on their block to have a new product; when that product arrives, it has a special badge or recognition that shows they were among the first 100 or 1,000 people to have purchased or donated to this campaign. Think about a museum or library; there's always a wall near the entrance that lists the major donors to that organization. The larger the name, the more money, time, or other services were given.

> The desire for recognition is the flip side of the feeling of belonging; it's the longing to be special or unique. Both pursuits are normal, and both are good. As someone about to embark on raising money from the crowd, you need to use this knowledge to carefully construct your campaign to appeal to everyone, no matter what their primary motivation may be.

Working toward the tipping point

In the past, when someone needed money to start a business, she went directly to her family and close friends. The people who agreed to help did so because they knew her. The challenge with crowdfunding is that you move beyond the people closest to you and include acquaintances or friends of friends. How do you convince them to believe in you when they barely even know you? One crucial way is to work diligently to gain traction with the people who *do* know you well. At a certain (and fairly well-defined) point in the campaign, called the *tipping point,* the folks who don't know you very well are more likely to climb onboard.

Here's what RocketHub says about this phenomenon: If you're crowdfunding, until you reach about 30 percent of your funding target, people who aren't your first-degree (or maybe second-degree) connections are very unlikely to give to your campaign. For example, if you're attempting to raise $30,000 for your film, the first $10,000 or so isn't likely to come from people who barely know you. But after you surpass the 30 percent mark, you demonstrate sufficient traction with your core group of supporters — you establish "social proof" that you're legitimate and people can support your campaign; you're the real deal. At that point, other people start trusting that you can reach your goal, and they're much more likely to open their wallets to help you.

Is the 30 percent tipping point always true? No, rare exceptions exist. In a handful of cases, effective public relations and social media buzz have propelled companies to stratospheric fundraising heights without the need to gain traction among close supporters first.

Gaining more insights from RocketHub

RocketHub has generously supplied the data we present throughout this section. Having raised millions of dollars from thousands of campaigns, RocketHub is an expert in the field of perks- and equity-based crowdfunding and worked tirelessly to support the efforts to legalize crowdfund investing.

Here's some additional information from RocketHub that sheds light on crowd-based funding activities:

- ✔ **Fraud gets nipped in the bud.** The perks-based platforms like RocketHub have created sophisticated algorithms to detect fraud in all aspects of the process. This technology (and the vigilance of the crowd) has resulted in no successful fraud on the RocketHub platform and no reported fraud on other perks-based platforms. Other equity- and debt-based platforms are likewise focused on doing everything they can to prevent fraud as well.

- ✔ **A campaign doesn't last forever.** A donation-based campaign tends to last from 30 to 60 days. Fundraising campaigns (like all things in life) need deadlines, which drive action. Campaigns that run longer than 90 days lose steam, so in crowdfund investing, RocketHub recommends aiming for the 30- to 60-day range.

- ✔ **The majority of campaigns fail.** On perks-based sites, about 40 percent of the campaigns reach their targets. This fact reminds us that the crowd performs due diligence and determines which campaigns are worthy of success and which aren't. Running a crowdfunded campaign isn't easy. Given the intense interest that people have in their money, the percentage of successful crowdfund investment campaigns could prove to be even lower.

Managing Your Social Network

Crowdfund investing is where social media meets online investing. In this section, we show you how to start your pitch (via your funding portal; see Chapter 7) by first engaging your core social networks. Then we explain how to nurture your pitch so it moves well beyond your first-tier contacts and reaches friends of friends of friends.

At the risk of nagging, we simply must remind you that what you post on your social networks may be seen by more eyes than you can imagine. Your potential investors don't want to see your wall plastered with drunk pictures or political tirades. (If an investor loves your concept but hates your politics, chances are, she isn't investing in you.) Treat the information on your social network like a résumé — because that's exactly what it is. Make sure nothing is on there that you wouldn't put on a résumé.

Building from your core social network outward

Chances are, you have at least one social network already. If you don't, you need to create one before you can attempt crowdfund investing. And if you do, now is the time to make your network(s) as robust as possible.

Consider the example of LinkedIn, the social network for the business world. (It was started by one of the most connected business people in Silicon Valley, Reid Hoffman, who was constantly asked to make introductions to his contacts. One day, Hoffman decided to make his life a lot easier and put his Rolodex online.) If you're on LinkedIn, you most likely have connected with all the people you've worked with in the past, people you went to school with, and anyone else who knows you professionally. Who else can you possibly tap to be part of this network?

When you're signed on, LinkedIn lets you see people's résumés. If you locate second- or third-degree connections who seem like strong potential investors, you can ask your first-degree connection for an introduction. For example, if you're about to launch a campaign to raise money for a food distribution company, you can easily see everyone in your extended network who has any experience in this field. Invite these people to be your first-degree connections.

Next, go into the related groups on LinkedIn and join the existing conversations. Make a name for yourself by posting relevant comments. Find the movers and shakers in the groups, and start conversations with them. When you're engaged in a conversation, you can add this person as your first-degree contact.

As you can see, this process takes some time. It's never too late to start, but if you haven't started already, start today. Set up a schedule for yourself with specific goals — for example, make ten new contacts each week or spend 20 minutes two times a day engaging people on social networks.

When taking these steps, do *not* spam people. There is a thin line between providing good content that people will enjoy and spamming people with things they don't care about. In the business world of social networking, everyone wants to gain fans or followers, but don't get so aggressive that you become a nuisance.

Be diligent about growing your social network. The larger and more comprehensive it is when you launch your project, the more potential people you'll have to invest in your business.

Supporting other companies for mutual benefit

While you're trying to grow your networks, remember that other companies are doing the same thing. If a company helps you out, make sure to respond in kind. In this section, we discuss how you can do so on some of the leading social media websites.

Sharing

Online *sharing* occurs when you repost something that someone else has posted. People usually post things because they want them to be shared; they want as many people as possible to see what they have to say. Businesses post things about their products or services, about upcoming events, and about other relevant content. By sharing something another business posts, you help it extend its reach.

The more you help other people and businesses by sharing their information, the more they'll return the favor. If you're consistently helping other people, they'll feel obliged to help you. Their appreciation will help you to grow your network so you can reach out to more potential investors. If an individual or business shares your campaign, all its contacts will be much more likely to look at your campaign because the information came from a trusted source.

Retweeting

Very similar to sharing, retweeting occurs specifically on Twitter. The unwritten spamming rules of social media are different for every social network, and on Twitter you can get away with a lot more than you can on Facebook. When sharing on Facebook, you need to make sure you aren't sharing too often. On Twitter, however, tweeting and retweeting multiple times a day is completely okay.

Find people and businesses that are related to what you're doing and repost their material. Learn how to tag them in posts that they may be interested in, and you'll start to see your list of followers grow.

Liking

Liking is what happens when you "like" something that someone else posts on Facebook. It's an easy, unobtrusive way to show your support for that person or business. Don't be shy with your likes — they can come back to help you.

One of your authors, Zak, has a chain of olive oil and balsamic vinegar tasting shops in the Northeast called Pure Mountain Olive Oil (`www.puremountain oliveoil.com`). When he opens a store in a new location, one of the first things he does is to "like" all the nearby restaurants and related businesses. Many of these businesses, in turn, "like" Zak's business Facebook page. When that person or business likes his page, they can see all his updates and make comments for all his followers to see. Zak is often happily surprised by the amount of engagement he can create by simply liking another business's page.

Commenting

If you were to rate what businesses like you to do on their social network pages, the most important thing would be to submit comments. That's because comments demonstrate a level of engagement with the company that goes far beyond just liking it.

When you post comments on other business's sites, make sure your grammar and spelling are perfect. (You don't want other professionals to read your comment and laugh at your lack of grammar skills or poor spelling.) Also, make sure that you're providing good feedback. Don't leave negative or long-winded comments.

Some social media platforms provide much more room for conversation than others, and sometimes these conversations can turn into arguments. Don't let yourself get sucked into arguments online! They look bad for all people involved. Your online reputation is extremely important when you're trying to raise money through crowdfund investing. Always keep this fact in mind when leaving a comment.

Realizing What Happens When Your Idea Goes Live

Make sure that everything related to your pitch is in place before it goes live. By *everything,* we mean your business plan, your video, your website, your social networks, your . . . everything! You can always postpone the launch date, but once your campaign is launched, it's launched. It will be live on your funding portal website for everyone to see and to share with their social networks. Potential investors can start commenting and asking questions on your project page. Potential business competitors can begin making comments as well.

When you reach this critical moment, the clock starts ticking loudly. The amount of time you have to raise your money can vary slightly depending on you and the funding platform you choose. But whether you have 30 days, 60 days, or something in between, the time will go by fast and things will happen quickly. Be prepared to be busy. Monitor your campaign like a hawk, because this is your time to shine! This section shows you how to act when your pitch hits the fan.

Reading crowd comments and responding to questions

You've spent hours writing your business plan, asking advice, interviewing similar businesses, and building your campaign. You've released your crowdfund investing campaign to the public, and now you're waiting for the money to start flowing in. You may feel that you can sit back and relax, but that couldn't be farther from the truth.

You need to be attentive to *everything* going on with your campaign. As we discuss in Chapter 6, you need to be constantly monitoring the chatter going on. People will be asking questions, and they want you to respond. Taking 24 hours to respond to a question is too long. Set a rule for yourself that you'll respond to every question within six hours.

Monitor the types of comments as well. If you're starting to see a theme of questions/comments, you may need to go back into your campaign and answer these questions before they start popping up again. The less time people spend on your campaign trying to figure out something that was unclear, the more time they'll be able to spend deciding how much to invest.

Watching your network grow through referrals

When someone invests in you, he's going to be tied to your success. It will be in his interest for your campaign (and later business) to be successful. Don't be shy — encourage your investors to help you. Having your investors share your project with their friends greatly helps you build both your network and your pool of investors. Every referral you get increases your network. Every addition to your network gets you that much closer to reaching your funding target.

Perhaps even more powerful than connecting with additional investors is if your investors introduce you to their network of people who can add value to your business. For example, when Zak was raising money for Pure Mountain Olive Oil (through traditional financing means), he received quite a few introductions to people who had successful backgrounds in starting and growing chains of retail stores. He didn't need the additional capital, but he always wants to hear advice and experience from someone who has done something similar. One such person he was introduced to during this process has been a great help. This person had started a multi-million-dollar chain of gyms in the Northeast and was the nephew of one of Zak's investors. The advice and insight that Zak got from this introduction has greatly helped his business.

Be ready to talk shop with anyone at anytime. As your network grows, research your new contacts, find something you can offer to your contacts, and identify something that you can gain from each of them.

Tallying your success

Ultimately, your success is completing your money raise. Expect this to happen; be confident that because you've done all the things necessary leading up to your campaign going live, you *know* you'll be successful.

As the money starts coming in, keep a close count of it. If it's trickling in slower than you wanted, be prepared to push your campaign out to more and more people. Prepare follow-up e-mails to your network, and if your tally isn't where you want it to be, reach out to them again. One of the biggest mistakes that people make in sales is not asking for the sale. You've done all the legwork, and people like you and your business; now it's time to *ask* them to invest in you.

In addition to tallying your money, tally the contacts that you're making. Organize your new contacts in a way that helps you to connect with them effectively and efficiently. Putting your new contacts into the following categories can help keep you organized:

- ✔ Marketing experts
- ✔ Product experts
- ✔ Law experts
- ✔ Tax experts
- ✔ Support experts

Demonstrating traction

The most important part of your campaign is your initial traction. As we discuss in Chapter 7, online funding portals that are registered as brokers rate your campaign through various algorithms. (Regular funding portals can't provide investment advice like this.) The higher a broker-dealer rates your campaign, the better chance you'll have at seeing your project placed in a prominent position. The more prominent a position you get on a broker-dealer's site, the more people will see your campaign.

Many lessons in life are learned in junior high school. One such lesson is this: Nobody wants to be the first one on the dance floor. The same is true for fundraising. If you do all the prep work and then send out your messages to every person in your entire extended social network on day one, you'll have a lot of people clicking on your campaign all at once. When they arrive on your page, they'll see an empty dance floor (zero dollars from zero investors). They may think "Hmmm . . . guess it didn't work out," and then it will be much harder to get them back to view your campaign again. If you have some core supporters on the dance floor when other kids arrive at the dance, the newbies will be more comfortable and more likely to stick around.

To avoid an empty dance floor, prepare a multi-wave marketing plan that moves in concentric circles out from you. Envision the circles as being based on how well the person knows you. Your family is at the core, and then close friends, friends, colleagues, acquaintances, business contacts, friends of friends, and so on. Create a schedule of when to contact these people so that you can start with your core supporters — and allow them to help you gain initial traction — before moving outward to people who don't know you as well.

Before you launch your campaign to the public, you'll surely have a group of people who have told you they want to invest in you. These are the people who will support you in anything you do — people like your mother, aunt, cousin, and college roommates. You know they'll invest in you, so make sure that doing so is as easy as possible for them. Give them detailed and bulleted instructions for how to invest on your funding platform and ask them to please make their investments within a specific timeframe (perhaps the first two or three days of your campaign). Explain why the money needs to be pledged so soon. (Go ahead and use our junior high dance floor analogy — we don't mind!) Be honest about the fact that you need to show traction early. Let these very close contacts know that even investing $100 is a great help to you.

After you've built a small base, then send the next wave of communication to the next group of people in your social network. Give each group at least a couple days to consider supporting you, and then repeat the process with the next group until you've completed the campaign.

Two of the most important factors that determine how your campaign is rated by the online platform are the number of investors and the amount of money you raise. Be diligent about your initial traction, and watch your campaign grow to completion!

Chapter 10

Troubleshooting Campaign Problems

In This Chapter

▶ Keeping your intellectual property secure

▶ Following the letter and spirit of the SEC regulations

▶ Dusting yourself off after a failed campaign

▶ Using common sense to avoid other issues

*R*aising money for your business is a full-time job. Building a crowdfund investing pitch (the focus of Chapter 9) takes a lot of time and energy, and going live with it means having major interaction with potential investors until you hit your funding target. At every step — before, during, and after reaching your target — you must follow SEC compliance rules (which we discuss on this book's website, www.dummies.com/go/crowdfundinvesting).

When you set out to raise money via crowdfund investing, you should expect to encounter some bumps in the road. This chapter helps you identify some of the most common bumps before you hit them and helps you maneuver around them whenever possible. In the case of the seemingly worst bump of all — the failure to meet your funding target — we offer advice for picking yourself up and maintaining momentum even in the face of disappointment. One failed campaign does not have to spell the end of your hopes and dreams!

Always keep in mind that crowdfund investing demands transparency, so approach any problems with an open mind and a willingness to share the truth with your supporters and potential investors. Keep the lines of communication open even when doing so means showing the world that you've made a mistake.

Protecting Your Intellectual Property before You Go Live

Intellectual property is the secret sauce that may make your product or service tick. It's something that's unique to your business — that no one else offers. Whatever that thing is, it originates from your creative mind and is rightfully yours.

When you start to share that knowledge, information, process, work, or invention with others, you may be afraid that someone will steal it. Patents, trademarks, and copyrights help you protect what you've created. If you have a patent, trademark, or copyright, anyone who tries to rip off your intellectual property can be sued. The three terms aren't interchangeable, and in this section we define what each means and briefly explain the process required to secure it.

Not every business requires securing a patent, trademark, or copyright. If what you're offering is a slight repackaging of a product or service that already exists — perhaps tweaking how it's delivered or lowering the price point compared with what's currently on the market — you likely won't need to secure a patent. And the nature of your business may determine whether a copyright or trademark is required. Definitely do some additional reading on the subject; *Patents, Copyrights & Trademarks For Dummies,* by Henri Charmasson (Wiley), is a good place to start. And ask your lawyer any questions on this subject *long* before you're ready to take your crowdfund investing pitch live.

Applying for patents

A *patent* is a type of property right; it's a document granting an inventor sole rights to an invention. It gives the holder the right, for a limited time, to exclude others from making, using, offering to sell, selling, or importing the subject matter that is within the scope of protection granted by the patent. In the United States, the U.S. Patent & Trademark Office (USPTO) determines whether a patent should be granted in a particular case. However, the patent holder must enforce his or her own rights if and when the USPTO grants a patent.

Securing a patent in the United States can cost as little as $5,000, or it can cost well over $20,000; the cost differences depend upon the type of patent (a process patent may be more expensive than a design patent, for example) and the degree of complexity involved.

The time required for a patent to be granted depends on the registration procedure and other factors that vary from country to country. In some countries, no examination as to the substance of the patent application is conducted, and the procedure generally lasts just a few months. In countries such as the United States, where the patent office conducts a thorough, substantial examination to check whether the patent meets the patentability criteria of "novelty, inventive step and industrial applicability," (per the USPTO website, `www.uspto.gov`), the entire procedure from application to grant can take well over three years.

You can apply for three types of patents:

- **Design patent:** Think of the famous Burberry design. According to the USPTO website, "A design consists of the visual, ornamental characteristics embodied in, or applied to, an article of manufacture. . . . A design for surface ornamentation is inseparable from the article to which it is applied and cannot exist alone." Design patents last 14 years.

- **Plant patent:** Think of Green Seedless Table Grapes. In very simple terms, a plant patent is useful for someone who has invented or discovered and reproduced (without fusing male and female cells together) a distinct and new variety of plant. Can you say, genetically engineered? Plant patents last 20 years.

- **Utility patent:** Think of a mechanical valve heart. A utility patent protects the way an invention is used and works. The word *utility* means that something has a purpose or a useful function. Utility patents are subdivided into mechanical, electrical, and chemical categories. In general, utility patents may be granted to anyone who invents a new and useful method, process, machine, device, manufactured item, or chemical compound — or any new and useful improvement to these same things. Utility patents last 20 years.

Two types of utility and plant patent applications exist in the United States:

- **Provisional:** An initial, temporary filing that grants you short-term rights. A provisional application is a quick and inexpensive way for an inventor to establish a U.S. filing date for an invention. A provisional application is automatically abandoned 12 months after its filing date and is not examined. An applicant who decides initially to file a provisional application must, within the12-month period, file a corresponding nonprovisional application.

  Filing a provisional application does not guarantee you a patent. It does, however, give you at least 12 months to decide whether to go for a nonprovisional patent and to seek crowdfund investment capital for your idea. You can file this application online for as little as $199 plus government fees.

✔ **Nonprovisional:** A full patent filing with long-term protection. A nonprovisional application is examined by a patent examiner and may be issued as a patent if all the requirements for patentability are met. Each year, the USPTO receives approximately 500,000 patent applications. Most of them are nonprovisional applications for utility patents.

In an effort to help people protect their intellectual property without having to wait three years for an answer, the USTPO has developed a new patent registration process called *prioritized examination*. Prioritized examination covers utility and plant patent applications. The goal is to provide a final answer within 12 months. A maximum of 10,000 requests for prioritized examination are granted each year.

If you seek one or more patents, let your investors know their status, including in which countries you have them. Investors want to know that the money they put into your business won't be wasted because you failed to protect your assets.

Securing copyrights and trademarks

Protecting any words and images you create to promote your business requires copyrights and/or trademarks. The familiar symbol © indicates that a copyright has been secured, and ® denotes a trademark. Copyrights protect books, songs, photographs, and other original works of authorship. (This book and its contents are covered by copyright.) And a trademark protects your logo.

Luckily, filing for these two types of protection isn't quite as cumbersome as filing for patent protection and doesn't necessarily require a lawyer. Websites such as LegalZoom (www.legalzoom.com) allow you to file for copyright and trademark protection online.

Securing a trademark for your logo is as easy as creating an online profile on a site such as LegalZoom, completing a simple questionnaire, running a trademark search to make sure no one else is using the mark, and filing it with the USTPO. For copyright protection, you follow the same steps but need to provide samples of your work.

For under $200, you can have your trademark protected. And depending on how much written material you have and how sensitive it is, copyright protection starts at around $150.

Playing Nice with the SEC

The U.S. Securities and Exchange Commission (SEC) is the governing body that oversees the U.S. securities markets. The 2012 JOBS Act (which we explain in Chapter 2) stipulates that the SEC makes the rules around which crowdfund investing takes place. For this reason, you must stay up to date on the SEC rules surrounding crowdfund investing.

Although this book's website (www.dummies.com/go/crowdfund investing) offers a great starting point for figuring out SEC regulations, you should also seek the most recent information from one of these three online resources:

- ✔ The SEC's website (www.sec.gov)
- ✔ The Crowdfund Intermediary Regulatory Advocates website (www. cfira.org)
- ✔ The Crowdfunding Professional Association website (www.crowdfunding professional.org)

Each site contains links to blogs and other pages where you can find the latest information about crowdfund investing regulations.

No matter where you find the relevant information, it's your job to live by the SEC rules. If you break one of them, you may forfeit your ability not only to close your current round of financing (if you're about to hit your funding target) but also your ability to seek crowdfund investing in the future.

The SEC holds sweeping power over all securities-related financial transactions and financial instruments, and its staff members are careful custodians of that power. The last thing you want to do is with your crowdfund investment campaign or your ongoing investor management is draw the attention of the SEC's enforcement division.

Do not break either the letter or the spirit of the laws and regulations on crowdfund investing. If you have a question about what's legal and what isn't, seek the professional advice of a securities attorney with SEC (and, ideally, crowdfund investing) experience. If the question is significant, your attorney can send a *no action letter* request for an official SEC opinion regarding a clarification of the regulations. The term *no action* applies because if what you're asking about is permitted, the SEC will say that no action will be taken against you if you carry out what you're asking about.

If you've already crossed the line (or maybe danced too close to it) and you've received a *cease-and-desist letter* or any other communication from the SEC, immediately consult with your attorney and follow the SEC's direction without fail. If you do break the law, you'll be spending all the money you raised on legal fees instead of on growing your business. Don't do it!

Handling the Disappointment of Not Meeting Your Funding Target

If you miss your funding target despite all your best efforts, you're going to be hugely disappointed. After all, as we explain in Chapter 3, failing to meet your target means that you get zero dollars for your efforts. (Crowdfund investing has an all-or-nothing provision so that investors who sign on early in the campaign don't find themselves funding a project that's a fraction of what was promised.)

What's your first step when facing such a disappointment? Take a couple days off and recharge. Chances are, you've been running hard and fast on your campaign for 60 to 90 days and working hard on your business idea for a lot longer than that. Take some time to relax, reassess, and reduce your stress.

Do *not* let yourself fall into a deep depression over this one failure. Almost all successful entrepreneurs have failures. In fact, in the Silicon Valley/San Francisco area, many angel investors and venture capital firms (which we explain in Chapter 3) are hesitant to invest in someone who has never experienced failure. One such investor recently remarked to us, "I want to see at least one failure and know what they learned from that failure. You learn much more from failure than you do success." We wholeheartedly agree. Each of us has faced adversity and experienced failure at some point in our careers. Some of the most powerful lessons that help us succeed today emerged from those difficult times.

In this section, we offer tips for making sure your campaign failure doesn't spell the end of your business plan.

Aiming for a constructive failure

People tend to think of failure only as a negative experience, but it shouldn't be. In the book *The Rainforest: The Secret to Building the Next Silicon Valley* (Regenwald), authors Victor W. Hwang and Greg Horowitt talk about the factors that create an ecosystem (or rain forest) of innovation. Here are three of the factors they identify as being the most challenging to bring to an innovation culture:

✔ Transparency in communication

✔ The ability to form trusting relationships with people you don't know well

✔ The ability to embrace constructive failure

We need more of all three factors in order to create more and better innovation, which leads to jobs and an improved economy.

How do you make your campaign failure a constructive one? Start by evaluating what happened. Ask yourself questions such as these:

✔ What are the lessons you can draw from this experience?

✔ What went right?

✔ What could have gone better?

✔ What will you do differently next time?

Try to be objective in your answers, and ask a good friend or business advisor/mentor — someone who tends to be very honest — to discuss what happened as well.

As we explain in Chapter 2, only about 40 percent of reward-based (perk-based) crowdfunding campaigns succeed. And because investors are considering a financial return, crowdfund investing may succeed at a similar or even lower rate. If you were unable to reach your goals the first time around, you can take steps to ensure that you have another chance at bat when you're ready.

Thanking your crowd

How you leave the field of play is just as important as how you enter it. As soon as possible after the end of your campaign, send a message to all the people who pledged to invest in you. Thank them deeply for their support, and let them know what you plan to do next. Even if you don't know what comes next, you can say something like, "Now I'm trying to learn the lessons from this experience that I'll apply to what comes next. I look forward to discovering those lessons and will let you know where I'm headed."

We also recommend that you reach out to the broader crowd, including those who didn't agree to invest, to thank them for considering your opportunity/ company/idea and let them know that you look forward to communicating with them again soon. Taking this step is very important because you don't want members of your crowd to feel awkward or uncomfortable the next time they see you or speak with you. (You don't want someone avoiding you, thinking "He probably hates me because I didn't invest in his company.") You must respect everyone's personal decisions regarding his own investments. There are a thousand reasons why someone may have chosen not to invest, and you can't take such decisions personally. Act in a way that demonstrates your maturity, professionalism, and sense of humor in the face of adversity — people will remember such grace.

Keeping your idea alive

You likely still believe that your idea is a great one, and you want to keep pursuing it even though you missed your funding target. We encourage you to validate your beliefs with others to determine where the disconnect exists between what you believe and what others see and believe about your company, product, or service. This exercise may be uncomfortable, but if you truly believe that your idea is worthwhile and you want to pursue it, you need to have this series of conversations.

Your goal here is either to refine your idea or your approach or to "pivot" to a new way of thinking. We put this word in quotes because it has a very specific meaning in the startup world. Essentially, it means that you were going to approach the market from one direction, and based on what you've discovered, you need to pivot to another direction in order to be successful.

Does pivoting sound like a copout or a concession? Consider this story: One of the most famous companies to pivot was originally known as Odeo. It was a podcasting company started by a couple of ex-Googlers. They had gained significant professional investors and a staff of 14 when, in 2005, Apple launched podcasting through iTunes, which made Odeo's product irrelevant. The founders and staff frantically began working in teams to create a new direction (a pivot) for the company. A couple of the engineers became interested in a technology to provide real-time updates from individuals out to the world. "Status updates" was the concept. They used their experience and talent to pivot their product to offer a way to update the world in real time, in just 140 characters. In 2006, Twitter was born, and we all know how that has turned out.

Many successful companies have had to pivot — some radically. Pivoting doesn't ensure success, but it shouldn't be a source of shame.

How do you begin to determine whether subtle refinement or a radical pivot is required?

1. **Talk with your supporters.**

   Find out why these people wanted to invest in you. Specifically, ask whether they would've invested if they hadn't known you. (Your mom may have a hard time answering that one.) If so, why? What aspects of your company, product, or service most appealed to them? Also ask about what *didn't* appeal to them — any concerns they had about the product or service, for example.

2. **Talk with a few friends or family members who chose not to invest.**

Try to identify people who will be brutally honest with you. You need to hear the negatives, the concerns, and the objections. (Case in point: When we were working on legalizing crowdfunding, one of our best friends was our biggest critic. We spent the most time with him trying to understand his argument. It turns out that was the most valuable time spent because we had thought through and had a clear, convincing counterargument in the end that we used over and over in Washington, D.C.)

3. **Consider whether the main problem was your pitch or your product or service.**

If the pitch was the problem, you likely can accomplish a lot simply by refining your presentation. But if the substance of the offer is the issue, you may have a pivot situation on your hands.

4. **Test-drive your new ideas.**

Whether you refine or pivot, seek input before you try to move forward. Ideally, get input from people who hadn't signed on to support you before. Find out if you've addressed their concerns and if they think they'd be more likely to invest now.

Avoiding Other Pitfalls

You must use common sense to make the most of crowdfund investing opportunities. Understanding why crowdfund investing exists, how investors and your supporters think, and how to act during your campaign is extremely important. In this section, we touch on additional bumps in the road that you must avoid.

Using crowdfund investing as a publicity stunt

The only reason to launch a crowdfund investing campaign is to raise money for your business. If you're looking for publicity and aren't serious about raising the money, don't put your idea on a crowdfund investing platform. There are plenty of better ways to get publicity:

✔ Create a group of videos and try and get them to go viral.

✔ Launch a series of press releases.

✔ Network your way into a few key news articles.

If you use a crowdfund investing campaign as a publicity stunt, you'll anger a lot of people, including folks in your online social network. People will spend time reviewing your campaign, asking questions, and thinking about the decision to invest or not. Don't waste their time by launching a halfhearted campaign for publicity purposes only.

Consider what happens if you get even a handful of people to support you with investment pledges. Say that someone in your network pledges $100 to your campaign within the first days after it goes live. Within a few weeks, that person likely has figured out that you aren't committed to the campaign and aren't doing what's necessary to raise the money. (Failing to answer potential investors' questions in a timely and robust manner would be a clue, for example.) Your investor gets disillusioned, and when the campaign period ends (in two or three months), he has a sour taste in his mouth for the whole crowdfund investing experience. Guess what? You just took that potential investor away from other people's legitimate campaigns. He'll be much less likely to take a chance on another startup or small business because of your lack of commitment.

On the flip side, if you're serious about raising money, you should absolutely try to use your campaign to create publicity for yourself and your business. Doing so helps you for two key reasons:

✔ Publicity helps your campaign go viral so you can raise more money.

✔ Publicity gets your business idea in front of many more people, which is a great help when your product or service is ready for the market.

A lot of eyes will be focusing on your campaign when it goes live, and you need to try to leverage this situation as much as you can. Communicate as much as possible with your investors and potential investors. Contact newspapers, blogs, and TV stations that have anything to do with your type of business. Write a story about what you're doing, and send the story and a link to your campaign to these media outlets. (After all, it can't hurt to do at least part of the work for them. Smaller media outlets sometimes run such a story with little modification, so make sure you've written something good!)

Pitting investors against each other

We make this point many times in this book: You must always show gratitude to your investors. Thank them honestly, sincerely, and repeatedly. Your investors are part of your team, and you want them to feel connected with you and with each other. Many investors come to the table with much more than money; they bring talents and skills that can mean the difference between your failure and success.

Unfortunately, some entrepreneurs try to create a contest among their investors. They point out certain investors' larger contributions in the effort to encourage smaller dollar investors to fork over more cash. Some entrepreneurs even single out their smaller investors to try to guilt them into investing more money. Obviously, this is a horrible idea! Doing so only creates resentment and ill will toward you and your business.

Crowdfund investing is designed to allow people of all income levels to participate. And because your goal is to get support from an entire crowd, each investment — whether at the minimum level you establish for your campaign or at ten times that level — is crucial to your success. You must be grateful for every investment. Doing anything other than showing gratitude will guarantee that you lose support from investors at all levels.

Violating a funding platform's terms of service

In Chapter 7, we walk you through the process of researching and selecting an online funding portal that will support your crowdfund investing campaign. You must read and fully understand a portal's terms of service (TOS) before signing a contract (and even before clicking the button that says "I agree" to the TOS). That's because after you've contracted with the portal, you *cannot* break the TOS. If you do, you may put yourself, your company, your investors, and the crowdfund investing platform in jeopardy of prosecution by the SEC or other federal authorities.

If you have questions about what is and is not permitted, contact the funding platform for help. And as always, we highly recommend you review all legal documents with your own attorney before signing any agreement. The Terms of Service on a portal or broker dealer site is written from their perspective — make sure you understand *your* rights and responsibilities.

Exploiting free labor

Free labor for a business is a wonderful thing. If you're in the pre-revenue stage, free labor may be the *only* thing keeping you moving forward! As you get ready to start a crowdfund investing campaign, you should definitely try to recruit some free labor so you can maximize the campaign's effects without needing to work twice as many hours as you already do. However, you must take pains not to exploit the people who step up to help you.

Campaign manager

As we discuss in Chapter 6, running a crowdfund investing campaign is a full-time job for at least two or three months. If you can't afford to hire someone to take on the job of helping you run the campaign, reach out to your network to see if someone is willing to do the work for the experience only (no paycheck). If you find someone willing to do so, be aware that she needs an incentive to put forth her best effort. For example, you may want to assure her that if your campaign is successful and she proves herself to be a solid manager, she'll secure a job with your company.

Whether this person will be a long-term partner or not, be extremely careful to limit what you expect her to do. Keep her focused on the campaign management duties, and don't ask her to pick up your dry cleaning, find a babysitter for your kids, or do any other non-campaign-related tasks. Just because this person is a volunteer doesn't mean you have carte blanche to demand her help with every aspect of your life. Avoid creating resentment; no one likes to feel taken advantage of. If your campaign manager starts to feel resentment, her communication with investors and potential investors (which is her number-one job) may reflect her attitude, which could spell disaster for your campaign.

Investor advisors

Throughout this book, we encourage you to tap the knowledge that your investors bring to the table. Doing so can add great value to your business. But always be aware that your investors have lives of their own and can't devote countless hours to answering your questions and offering advice. Just because your number-one priority is creating a successful business doesn't mean that your investors share your sense of urgency. They have families, businesses, and jobs of their own; respect that what they can offer you is limited by the time they have available.

Ask investors if they're interested in offering help and guidance. If someone says yes, find out what his expertise is, and request small amounts of help related to this expertise. Don't overwhelm him, or he'll feel exploited and will react by not helping out at all.

Changing your mind

Part of being an entrepreneur and the leader of a company is being decisive and sticking to your decisions. In the fast-moving world of launching and running your own business, you don't have the time to be constantly second-guessing your decisions. When you make a decision, you should stick to it. That includes the decision to launch a crowdfund investing campaign.

Canceling a crowdfund investing campaign damages a lot of people, so don't make a haphazard decision to launch a campaign. It's much better to change your mind in the days and weeks leading up to the campaign launch than to do so after your campaign goes live.

But what if, in the worst-case scenario, something happens and you absolutely need to pull out of your campaign? Do so responsibly. Send immediate communication to your investors apologizing and explaining to them why you're pulling out. (With first-degree supporters, such as friends and family members, you may want to invest the time to make phone calls.) Be transparent and honest. Make a public post on your campaign page (via your funding portal; see Chapter 7) explaining what happened that led you to change your mind. Thank all your investors, apologize to them, and move forward.

Delaying your plans

There's nothing wrong with delaying your plans to launch your campaign. After all, everything business related always takes longer than expected. If you don't have all your ducks in a row before you launch your campaign, you won't be able to give the time and energy needed to manage your campaign effectively. No one will be harmed if you need to delay for a week or a month before you launch your campaign.

However, delaying your plans when you're mid-campaign or — even worse — after you secure your funding is a sure-fire way to alienate investors and miss the key milestones that you set out in your business plan (see Chapter 5). Therefore, you must make sure that you're ready to hit the ground running the second that campaign goes live. If you're not 100 percent ready, wait until you are. The initial traction that you get in your campaign (which we explain in Chapter 9) is crucial to your success. If you're still trying to get organized in the first few days or weeks of your campaign, you won't secure your funding. And if you're not ready to act like a business owner the minute your campaign is successful, you'll be doing yourself, your staff, and your investors a serious disservice.

Chapter 11

Moving Forward When You Reach Your Funding Target

. . . .

In This Chapter

▶ Getting prepared to receive the funds

▶ Showing appreciation to your crowd

▶ Taking the first steps post-funding

▶ Leveraging your crowd's talents

▶ Heading into the second year of business

▶ Reaching out for more crowd funding

. . . .

*W*hen you hit your funding target, you should definitely take time to celebrate. Not every campaign is successful, so success means that you've done some great work on your business plan and your pitch.

Of course, the celebration can't last too long (and *definitely* can't be funded by your campaign investments!). With dollars committed to your venture, you need to get to work to prove that investors made a great choice by supporting you. The task before you is to put concept into practice — to turn all your ideas, research, and business planning into a tangible reality.

In this chapter, we start with the most basic topic: getting your hands on the money. Then we help you figure out how to start executing your plans (which is similar to starting a new job and needing to decide what to do first).

From there, we look at your pool of supporters and how to leverage them to achieve your goals. Then we discuss options for raising additional money (if and when you need to do so), get you prepared to end your first fiscal year, and remind you what you need to do to be compliant.

This chapter is important. It keeps you on the straight and narrow and provides you with tools to help you be credible with your crowd. With a great business comes great responsibility, and we prepare you to perform like a superhero.

Collecting the Money!

Ahhh, this step sounds so sweet! When you meet your funding target, all your hard work finally translates into the dollars you need to turn your ideas into real products or services. But because you're potentially receiving small dollar amounts from lots of different investors, how do you actually get the cash into your hands? In this section, we begin by explaining the steps you need to take before your campaign even begins. We then demonstrate how money flows from the investors through an intermediary and into your company's bank account.

Preparing well in advance

In Chapter 7, we explain that before you can start raising money via crowdfund investing, you need to incorporate. Lots of websites are available that make the incorporation process easy and relatively inexpensive. (Many crowdfund investing funding portals provide links to this type of service.)

When you receive incorporation documents, you also receive a form to create a federal tax identification number. You must file this form with the federal government. You may also need to file documents with the state where you've incorporated and apply for a business license.

When all these forms are signed, sealed, and delivered — ideally, before your campaign even goes live — you should take them to your local bank and open a business checking account. Doing so is critical because, without a bank account, you can't collect cash.

Working with an intermediary

The type of funding platform you use for your crowdfund investment campaign determines how you receive your money:

✔ **Online funding portal:** Most likely, you registered with an SEC-approved online funding portal that exclusively hosts crowdfund investment campaigns (see Chapter 7). These portals are required by law to outsource the cash management process to a third party. That's because funding portals are recent startups (they didn't exist prior to the 2012 legislation that legalized crowdfund investing). Startups carry some risk, and if your particular funding portal goes out of business for some reason, this requirement reduces the risk of your cash disappearing. The third party is an *escrow agent* that moves the cash into your business bank account.

✔ **Broker-dealer:** If you register your idea with a broker-dealer, which is more expensive than using an online portal (see Chapter 7), this person or company manages (holds) the cash for you without the involvement of a third party. That's because broker-dealers (unlike funding portals) are generally established entities with long company histories. (The risk of one of them shutting its doors is not very high.) The broker-dealer itself moves the money into your account.

How can you be certain where your money will come from? Before you list your pitch with a funding platform, you need to find out what kind of portal it is. The platform's terms and conditions or its "About Us" page on its website should tell you.

The JOBS Act prescribes a 21-day window between your campaign pitch going live and your ability to collect your cash. If you're extremely lucky and you hit your funding target on Day 10 of your campaign, for example, you won't be able to get any cash until Day 22. Why does this provision exist? It gives investors time to uncover any attempts at fraud and offers investors the right to change their minds and get their cash back. However, if you hit your funding target on Day 45 of your campaign, you can immediately get your cash from either the escrow agent or the broker-dealer. (If anyone is trying to swindle the crowd, a few weeks should be sufficient for potential investors to root out the fraudulent intent, spread the word, and shut down the campaign.)

When you first sign your contract with the funding portal or the broker-dealer that will host your campaign, ask how long it takes to get your cash after you hit your funding target. The terms differ from escrow agent to escrow agent and broker-dealer to broker-dealer. You also want to find out whether the cost of transferring the money is included in the success fee that the platform charges when you hit your funding target (see Chapter 7) or is a separate fee. If it's a separate fee, make sure you know how much the money transfer is going to cost so you aren't facing any surprises.

You also want to confirm with your bank whether it charges any fees related to receiving the money into your account — particularly if the money is wired. Again, you want to be sure you're prepared for the true costs associated with your venture so you don't face any unpleasant surprises.

Thanking Your Investors

At the risk of sounding like Miss Manners times three, we must remind you to thank your investors when your campaign is a success. (You thank them if it fails also, as we explain in Chapter 10, but here the focus is on success!) What type of thank-you is appropriate for the people who are helping make your dreams come true? You may be tempted to shower your crowd with gifts, but don't do it! Every dollar you spend from here on out is going to be scrutinized by your investors. Don't give your crowd any reasons to worry that you're being less than careful with your finances (which are *their* finances as well).

Here are some less costly ways to accomplish a heartfelt thank-you:

- ✔ On the online funding platform, write a thank-you note to all your investors (and even to the people who didn't invest in your idea).

- ✔ Create a short (perhaps one-minute) video to post on the funding platform. The video can explain how excited you are to have hit your funding target, that you're ready to jump in with both feet, and that you couldn't have made it this far without your investors. Then you can tell them the first two or three things you're going to do as a new or expanding business owner. (Not sure what those two or three things will be? Be sure to read the next section of this chapter.)

- ✔ Feeling ambitious? Really want to win over the hearts of your investors? Write personal thank-you notes by actually putting pen to paper, sealing notes in envelopes, going to that very bureaucratic building known as the post office, and paying for stamps. "But no one does that anymore," you're thinking. Exactly the point! The act of writing an actual note will make a huge impression.

  Of course, if you have 1,000 investors (or even 200), we aren't implying that you send 1,000 (or even 200) thank-you notes. You're too busy for that! Be strategic about it. Consider sending thank-you notes to your largest investors and to those people who worked hard on your behalf to get their social networks to back your idea.

People remember a simple thank-you note for a long time. Unfortunately, they remember *not* receiving a thank-you for a lot longer.

Year One: Living Out Your Business Plan

Okay, so the excitement of hitting your funding target has subsided a bit, the cash is in the bank, and you've reached out to your crowd to thank them for believing in you. What comes next?

First, take a deep breath and remind yourself that you've already proven you can do a great job. (If you were a lousy manager or communicator, or if you had a weak vision, the crowd wouldn't have funded you.)

Next, learn the most important word in your vocabulary from now on:

EXECUTION

Do *not* go out and kill someone. Instead, execute your plan. Thomas Edison once said, "Vision without execution is hallucination." You've already got a great vision, and you don't want your business to be a hallucination, so you need to follow through.

Here are five steps to help you execute:

- ✔ **Think micro.** When you were sharing your vision with the crowd, you were thinking macro — explaining the big picture of what you want to accomplish. Now it's time to think micro — to shift your attention to the details. You don't want to get bogged down in micromanagement, but you must think about what you need to accomplish and break each big step into smaller tasks.

- ✔ **Build your team.** When you have a sense of the tasks at hand, find people who can help you complete them. If you've budgeted to hire staff members, now's the time to run a search. If you don't have the budget to pay people, locate supporters who are willing to volunteer. Whichever situation applies to you, pick the best possible team and don't compromise. Get comfortable asking people for help and delegating responsibilities. A great leader knows how to delegate. Just don't make everyone else do *all* your work!

- ✔ **Be flexible.** Starting a business is never a smooth endeavor. No matter how diligently you try to prepare for what's next, "more important things" will invariably pop up that demand your attention. Be prepared for this situation by charting a clear course but being flexible enough to change it and recalibrate if need be. And if you do change course, be sure to let the people on the ship (your investors) know what you're doing. If they think you're heading in one direction (the equivalent of sunny Hawaii), and you arrive somewhere else (that may look like freezing cold Alaska to them), they won't be happy unless you've prepared them for the change.

- ✔ **Always strive to do your best.** Don't overpromise and underdeliver; you'll only set yourself up for failure. Instead, be honest with yourself about your capabilities, and strive to exceed your investors' expectations.

- ✔ **Think before you act.** Deliberate action and speech are crucial because you don't want to make rash decisions, put your foot in your mouth, or behave in any other way that rattles your investors. Try to be a steady force at the helm of your endeavor.

Striving to hit your milestones

You can't complete 100 percent of your goals in a day. However, if you work on completing 1 percent of a goal each day, by Day 100 you'll have accomplished what you set out to do. This type of thinking should guide you when it comes to hitting your milestones.

In your business plan (see Chapter 5) and in your crowdfund investment campaign pitch (see Chapter 9), you told the crowd what you needed to do, when you needed to do it, and how you were going to do it. Those are your milestones. Summarize them into bullet points and put them on a piece of paper.

In his book *Mastering the Rockefeller Habits* (Gazelles, Inc.) — which is a great read, by the way — entrepreneur guru Verne Harnish uses a very simple tool to help entrepreneurs hit their milestones. He tells them to take the list of milestones and break it into priorities. Figure out your Top 5 priorities, and then identify one priority that supersedes the others — the Top 1 of the Top 5.

For example, if you're starting an organic farm, some of your tasks include getting the seeds and animals, buying equipment, and signing the lease on the land. Your first priority should be signing the lease; it's your Top 1. Within that priority you have various tasks: contacting the land owner, reading the documents, having them reviewed by attorneys, and so on. You need to spell out and prioritize each of these tasks (even the very mundane ones). Checking off these items (working on 1 percent at a time) will make you feel like you're progressing. That's what the Rockefeller Habits are all about.

Work on that Top 1 until it's done, and then move on to the second priority. Tell people about your Top 5. Make it a game. Share it with your crowd. They'll appreciate the fact that you have a game plan in action.

If you need help deciding what to do and when to do it, use the chart shown in Figure 11-1. It helps you prioritize your tasks based on their importance and urgency. On the vertical axis, you have Urgency. You assign each task a number from 1 (not very) to 10 (very) based on how urgent it is that you get this task done quickly. On the horizontal axis, you have Importance. For each task, you assign a number from 1 to 10 based on its relative importance to your overall vision.

After you chart your tasks, the upper-right quadrant of the chart is where you find the most urgent *and* most important thing(s) you have to do; anything that falls in that quadrant is a Top 5. Moving left, you have urgent but not so important things to do. In the lower-right quadrant will be tasks that are important but not so urgent. And finally, the tasks that are not very important or very urgent will appear in the lower-left quadrant.

Do this exercise now, and organize your tasks based on your results. This is now your game plan for where to focus your attention.

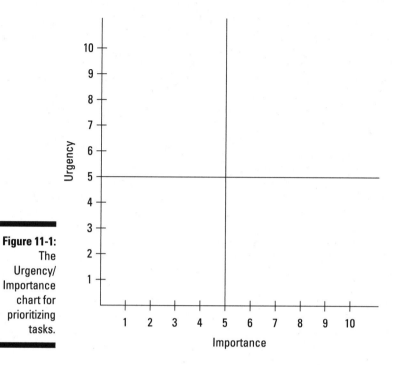

Figure 11-1:
The
Urgency/
Importance
chart for
prioritizing
tasks.

Staying faithful to fiscal responsibility

When you start a business, you may feel like there are unlimited demands on your time and financial resources. There's good reason to feel that way! The reality is that you have a very limited amount of time to do all the things required to start a business and (most likely) very little money to do it with. We don't discuss time management here (plenty of other resources can help you with that); our focus for the moment is on money management.

No matter what funding source you use for your business, you have to be careful with your spending and try to make it last. But when you add equity or debt investors into the mix — people who expect to see a return on their money and expect you to use their money very prudently — the financial pressure increases.

Let's talk first about what not to do. A professional investor we know in the western United States once invested in a small business that was run by two individuals who convinced him to make a six-figure investment. A week after that investment was completed and the money was transferred to the business owners, the investor stopped by the business office for a visit. When he arrived, he was surprised to see two brand-new BMWs parked in the spots used by the business owners. He asked, "Who bought the BMWs that are out front?" The business owners replied proudly, "Oh, we did! We thought it would be good for our business reputation." These idiots had taken precious capital meant to help them build a business and used about $80,000 of it to buy two depreciating assets that offered zero value to the business. Just imagine how you would've felt at that moment if you were the investor.

Investors have expectations. They expect you to be a careful custodian of their money and to deploy it in the best ways to achieve your business goals. For this reason, you don't want to schedule a Caribbean vacation two weeks after your funding campaign closes and then post lots of photos from extravagant locations on Facebook. Even if you had saved for that trip for ten years and every expense was paid for strictly from your personal finances, the perception wouldn't be good. You'd have to spend precious time explaining to some investors where the money came from and why you thought the timing would be appropriate.

What can you do to demonstrate to your investors that you're carefully deploying their capital? With every task you undertake, ask yourself questions like these:

- ✔ What is the return on investment (ROI) for this? How soon will I get the money I spent back in the form of new sales?
- ✔ How can I do this cheaper?
- ✔ How can I negotiate a better discount?
- ✔ Do I really need to spend this money now, or can I delay the expense?
- ✔ Could I do what I'm thinking about by exchanging in-kind services?
- ✔ How can I test this with a small experiment before I spend big?

This last point requires some additional explanation. Whenever you can test a strategy in a small way before you launch a major initiative, you should do so. That way, you learn from the experiment so that when you launch your major initiative, you'll be right on target and achieve the intended outcome. The mantra here is "Fail cheap and fast, and then track in on success."

When cannons were used in wars, the cannon officers would start by testing the aim of the cannon with very small munitions — just large enough to see where they were tracking. Then, when they had learned just how to aim the cannon to reach their intended target, they would use their heavy munitions to destroy the enemy. You aren't aiming to destroy anyone (we hope!), but try to think in a similar way. Use this tactic when you're considering a new sales and marketing strategy, a new product line, or other innovations. If you try small experiments and they fail, they fail quickly and cheaply, which is much better than launching a major initiative (that consumes significant resources) only to discover something at the launch of your business that dooms you to failure.

Communicating your actions to investors

We devote all of Chapter 12 to the topic of communicating with your crowd. Consider this section your sneak preview.

During your crowdfund investing campaign, you used all the communication tools at your disposal to express your need for capital. When the campaign is complete and the capital is in hand, you must continue to find and use tools and services to communicate in scalable ways with your investors.

What do we mean by "scalable"? You're trying to build a business, and you just raised money. You don't have time for individual conversations with hundreds of people on a regular basis. Therefore, you need to set expectations with your investors immediately about how and at what frequency you'll communicate with them. In doing so, you create a *communication cadence.* If you promise to send a monthly e-mail, then send a monthly e-mail. If you're more comfortable sending out LinkedIn statuses to a private group weekly, then do so. If you're going to have a semiannual conference call or meeting in your store, then hold it on schedule. The frequency or the mode of communication isn't nearly as important as your follow-up; do whatever you say you're going to do, so investors don't get spooked by unexpected silence.

In your first investor communication (whatever form it takes), explain your business plan again to investors and make sure you mention that you'll follow this plan until or unless circumstances change. Investors must understand that change may happen, so you should explain that early-stage businesses or small businesses have to be nimble and sometimes react to changes in the market. Commit to communicating changes to investors as soon as possible, in addition to explaining the reason for any change.

Revising and improving your plan

In all small businesses and early-stage companies, plans change based on the development of the business, based on competition, and based on the market in general. Sometimes these changes occur in response to a new opportunity, and other times they reflect crisis management. Sometimes you make modifications to a plan, and other times you make a very large change in direction that is called a *pivot.*

Modifications to a plan tend to be tactical in nature. Here's an example: "Instead of launching our second store in August, we'll launch in September." Or, "We've decided to change our pricing on Item A from $8.99 to $9.99 because our competition has raised theirs to $12.99."

As we explain in Chapter 10, a *pivot* is a significant change in strategy that may seem jarring to investors. You need to have strong rationale for a pivot, but if you do — if you really believe a significant change is the right thing to do for the business — then pivot you must. In Chapter 10, we explain that Twitter arose from a pivot. Here are two other examples of famous pivots:

> ✔ A video dating website pivoted to become the go-to location for posting videos online. The company name? YouTube.

> ✔ Confinity began as a cryptography company that was supposed to exchange money via PalmPilots (the precursor to iPhones). That company pivoted and became PayPal.

Whether you're making a minor modification or a big-time pivot, the most important thing you can do is *not* surprise your investors. As long as you communicate fully and give your reasons supporting the change, most investors will appreciate your rationale. (Those that don't appreciate it will likely seek an exit after the first year of owning your stock; until that time, they're required to stay put because of the SEC's 12-month holding period on crowdfund investments.)

Tapping into Your Investment Community

Investors supporting a company at the *seed stage,* or early stage, as well as local investors, usually care deeply about the companies and people they're investing in and want to be involved. Many of them invest with their hearts as well as their brains; this is especially true for investors in local, Main Street businesses.

Don't underestimate the value of this level of investor commitment. Take a look at your investor list, review it carefully, and find people who can help in different ways. Do you have any potential beta testers among your investors? User interface (UI) testers? Market researchers? Taste testers? Think about the services that small businesses have to pay for, such as advertising, marketing, research, hiring, and sales. Which of these things can your investors help you with?

As always (and as we discuss at length in Chapter 6), set very clear expectations: Investors need to know that not everything they suggest or create will be used; sometimes you'll listen to their advice but choose to go a different direction. When deciding which of your investors to approach for assistance, you want to focus first on the people you know and trust to accept this business reality — as the owner of the business, ultimately you must do what you think is best for the business.

In this section, we suggest three of the most common ways you can tap into your crowd's expertise for support in the early days of your operation. Of course, you can be creative and find countless other ways to use their skills as well.

Establishing a board of advisors

The difference between a surviving business and a booming business is the quality of the team of people running it. That's why you should always try to hire people who are smarter than you, and it's why you should try to build the best board of advisors that you can.

A board of advisors is different from a board of directors. A board of directors is the entity that the CEO of an organization reports to — a group comprised of elected or appointed members who oversee a company's activities. A company's bylaws grant its board of directors specific powers, duties, and responsibilities.

A board of advisors doesn't supervise you. Instead, it's a group of individuals — the smartest, most well-connected people you can find — who can become your biggest supporters and advocates. These are people with 500+ high-quality LinkedIn connections who are willing and able to make introductions to those people to help you get connected. One of your authors, Jason, was once at a dinner in Stockholm, Sweden, and spoke to the gentleman who brought cellphones to China. This man said that what matters to a business isn't "know how" but "know who." Your advisors should be people who can help you to connect to strategies, customers, partners, resources, and ideas.

Of course, the more connected someone is, the busier he or she is, so be careful with your advisors' time. Don't trouble them with mundane tasks. Focus them on big problems or targeted "asks" so they can help you and get back to their own priorities.

Asking investors for marketing support

How can your investors help you market your brand in your community? Be strategic as you review your list of investors and their LinkedIn and Facebook profiles. This step is important so you know all the potential strengths and opportunities that your investors may bring to help you build your brand.

Are there a handful of your investors who could become your "brand evangelists"? These are people who love your brand and your company so much they can't stop talking about it. Likely, you'll find only a few of these among your supporters, so think about how to use them wisely. For example,

✔ Could they be interviewed by the press regarding an issue related to your brand?

✔ Do they use social media, and would they like to share information about your brand via those channels?

✔ How can you direct these investors in ways that reinforce their connection with your brand and drive awareness and sales?

The majority of your investors won't be your evangelists. For them, you may want simply to suggest ways to mention your brand at appropriate times in conversational ways. Maybe they'd be willing to forward, repost, or retweet articles about your industry that mention your brand. Start small. Select five to ten of your investors who are rabid social media users. Try to engage them more deeply in your brand, reminding them of why your brand is relevant to them so they can help you drive awareness and sales. Then, after the first group is onboard and helping you with marketing efforts, select another group of five or ten people and take the same steps.

Encouraging investors to become passionate customers

Have you ever made an investment in a public company that sells a product or service that you love? Sometimes the product or service may be the primary reason for the investment. Do you believe in Apple? Coca-Cola? Disney?

One of the powerful things about crowdfund investing is that it enables you to turn your investors into your most passionate consumers. If you live in a town with five car washes and you're invested in one of them, which car wash are you going to use every time your car gets dirty? The one you invested in, of course! You're proud of your investment in your community, and you want to see how the store looks and check out how busy it is. You want to see if the manager is on duty, if the owner is onsite, and if the technicians do a great job on your car. Then, when you go to a business meeting and are talking with colleagues, you might mention, "Jimmy's Car Wash is running a special today. You should check it out."

This scenario may sound a bit silly, but just think about all the things you've purchased or done because someone you knew recommended them. If you're an investor, you'll do what you can to support that company and drive business to it whenever possible. How great would it be to have hundreds of salespeople (investors) in your community talking about your service or product every week?

You can do exactly that, but you need to make it easy for your investors to tout your business. Come up with a list of three to five things you want each of your investors to know about the business. Write them in bullet points, and send them to every investor. Ask your crowd to share this information with their networks. For the local car wash example, here are some ideas:

- ✔ Every Tuesday, Jimmy's Car Wash gives a 20 percent discount.
- ✔ Jimmy's Car Wash gives 5 percent of its profits to the local Boy Scout chapter.
- ✔ A lot of the soaps that car washes use are bad for the environment. Jimmy's Car Wash uses only environmentally friendly soaps.

Getting your investors to be passionate customers and brand evangelists can be as easy as keeping them updated about your business. Everyone likes to know something that other people don't know. When a new band hits the scene, people like to say, "I knew about these guys before they were popular" or "I've been listening to these guys for months." Keep your investors up-to-date about your business, and chances are, they'll enjoy sharing their "insider" information with all their friends. Doing so makes them look like they're in the know and, of course, helps ensure that their investment will pay off.

Year Two: Preparing for the End of the One-Year Stock Holding Period

A 12-month holding period exists on the shares you sell to equity investors during your crowdfund investing campaign (see Chapter 4). As the 12-month period comes to an end, make sure that you're ready for it. Investors will be reevaluating your company and the progress you've made. At around the ten-month mark, you should start getting solid data together to show your progress and the ROI you've created for your investors.

You definitely want to avoid any sort of mass exodus of investors. If too many people try to sell off your company shares as soon as the 12-month period ends, you'll be stressed and distracted from running your company. The better you communicate with your investors throughout the first 12 months, the better positioned you'll be to keep more of them around.

Your job as the head of your company is to create as much revenue as possible, but you must think about revenue in the long run. Putting investor communication in place early on will save you distractions down the road. Communicate clearly and often with your investors. Make sure you're answering their concerns and taking their advice when warranted.

Expecting some investors to depart

No matter how good of a job you do, how well you communicate, or how much money you create for your investors, some of them will undoubtedly depart at the end of the 12-month holding period. Even if you've done an amazing job, some people will just simply need the capital for other expenses in their lives.

Be prepared for this reality, and don't take it personally. Seeing investors depart could be rough on your self-esteem. Don't let this get in the way of your running your company. If you've done everything that you were supposed to do and investors are still leaving, take things in stride and continue to create more revenue for your company.

Anticipating the need for new stockholders

Knowing that some of your investors will undoubtedly depart after the 12-month holding period, you should anticipate the need for new stockholders. The investor is responsible for selling her own shares, so you don't need to worry about that. However, you should keep your ears open for potential new stockholders who could buy those shares if they can add value to your company.

For example, say that you have some advisors who've been helpful to you over the last year, and they aren't currently equity holders in your venture. They would be a good place to start. If they were helpful without any skin in the game, think about how much more help they may give if they stand to gain financially from the advice they're giving you.

Reaching Out to the Crowd for More Money

At some point after your initial crowdfund investing campaign has succeeded, you'll likely find yourself thinking about tapping into this funding source again. You don't want to do so too quickly; starting a new campaign a month after the first one ended demonstrates a serious lack of financial planning and likely won't result in a repeat success.

But if a year or more has passed, and if you've done a good job communicating with your investors and you've turned their money into a revenue-creating company, you may be in a position to reach out to them for more support. In this situation, if you're looking to raise more money, your initial crowdfund investors are a great place to start.

Plan out carefully how you're going to reach out to them. You want to inspire confidence, not fear. As always, be honest and transparent with your investors (and yourself and your employees as well). Show them the successes you've had since the first funding round closed — milestones reached, revenue created, investor ROI. Lay out why you need more money and, just as you did the first time around, your sources and uses of funds.

Before posting your campaign pitch for the world to see, send out a communication to your investors to test the waters and see how interested they'd be in investing more money in you and your company. Your investors will likely have a series of questions that they want answered. Answer these questions sufficiently, and then use the answers to craft your new crowdfund investing campaign.

Your second crowdfund investing campaign should be much smoother than your first. That's because, as we explain in Chapter 9, your initial traction is crucial to the eventual success of your campaign. If you can get all or most of your existing investors to reinvest in your company as soon as your project goes live (by encouraging them to invest by a specific deadline within the first few days after you go live), you'll benefit from some terrific online visibility. More visibility should equal more investors and more money.

What happens if you reach out to your investors to test the waters and they aren't interested in investing more money? In this case, you need to reevaluate your plans. If you go forward in launching a new campaign and people see that the initial investors aren't lining up to reinvest, the potential investors will think (and rightly so) that there's a problem either with you or with your business. If there's some other valid reason why your investors don't want to give you more money, you need to communicate this reason clearly in the campaign pitch so potential investors won't be scared off.

Part IV
Running Your Business with Your Investors in Mind

The 5th Wave   By Rich Tennant

"I know you're passionate about crowdfunding, but I wish you wouldn't refer to my family as your investors-in-law."

In this part . . .

When you choose to seek crowdfunding investing for your startup or growing business, you take on responsibilities to your crowd of investors. This part helps you do right by your crowd, starting in Chapter 12 with communicating clearly and regularly (whether that means once a week, once a month, or once a quarter — you set the pace).

Chapter 13 warns you against making certain mistakes that could lead your investors to revolt and shows you how to win them over again if the worst-case scenario happens. Of course, the best laid business plans some-times go astray, so Chapter 14 offers advice for keeping your investors happy even when your business goals change or your plans are delayed.

Chapter 12

Communicating with Your Investors

· ·

In This Chapter

▶ Tapping into what makes your investors unique

▶ Sketching an outbound communications plan

· ·

Shhh. What's that? Silence. Not good. A strategy of silence and not engaging may be good when you're deep in meditation and trying to escape the noise of your life. But when it comes to running a business, silence is never golden.

Leaving your crowdfund investors out in the cold is not smart, and it's actually illegal. According to the JOBS Act, you have to communicate with your investors through written documents in the prefunding stage (via your business plan), through open dialogue during the funding process (via an online funding portal, which we describe in Chapter 7), and through reporting after funding has been secured (via annual reports). You have a responsibly to tell them what's happening, whether the news is good, bad, or something in the middle.

In this chapter, we help you understand how to communicate with your investors post-funding. First, you need to understand how crowdfund investors differ from the typical Wall Street or even venture capital financiers. We also help you deal with investors who may become more difficult to deal with.

We show you how to develop a communication plan so that you're never leaving your investors in the dark. And we help you stay compliant with the communication requirements built into the JOBS Act.

Recognizing Some Crowd-Specific Opportunities and Challenges

Prior to the legalization of crowdfund investing, U.S. investors were divided into two categories: accredited and unaccredited. In Chapter 2, we explain that accredited investors are those with a net worth over $1 million or an annual income over $200,000 per year. Federal securities laws consider those folks sophisticated and able to make serious financial decisions. (Apparently, the people making these laws never met Britney Spears.) The federal laws assume that accredited investors understand the challenges and stresses of starting and investing in a business. (We know this isn't necessarily true.)

Although these two categories still exist and control how investors can engage with private companies, we'd like to discuss a new distinction that can be applied to investors who consider participating in crowdfund investing: *educationally accredited* and *educationally unaccredited investors.* Educationally accredited investors understand the challenges of growing a business, the risks of investing in startups and small businesses, and the rewards of the potential upsides. They may or may not be financially accredited, but they understand the fact that a dollar invested into a business today doesn't turn into a million dollars tomorrow. The more experience they have, the more likely that they'll challenge you (such as by sharing experiences they've had when dealing with a similar issue) and encourage you to leverage their knowledge.

Your educationally unaccredited investors may provide the greatest challenge. These people don't have degrees in finance, and they likely never have run a business before and don't understand the challenges. Their passion about your product or service may compel them to speak out more than you'd like, and their lack of knowledge and experience in relation to what you're trying to accomplish will be frustrating. Nonetheless, you have to pay attention to what they say because they're part of your team.

In this section, we address some of the big-picture issues you need to consider when communicating with your investment crowd. Your goal is to size up your investors quickly, understand where they're coming from, work quickly to address their concerns (without attacking them), and utilize the power of others in your crowd to help you address or calm rabble-rousers so that you can focus on running the business. The information in this chapter can help you achieve that goal.

Many times, people will want to know why you made a certain decision. An easy answer is that you discussed it with your board of directors and they told you it was a good strategy. (This answer can work even if your board consists of just you and two or three friends or trusted advisors.) However, you don't want to rely on this pat response too often; your investors deserve better.

Understanding why your investors differ from other stockholders

People invest in the stock markets because putting cash in a mattress doesn't earn them any money. (Plus, as the costs of products increase over time, the value of a dollar in the mattress stays the same.) Most investors make investments through retirement funds such as IRAs and 401(k)s, and many of them follow the advice of advisors and/or put their money into index funds. The majority of these investors aren't playing a very active role in the investment process.

A crowdfund investor acts differently from the typical stock investor because of the relationship he has with the entrepreneur. After all, how often does a stockholder actually know the company founder, receive direct communication from that person, and have the chance to invest in a company from day one (or at least very early in the company's life)? Crowdfund investors put their hearts into their investment choices.

What does this difference mean to you, the business owner? Your crowd will share a sense of pride and ownership in your business. They'll want to be more proactive than a typical stock investor because they understand that their voices actually can make a difference to your business. Therefore, they'll be much more likely to try to drive traffic to your business. They'll be much more likely to use social media to share news about what you're doing. Leverage that enthusiasm every chance you get!

Keeping your crowd engaged even if your progress is slow

Okay, so you have engaged investors, you start to work your business plan, and you hit a wall (or two, or ten). Don't get too frustrated, and don't clam up! Even if you're experiencing problems, your investors can handle the turbulence as long as you're honest and forthright. Whereas a typical stockholder (whose heart isn't involved in her investment decisions) may pull out of a company at the first sign of trouble, a crowdfund investor is much more likely to stay on your side and help push you forward — as long as you give her the chance to understand what's happening.

Therefore, if you're experiencing problems, you should let your crowd know. But don't just whine about the problems and throw your hands up in the air. Communicate with a purpose. Here's how:

1. **Make sure you fully understand the problem and consider some potential solutions.**

2. **Present the problem to your crowd, offer your ideas, and ask for their feedback.**

   Chances are, most of your investors will appreciate the request and will do their best to brainstorm potential solutions.

We encourage you to keep a journal (whether online or offline) that tracks what happens each day in the early life of your business. If you receive useful feedback from an investor, make note of it in your journal. Later, you can indicate whether you used that feedback, including how and why. Keeping this record is important because when you report to your investors, you can acknowledge and thank the source(s) of the feedback you used.

Balancing crowd feedback with your own ideas

When you reach out to the crowd for help, keep in mind that these people have a vested interest in your success. They'll offer suggestions that they think will be best not only for your business but also for their investment. Your job is to read or listen to their feedback, consider where they're coming from, consider their experience with similar problems or opportunities, and choose the bits and pieces of advice that make the most sense to you. Ultimately, only *you* are responsible for running your business, so you can't ever give up control to your investors.

If you don't agree with someone's suggestions, don't be rude or snide. The last thing you want to do is bite the hands that feed your business. Also, be prepared to defend your decisions. And if you make a wrong decision, be honest and upfront about it. Investors can't argue with a sincere apology, but they definitely can argue with someone who is too arrogant to listen.

Juggling the bad apples

At some point, you're going to get *way* too much advice from a specific investor. It happens to all entrepreneurs. You'll think to yourself, "Do you have a day job? Or is your job to make my life miserable?" Your job is not to attack a bad apple. (It doesn't smell so good when it's smashed all over the place.) After all, you'll likely find that his heart is in the right place; he just wants you to pay attention and acknowledge what he can offer. A little "Hey, I hear you" will go a long way.

If you've got a bad apple in your crowd, give him a project. You may find that this person has a lot of time on his hands. Tell him that you're genuinely interested in what he has to say but your time is constrained. Ask for his help in preparing a report on his idea — detailing the who, what, when, where, how, and why of it. Ask how that idea would be implemented. Let him know that you want to present the report to your advisors. Gently remind him that a plan (idea) is nothing without execution, and execution is where you need help. He'll either step up to the plate or leave you alone.

The idea is to put the ball in this investor's court. And who knows? Maybe this person actually has a brilliant strategy for you to consider.

Making Outbound Communication a Priority

Outbound communication is the kind that you initiate; it's not communication solely in response to questions, demands, or emergencies. Your goal in creating an outbound communication plan is to make it *scalable*. Think of it this way: If your communication plan were a mountain, could you climb it? If it's too tall or steep or rocky (the communication plan is too demanding and overly ambitious), you won't scale it. You have to know that you're capable of pulling off whatever's in your plan.

Communication takes a lot of time and a lot of repetition. Your investors and potential investors may need to hear something from you multiple times before it sinks in. Therefore, any communication plan you create must be founded on consistency; your investors need to know when and how you'll share news with them.

As we note throughout this book, your goal at every stage is to manage your investors' expectations. That means being realistic about what you can do and then actually doing it. Don't promise an e-mail update every week and then send an update only once a month. Instead, anticipate upfront that once a month is your preferred time frame. Then consistently follow that time frame so your investors' expectations are met.

In this section, we offer a few more detailed ideas about what your outbound communication should look like.

Heaping praise on your supporters

As often as you can, and in as many ways as you can, you need to communicate praise to your crowd. You can never say thank you too many times. (Do you feel like you've read this same sentence a dozen times already in this book? See what we mean about the necessity of repetition to drive home the really important points?) Your investors opened their wallets to you because they opened their hearts to your business idea. They believe in you enough to assume an equity interest or a debt-based investment in your idea.

You owe your crowd a debt of gratitude for their willingness to help a small business person achieve a dream. Thank them at every opportunity because it's the right thing to do and because if things go wrong (you make mistakes or your business fails), they'll be more likely to trust that you did everything possible to make it work.

Updating them regularly

Set clear expectations for when communication to your crowd will occur, and then meet those expectations. In this section, we offer some specific suggestions.

Some of your investors will read or listen to every word, and others will check in only occasionally. Regardless, you want to have a trail of communication so if questions ever arise about how fully or frequently you communicated with your crowdfund investors, you're prepared to show everything to anyone who asks.

What to do each week

First and foremost, investors expect you to focus on your business, so you don't have to spend five or ten hours a week on communication. Instead, take one hour per week to scan e-mails that investors have sent you and look for common themes of questions or issues. Create a spreadsheet so that each week, you can quickly jot down the top five (or even two or three) questions/issues/concerns/successes of that week that you heard about from investors. Then respond to these items in a brief weekly update. (Depending on your business pace, you may determine that you can send this type of e-mail every other week or even once a month; only you can determine the most appropriate frequency.)

Spend no more than 30 minutes writing your e-mail update. After all, your investors are busy people, too, so you want to create something concise. Don't include filler content, and don't repeat information you discussed in a prior update. Keep the e-mail short and simple. Use bullet points to make it easier to read (and write). Bullets also give your writing a more action-oriented feel. Here's an example of the kind of weekly update you might provide:

Dear Investors:

It has been a week of ups and downs, and as always, I will let you know the bad news first, and then the good news.

• One of our top salespeople quit this week. He had to move his family to a different town, and we'll need to quickly find someone to replace him. If anyone knows a top-notch salesperson in town, please let them know we have an opening and to send their résumé as soon as possible. Thank you for your assistance and support.

• Budget cuts have put the deal with the school board on hold. We were hoping to close this deal this quarter, but it won't happen. This revenue is no longer projected for this year. However, because we knew this was a strong possibility, we didn't factor it into our budgets (which means that it won't force us to cut planned expenditures).

• We closed 18 more deals last week! That's a record for a week, and we're very pleased! Having our top salesperson leave will impact sales in the short term, but it usually takes only about six weeks to get a salesperson up to speed, and I'll put the sales hat back on and hit the streets until that person is ready to sell.

• Per investor suggestions, we completed two new customer success stories that we'll use in sales efforts starting next week.

• In response to several questions: Customers are reordering products about 9 percent faster than we anticipated. If this pace continues, we should end the quarter 2 percent to 3 percent ahead of revenue forecast.

Thanks again for your investment, for your ongoing support, and for all that you do to help our company reach its goals! We appreciate you!

Warm Regards,

J. Jones, ABC Corp.

What to do each month or quarter

A monthly or quarterly review should be an opportunity for you to look at your long-term goals (which, for a small business, may extend out a quarter, six months, or a full year — but probably no further). Use this monthly/quarterly communication to talk about the progress you made toward those long-term goals. Your weekly e-mails are giving investors details about company activities already, so focus this monthly or quarterly communication on bigger-picture updates. Examples may include

✔ The status of a marketing campaign.

✔ An update on monthly sales and expenses, year-to-date sales and expenses, and how actual results compare to what you planned to achieve.

✔ Information about the development of a new product or service.

✔ A tally of how many net new customers you added for the month. (This number is particularly important for Internet businesses that have software as a service offering.)

✔ The hiring plan for the next three to six months and what open positions you have. (Feel free to engage your crowd in hiring.)

✔ A request for feedback from investors regarding what they're hearing about a new competitor in the market.

This review could be presented in e-mail format, it could involve a conference call, and/or it could be an opportunity to have local investors come to your store or office for a meeting after business hours. The format of the communication is up to you because you know your investors better than anyone. If most of your investors aren't local, an in-person meeting may not work (or, at a minimum, must be supplemented with another type of communication). If you tend to get the most useful feedback from investors when you're talking with them rather than via e-mail, a call or in-person meeting may be best.

So, which is better, monthly or quarterly? Again, the right cadence for your business is up to you. You may even decide that you want both monthly *and* quarterly special updates. Whatever you decide, just make sure you can keep it up — make sure it's scalable.

Crafting a useful annual report for investors

After you make it through a full year in business (with investors onboard to boot!), you get to create an annual report that reflects what you've accomplished. If you're familiar with the slick products generated by Fortune 500 companies, fear not: Your annual report doesn't need to be anything that fancy. You could cover everything you need to in a few pages of text with some graphs or spreadsheets.

We recommend talking with an accountant or a lawyer to get some advice about what to include in your annual report. Essentially, you want to thank your investors, provide them with the full year's results of the business, show growth (you hope) in the business they invested in, and talk about the opportunities and challenges ahead and how you intend to reach new goals for the next year. Here are a few specific suggestions for what to include:

✔ A list of accomplishments for the year

✔ Full-year financial statements (a balance sheet, statement of cash flows, and income statement) that compare your estimated budgets and actual results

✔ What you see as the big opportunities for growth in the next 12 months and how you'll prioritize achieving them

✔ What you consider to be the big risks for the business in the next 12 months and what you'll do to mitigate them

✔ A request for any help that your investors can provide to assist you in reaching your goals the next year

Need more guidance? Consider picking up *Accounting For Dummies,* 5th Edition, by John A. Tracy, CPA (Wiley).

Submitting an annual report to the SEC

Not less than annually, you need to file with the Securities and Exchange Commission (SEC) and provide to your investors reports of the results of all operations and financial statements of your business. When you're getting ready to file your annual report with the SEC, you need to check its rules for what it deems appropriate to be included in this report.

Chapter 13

Crowd Mentality: Staying Afloat in the Face of Investor Revolt

. . . .

In This Chapter

▶ Stepping around potential pitfalls

▶ Firing up your communication engines in the face of poor PR

▶ Facing legal problems head-on

▶ Convincing your crowd to trust you

. . . .

*A*s we discuss throughout this book, the beauty of crowds is that they can provide tremendous support as you create a new business or grow your small company into something larger. But crowds aren't one-dimensional, and if you make too many missteps after a successful crowd-fund investment campaign, your crowd could turn against you. We certainly *hope* that won't happen to you, but we've written unlucky Chapter 13 about the possibility of investor revolt: what could create it and how it must be managed so you can emerge with your company intact.

Even if you know most of the people who invest in you and can't imagine them ever getting surly, we encourage you to read this chapter. You want to know what *can* go wrong so you've always got a little voice in the back of your head that stops you when you're about to do something the crowd may not like. And at the first sign of any trouble, you want to recall that you've got a resource to turn to that can help you calm your crowd before the situation gets ugly.

What would an ugly situation look like? Ask anyone who has been on the receiving end of a lawsuit, and they'll tell you how emotionally draining legal and public relations problems can be. Your entire life is consumed by what people are saying about you. The focus of your attention moves away from your business to the lawsuit. It consumes your time, your emotional energy, and your money. (And you'd better believe that the media will eat it up!)

Always keep in mind the impressive power of social media. Managed wisely, that power can take your company into amazing new territory. Mismanaged, it can lead to revolt. (Just ask the Middle Eastern governments whose leaders were ousted during the Arab Spring in 2011. Their undoing began with a series of tweets.)

Avoiding Common Business Blunders

Here's the good news: Lots of business owners have made mistakes in the past, and the chances of you coming up with a new one are slim. Those unlucky folks paid the price for their mismanagement, and you get to learn from their mistakes.

As you read this section, put yourself in the mindset of an investor — a member of your crowd. If you can figure out why each situation has the potential to rub the crowd the wrong way, you'll be much less likely to engage in these mistakes.

Pivoting without telling your supporters

Pivot is a buzzword these days, sort of like *re-engineering* and *business disruption*. Stick with us, and we'll teach you how to use these terms like a pro!

As we explain in Chapter 11, pivoting means changing your direction or tactic in response to changing markets, increasing competition, or any other business reality. Pivoting can be a good strategy if it's handled well. (Twitter and YouTube both emerged from pivots.) But if you pivot — if you change the core of your business — you absolutely *must* share the news with your investors. You definitely don't want a fundamental shift in your business to be a secret from the people supplying the cash.

Investors have jumped onto your ship because they believe in you and like the direction you're going. They like the vision that you created and want to be a part of it. Pivoting away from that direction or vision without letting your investors know is bad business and leaves them feeling insecure and uncertain about how their money is being used.

However, don't just assume that you can make a statement to your investors about a pivot and they'll smile and nod. If you've been trying to establish an organic farm, you can't simply say, "I've decided to focus on grain-based, clean-burning fuels instead." Your new idea may be the greatest one in the world! It may carry the potential of saving the environment and making huge profits at the same time! You may be hitting yourself in the head for not thinking of it years ago! But no matter how jazzed you are about the new idea, you can't assume that people will follow you onto a new path with just a quick, one-sentence message.

Instead, if you're going to pivot, you must *socialize* the idea first. That's a fancy way of saying that you need to talk to people about it. Some of those people must be your key investors and supporters. You need to bring them in on the conversation early, let them point out potential flaws or weaknesses in your plans, and ask for their help to conduct research and generate talking points about the new possibility.

What happens if you aren't upfront with your investors about a pivot? Well, then the *buzz* about your business is that you just *disrupted* the process and you're going to need some serious *re-engineering*. Not cool. Your relationship with your investors is long-term, and as with all long-term relationships, communication is the key to success.

Choosing the wrong results

When you're creating a business plan (as we explain in Chapter 5), you have to determine what results you're aiming for. In the case of a brand-new or very young business, chances are, those results center around growth markers: increased sales, an expanding customer base, and so on.

Unfortunately, what you envision when you're in the planning stages isn't always the best result when your business is actually up and running. Maybe your growth projections were so aggressive that the quality of your product or service is melting down in the effort to meet them. Perhaps you realize that for the long-term health of your venture, you have to adjust your short-term desired results. (The same thing happens in our personal lives. Have you ever gone on a diet with the goal of losing some outrageous amount like ten pounds in a week, only to realize that you're doing more damage to your body than good?)

Choosing the wrong results is a painful thing to admit; no one likes to be wrong. But it happens to lots of businesspeople — even really good ones! The way to make sure you're one of the good ones isn't to avoid mistakes altogether; you can't. Instead, it's to be proactive in the face of a mistake.

Here are four things to do when you choose the wrong results:

- ✔ Be humble and tell yourself that you were wrong.
- ✔ Try to figure out why you made the mistake.

✔ Pinpoint what you've learned from the mistake.

✔ Inform your crowd as soon as possible about the mistake, what you've learned, and how you'll correct the situation.

As we note repeatedly in this book, crowdfund investing demands transparency. Investing in a startup or a small business is a huge risk; if someone invests in ten such companies, statistics tell us that five of them are likely to fail. You must do everything possible to be open and honest with your crowd so that they trust you. Otherwise, if someone in the crowd smells a cover-up, the suspicion will spread quickly, and you may find yourself face-to-face with an investor revolt.

Responding to problems with inaction

The price of inaction is far greater than the cost of making a mistake.

—Meister Eckhart

Sherwood loves to watch what happens when politicians do something wrong and try to deny or avoid it. The media goes crazy — particularly when they dig up nuggets of information that show the politician was wrong. In a way, the public doesn't want politicians to come clean because then we have to forgive them. It's much more entertaining to watch them squirm and dig themselves in deeper and deeper holes.

But what's entertaining in one situation is infuriating in another. If you're an investor who suspects that a business owner has done something wrong, you can't tolerate inaction.

The decision not to act when things are going awry causes confusion and frustration in your crowd, which can be shared in an instant if one or more of your investors decide to express their fears online. Therefore, if something bad happens that threatens to derail your business plan, doing nothing is not a strategy. Ideally, you want to engage in thoughtful action after conferring with your key supporters. But if the pace of disaster is too quick for deliberate action, don't wait for a perfect plan to emerge before you do something. In the eyes of your crowd, any action may be better than no action at all.

Racking up unexpected costs

When you first get your hands on the money raised via your crowdfund investment campaign, you may struggle to control the impulse to reward yourself. And hey, a small reward is in order — you just accomplished something amazing! But there's a big difference between eating a nice meal with your business partner and buying yourself a yacht.

Likewise, there's a big difference between following the expenditure strategy laid out in your business model and deciding to increase your expenditures exponentially because you think doing so may make your job easier or more profitable. ("If three salespeople bring in $20,000 per week, why not hire nine and triple my earnings?") Making a significant change to your spending strategy (such as by hiring three times as many salespeople as planned) qualifies as a pivot. And as we explain in the earlier section "Pivoting without telling your supporters," any pivot must be well thought out and carried out only with investor approval.

Think you can get away with spending more than planned? Keep in mind that every year you need to report to your investors, the IRS, and the Securities and Exchange Commission (SEC) exactly what you did with the company's money that year. (See this book's website, www.dummies.com/go/crowd fundinvesting, for the SEC financial reporting requirements.) The minute you decided to raise capital from outside investors, you gave up the right to make money decisions in a vacuum. No matter how small someone's investment in you may be, that person owns a piece of your company and has the right to know how you spend money. You cannot incur unexpected or frivolous expenses. You simply don't have the right.

Your best bet when spending the company money is to ask yourself whether you'd spend it if it were your own cash from your bank account. Would you buy a new computer to replace one that's running a bit slow if the $1,000 were coming from your own coffers? Or would you get the old one repaired instead and spend a fraction of the money?

Lessons learned from the Facebook IPO debacle

The Facebook initial public offering in May 2012 was the third-largest IPO in U.S. history and created the highest trading volume for an opening day on NASDAQ. Everyone — experts and novices alike — had something to say about the amounts of money involved. The public relations and communications issues surrounding the IPO were almost as massive as the dollar amounts involved. Many case studies will be written about the problems that occurred leading up to the IPO, as well as the debacle of the launch day and the days that followed.

The biggest problem with this IPO was that information known by a few was not shared openly with the masses. Tucked pretty deep inside its prospectus, Facebook made reference to the fact that it might not hit its numbers, but its representatives didn't discuss this possibility when they went on their roadshow. Having "disclosed" the possibility in a lengthy document but not referred to it in public when speaking about the future projections turned into a PR nightmare. Lesson: Don't try to disclose the truth by hiding it deep in the pages. People expect to be told.

Regardless of the size of your organization, when things go wrong or you find yourself in a crisis situation, the more information you can put out to your investors and/or the public, the better. When in doubt, disclose it . . . the sooner, the better. Transparency is a powerful weapon.

Investors love to hear words like *frugal, strategic, lean,* and so on — words that imply not going crazy with money. Treat other people's money as your own, and always ask yourself, "Is this a nice-to-have or a need-to-have?"

Dealing with Bad Publicity

Not so long ago, if you wanted to know about the quality of a restaurant, you could read a review in the newspaper or ask a friend who had already eaten there. Today, you can go to Yelp (www.yelp.com) and find out which restaurant within five blocks of you is the best rated. Instead of rolling the dice when choosing a hotel to stay in, you can go to Trip Advisor (www.tripadvisor.com) to discover the best hotel in Miami Beach. If you need a mobile app to help you exercise more regularly, you can find out which of the 45 apps available for that purpose are the highest rated and why, as well as when the last update to that app occurred and what the update was. Welcome to the transparency of the web!

At any moment, you can choose from hundreds or thousands of opinions about any business or experience, all within seconds of asking the question. This access can serve as incredible free marketing for your business, or it can be a horrible nightmare to deal with, depending on how your crowd rates you. (Many small businesses have blamed online rating sites for their demise.)

Bad publicity used to mean photos of you in handcuffs on the front page of a newspaper. That still qualifies as very bad publicity, but many other (more subtle) forms of bad publicity exist today. Business customers and investors can now visit an online review site and write anything they want about their customer experience, your product, or your service. You can survive a small percentage of negative ratings (because the positives outweigh them), but if you begin to trend in the wrong direction, you can find yourself with a crisis on your hands — especially if your investors join the negative chorus.

The only thing more damaging to your company than an unhappy customer is an unhappy investor. An unhappy customer may cost you some sales, and that's pretty bad. An unhappy investor who has legitimate grounds to be unhappy may shake the confidence of your entire crowd, and that's potentially catastrophic.

How do you ensure that an unhappy investor doesn't take to the web and throw you to the wolves? We need to divide the answer into two broad possibilities:

  ✔ **You have a legal problem.** If your investor is responding to the fact that you've actually broken the law, you must seek legal counsel. We aren't lawyers, so we can only tell you that you need help — fast.

> ✔ **You have a communication crisis.** This possibility is more likely, and it can occur because you've made a mistake or — very often — through no wrongdoing on your part. If this is what you're facing, we can help.

In this section, we offer some common-sense steps you can take to tackle bad publicity, always keeping in mind that your goal is to achieve transparency and honesty with your investors. If you haven't done anything wrong, your initial response may be emotional; you likely feel angry or hurt by what's being said. But if you follow our advice, you can transcend those emotions and respond like a true professional — someone worthy of your crowd's ongoing support.

Letting naysayers speak (or type) their minds

Your first step is to remind yourself that anyone can send an e-mail, respond to a blog post, or post on a site like Facebook, LinkedIn, or Twitter. You can't stop them, so don't spend any energy trying. Accept the fact that some people thrive on stirring things up, and they may even be trying to engage you in a public (online) confrontation. Don't take the bait.

We aren't suggesting that you ignore what's happening. (That would be inaction, and as we mention earlier in the chapter, inaction is bad. Very bad.) If your investors begin to go negative in the discussion forums on your online funding portal (see Chapter 7), in e-mail threads, or on their social media sites, you must take their complaints seriously. Just don't let your fingers start typing responses before you've had a chance to step back and think through an appropriate communications strategy. If you hit Send when you're seething with anger over someone's false statements, you'll likely regret it later.

Responding with the facts

If you're operating in a transparent manner, you always have the facts on your side. Make sure that you track your own investor communications (such as those we outline in Chapter 12) because they can support you in times of crisis. Keep a record of all your investor updates, your online discussion forum posts, and your blog/Facebook/LinkedIn/Twitter posts. That way, if someone misunderstands or misinterprets what you wrote, you can reread your comments and clarify what you meant.

When a customer or investor makes a false statement online, take your time and respond with facts you can support. You don't want *too* much time to pass before responding, but you should give yourself a chance to feel certain about what you're saying. And if you can ask one or more of your supporters to read what you've written before you post or send it, even better; they can help ensure that you're writing in a calm, professional way that will soothe fears — not add fuel to the debate.

If you always rely on facts, you never have to remember two or three versions of the "truth." (For most of us, just accurately remembering what actually happened is hard enough!). You also save a lot of time and mental strain. We hope this advice seems obvious to you; if it does, you likely won't have any trouble managing some bad PR. But time and again we see examples of how things snowball: A small lie is covered by a medium-size lie, which is covered by a large lie that eventually gets blasted to bits. In extreme cases (think Enron and Bernie Madoff), the lies defraud stockholders of millions or billions of dollars. But even in smaller doses, lies hurt investors and companies alike. Make it your policy always to tell the truth about your business — *always.* That way, you'll never lose your investors' trust.

Involving your crowd proactively

The best defense is a good offense. If you follow our recommendations in Chapter 12, you'll already be proactively and voluntarily interacting with your investors via consistent communication. Doing so helps you build strong social capital with them; your investors will feel like they're on your side and will defend you from outside attackers.

If, on the other hand, you fail to keep your investors apprised of what's going on at your company — if you fail to communicate regularly with them and overlook the need for transparency — they may be shocked when they read something negative about you or your company online. They won't automatically jump to your defense because your silence may suddenly feel very suspicious. And if your own investors don't come to your defense, you may end up with a PR snowball that knocks you flat.

Your investors will be your best advocates if you involve them proactively. Don't underestimate the value of consistent, honest communication.

Remaining honest

Think of a recent scandal involving a public figure. (Politicians and sports stars make sure we always have a crop of such stories to consider.) What made that story so juicy? Why did the public eat it up? Chances are that the facts of the story were only one part of its appeal. In most cases, the attempted cover-up is equally fascinating and keeps the story in the news cycle for weeks instead of days.

We hope that you never have to manage a celebrity- or politician-sized PR scandal, but you can learn from their mistakes nonetheless. The most important lesson to take home from this chapter is this: Be honest! If you make a mistake, admit it. If your investors are justifiably upset with you, acknowledge what really happened and offer assurance that you won't repeat the behavior. If you try to cover up the truth, you'll only prolong the pain.

Steering Clear of Legal Woes

As you add stockholders, you may want to consider including mediation and arbitration clauses in your stockholder agreements. This is a topic worth discussing with your attorney. Mediation and arbitration can be fair, effective ways to settle disputes among parties, and both methods are usually dramatically less expensive and much faster to complete than a legal action in court. They provide a mechanism for an impartial third party to help those in dispute to come to an agreement and move forward.

Starting and running your own business should be rewarding, but it will also be very stressful. Running your own business is very different from having a traditional job because you'll be thinking about your business every waking minute. Sometimes, when the stress gets overwhelming, you may be tempted to take a shortcut here or bend a rule there. Taking that path is never wise and could result in an all-out investor revolt. In this section, we explain why.

Playing loose with your cash

If you're running a retail establishment, one of your greatest temptations may be to take in some cash off the books and perhaps keep certain people off payroll (paying them in cash instead). You may convince yourself, "Everyone hides a little cash. It's not a big deal."

If you're running a different type of business, you may be tempted to cook the books a bit — hiding some profits here, ignoring some expenses there. After all, does the SEC really have time to study every line of every company's annual financial report?

Do *not* fall to this kind of temptation. When you start down this path, it's hard to get yourself back on the right track. If you think you're stressed out now, think about how stressed you'll be doing all the same things you're doing now and getting audited on top of it. (If you haven't broken any laws, getting audited is very stressful. If you have broken laws, getting audited is an absolute nightmare.) Taking the less-than-legal path is never worth it. You must always be thinking long term.

When the little devil sitting on your shoulder tries to get you to take the wrong path, remind yourself that you don't own your business all by yourself. You have a much bigger responsibility. When you made the decision to do a crowdfund investing campaign, you took on a crowd of investors; you're responsible to each of them. And getting entangled in legal woes can only undermine their investments and cause harm. Don't do it.

Lacking patent, copyright, or trademark protection

You have to protect yourself and your business as much as possible, for your investors' sake as well as your own. In Chapter 10, we explain how and when to secure your intellectual property (a product design, logo, slogan, and so on) with a patent, copyright, or trademark.

Here, we simply want to remind you of the importance of considering intellectual property (IP) issues *before* someone tries to duplicate your efforts and steal your business thunder. If you lack IP protection, you may be putting your entire business at risk.

When cash is tight (as it always is when a business is just getting off the ground), hiring an attorney and paying the requisite fees for IP rights may not seem like the best use of funds. But try to imagine the costs involved (in cash and in your time) if you have to seek legal redress to stop someone from duplicating your product or service or using your company name or logo. If this situation happens in the early stages of your venture, it very well could put you out of business. Don't run this risk. There are plenty of things out of your control that can harm your business. Securing IP rights is something within your control, so control it and get the protection you need.

Facing a cease-and-desist order

If you receive a *cease-and-desist* letter — a communication that demands you stop creating your product or service or else face legal action — you may have a serious situation on your hands. Don't try to ignore it, and don't try to hide it from your investors. As we say throughout this chapter, rely on the facts and aim for complete transparency. Doing so is your best tactic for addressing whatever concern prompted the letter.

Maybe the person or company serving you the letter has absolutely no grounds to do so. (Perhaps a company claims that you stole its product design, but you've never even heard of the company, and you've got a patent to back you up.) Regardless of the situation, seek out the advice of an attorney immediately. You're in a much better place starting the conversation with an attorney as soon as the letter arrives than if you're served with a summons to appear in court.

The worst thing you can do is ignore the cease-and-desist order and hope that it just goes away. Problems like these don't just go away — ever! Be proactive. Write an e-mail to your investors explaining what's happening, why the letter is not a threat, and what action you're taking. Do whatever you need to do to make sure your business operations are not affected.

Trying to Win the Crowd Over Again

If you mismanage a difficult situation and lose the support of your crowd, don't give up. You can win it back if you're willing to work at it, but you're going to have to start doing some things differently.

Whatever you do, accept the fact that an entire crowd is rarely wrong. If you have 200 people who are unhappy with the way you're running your company, chances are, you should take a hard look at what you're doing and talk with a few of your investors about what you could do differently.

Honesty, honesty, and more honesty is required. You need to communicate with your investors and let them know that you realize you messed up. Put your cards on the table, and ask for your investors' help to figure out a better way forward. Keep in mind that if their money is still invested (which is a given if the problem occurs within the first 12 months of the crowdfund investment campaign; see Chapter 4), they still want you to succeed.

Realizing that a revolt happens for a reason

Admitting your errors to yourself and to your investors is an important first step toward repairing investor relations. Reach out to your mentor and/or key supporters and let them know the problem you're having. Seek advice from people who aren't afraid to be frank with you. Then listen to what they say and don't get defensive and make excuses. Someone sitting on the outside will be able to see things that you can't see.

When you understand why the revolt happened, you're ready to start fixing the problem. Again, the most important thing to do is listen. When you send out a communication to your investors, be prepared to sit back and listen to what they say. You may hear a lot of frustration, but you'll likely also hear some truly helpful advice for turning things in a more positive direction.

Often, people simply want you to listen to them. If you respond to every frustration with an explanation, your investors may get even more frustrated because they'll think you're not listening to them. And the truth is, if you have an answer for everything and an excuse for every problem, you aren't actually listening.

Rethinking your plans

After you really listen to your mentor, your key supporters, and your investors, you're ready to start rethinking your plans. If you've had a big investor revolt, you obviously need a new plan for how to communicate with them. Take a long look at their frustrations. Chances are, all the frustrations can boil down to a few main issues, some of which may include how you communicate with them and others that relate to how you're running the company.

In this chapter, we talk about following the law, spending money correctly, and being honest with your investors. Use this chapter to help you outline your new plan. Write down some action steps, and ask your mentor to look over the plan and give you blunt feedback. If you haven't pushed far enough, you want to know that before presenting your plan to your investors. You've got to make sure you're ready to assume a leadership position in their eyes again, so don't present a half-baked idea.

Making a new pitch for support

When you're ready to make a new pitch to your investors, tell them again that you know you need to fix some problems and that you're going to be doing things differently. Apologize for your past actions, thank them for bringing the issues to your attention, and ask for their forgiveness.

Lay out your new plan and let them know that you're going to be held accountable to sticking to it. Ask for their thoughts, including whether they believe the new approach will alleviate their frustrations.

Assuming that you win back their support, that's when the hard part begins: sticking to your plan. Your investors may be wary of you for a while. They'll want to make sure you're doing what you said you'd do. Hold yourself accountable, and ask other key supporters to hold you accountable on an ongoing basis. You only get so many chances. Make this one work!

Chapter 14

Knowing Your Options If Your Plans Go Astray

. . . .

In This Chapter

▶ Deciding to cancel a project post-funding

▶ Stopping your campaign midway

▶ Figuring out the best way to postpone your plans

. . . .

*Y*ou spend three months (or six months or longer) conducting research so you can carefully craft a watertight business plan. You spend a month writing said plan and vetting it with people who know a thing or two about running a business. You investigate how to protect your intellectual property before presenting it to the world. You emerge with a concept, a set of goals and milestones, and financials that you feel confident will be solid for the first year or more of operation. You run a crowdfund investment campaign to raise a portion of the funding necessary to support your plan, and you succeed. Things are really going your way!

Then, one day, you get a call or e-mail or text that makes the hair on the back of your neck stand up. Maybe someone has spotted an ad for a new product coming to market that makes your product obsolete. Or your manufacturing facility flooded, and all your shiny new inventory is floating across the warehouse floor. Or your lawyer has determined that a cease-and-desist letter from someone claiming that you've broached intellectual property rights actually has merit. (Gulp.)

Just like the rest of your life, your business life will not always proceed smoothly. Most problems you encounter will be small enough not to interrupt operations, and you won't need to share each and every one with your crowd. (They care about your business, but they don't need to hear from you every time a toilet overflows.) But you have to assume that a major problem may emerge at some point, and perhaps even at some point very early in your company's life when you're still working out the kinks of your operation.

What do you do? How do you address the problem itself, and how do you handle communication with your crowd so they don't revolt (which is the subject of Chapter 13)? Do you just return every investor's money and say "Thanks, but it didn't work out"? Maybe, or maybe not.

In this chapter, we help you consider how to respond in the face of a major issue that forces you to cancel, interrupt, or postpone your plans. We offer guidance for keeping your investors calm and remaining compliant with federal government regulations so you don't pile any additional problems on your plate.

Canceling a Project Immediately after the Crowdfund Investing Campaign

Say you make it all the way through your funding campaign and then you experience a life-changing event (such as a health issue or a sickness or death in your family). You realize that you can't focus on starting a new business right now, but what choice do you have?

First, consult your business mentor and other close advisors and seek their input. Tell them where your heart is, and listen to their counsel. Depending on the circumstances, they may encourage you not to give up but instead to seek the assistance of your crowd. After all, these people have rallied around you already because they believe in you. Your advisors may suggest that you ask whether people from your crowd will take over some of the responsibilities to lighten your load. Or they may agree that you should cancel your project outright.

If your advisors agree that you should cancel your project, immediately do so and return your investors' money. You must work with your online funding portal (see Chapter 7) to accomplish this step. Keep reading to find out how the refund process will likely work.

At the same time, you must tell your investors *why* you're returning their money. You don't want to surprise them with the refund because you want to do everything possible to maintain their trust and respect. In the upcoming section "Being upfront with your crowd," we offer an example of the type of communication that fills the bill in this situation.

Have faith in your crowd, and chances are, they'll live up to your expectations. Crowds don't revolt when life circumstances change plans; you shouldn't face any horrible public relations crisis as long as you communicate effectively. If you share what's happening, you'll actually build trust with your crowd. And you may be shocked by how many people reach out to see how they can help you both with your dilemma and with your business if you decide to continue pursuing it.

Taking the necessary steps to appease the SEC

When you make the decision to cancel your project, you need to take the appropriate steps to make sure you're compliant with the Securities and Exchange Commission (SEC). Consult an attorney who has securities experience to ensure you have guidance that is specific to your situation. The SEC's number-one concern here is that fraud didn't take place. One way to protect yourself from any suspicion of fraud is to consult with your attorney, and visit this book's website, www.dummies.com/go/crowdfundinvesting, to learn about the process that the SEC has determined you must follow to be compliant with its regulations.

This means that you'll absorb all the costs related to posting your campaign on the funding portal. Any money that you spent on producing a pitch video (see Chapter 9), as well as money you paid to the funding portal for its services (which could include a background check fee, success fee, escrow fee, and transfer fees), can't be reimbursed by investor funds (which may have been part of your original financial plan). You most likely will have to pay the *escrow agent* (the third party that collects investor funds; see Chapter 7) another fee to return all the money. It's important to realize that this is *your* financial responsibility — not the responsibility of your investors.

Here are the steps you must take to ensure SEC compliance in the event of a cancelation:

- ✔ **Contact your online funding platform and seek guidance from its staff.** Consult its Terms and Conditions, which likely contains a section letting you know what to do if you need to cancel a project. Don't make any assumptions. Find out from the platform what its specific rules and procedures are.

- ✔ **Notify your investors of what you're doing and why.** As we explain in the next section, doing so is important to maintain your crowd's trust. But it's also important so the SEC knows you're sharing appropriate communication with your investors.

- ✔ **Take the appropriate action to return the cash to your investors and get their equity shares back (if your campaign offered equity participation).** If you used an escrow/transfer agent to collect the money and distribute the shares in the first place, you'll likely have to engage that entity again. Your funding portal is your information source for how to accomplish this step.

✔ **Request confirmation from the escrow/transfer agent and/or from your funding portal that all the investors received their money back.** You want to have documentation on file that demonstrates that every dollar has been returned.

✔ **Inform the SEC by phone that the project has been canceled and the investor money returned.** Your funding portal reported information related to your campaign and how much money you raised to the SEC when you hit your funding target. The SEC thinks you've got that cash until you tell it otherwise.

The SEC Office of Compliance and Inspections is your main point of contact here. Reach out to them, introduce yourself, and tell them what's happened. Let them know the steps you've taken, and ask what else you need to do to be fully compliant. Keep a record of who you spoke to and when, as well as of the nature of your conversation and any follow-up steps that were suggested to you.

✔ **Write a formal letter to the SEC repeating the information covered in your phone call.** Reference the date and time of your call to the SEC, as well as the name of the person you spoke to. Reiterate that all the money has been returned to your investors, and provide your complete contact information.

Keep a copy of this letter. Send the original via Certified Mail, FedEx, or UPS for delivery confirmation. You want to have a record of receipt so you know that you've done everything necessary to let the SEC know you canceled your project and are in compliance with the law.

Expect that both the SEC and the funding platform will follow up with you to make sure all appropriate steps have been taken.

If you don't follow these steps, in addition to dealing with your life-changing event, you'll probably be dealing with a lawsuit from your investors and one from the SEC. Trust us: You don't want this. Consult with your attorney. Be transparent, be efficient in your communication, and stay above the law.

Being upfront with your crowd

As we say repeatedly in this book, your crowd demands and deserves transparency and honesty. Even when you're dealing with difficult life circumstances and a campaign cancelation, don't skimp on the crowd communication. After all, in the future you may want to approach the same people again about funding a business (whether the same business or a new one), and you don't want to alienate any potential supporters. In addition, as one of the crowdfund investing vanguards, you don't want to alienate investors from the entire crowdfund investment process. Someone who is left in the dark when you cancel your project may decide never to trust another investment campaign again, and then other entrepreneurs and business owners suffer for your mistake.

Depending on your reasons for canceling, you may not want to provide personal details to your crowd, and that's fine. But you do need to give them a clue what's going on. Otherwise, you risk their assuming that you simply weren't prepared to run a business. You should express understanding of their potential dismay about the change of plans, and you should try (if possible) to give them a sense of whether you anticipate starting or growing this business at some point in the future when life circumstances calm down.

Do everything in your power to keep your investors informed. Specifically,

- ✔ Update the comments section on your online funding platform.
- ✔ Send all your investors an e-mail.
- ✔ If possible, make phone calls to the people who have supported you most, whether financially or with their expertise.
- ✔ If possible, create a video to post on your funding platform in which you talk directly to the investors.

Doing all these things shows you're trying your hardest to reach out so they know what's going on.

Here are the key things you need to do when communicating your plans to your investors, whether in writing, on the phone, or by video:

- ✔ Be honest, sincere, and transparent.
- ✔ Get to the point quickly.
- ✔ Let them know what your future plans are (or could be, if you're facing a lot of uncertainty).

You could communicate something like this:

> Dear Investors,
>
> I have been dealt a (huge challenge, terrible tragedy, wonderful opportunity, or whatever phrase applies). Prior to the funding campaign, I couldn't have foreseen how this event would affect my life. Rather than risk dealing with this (challenge, tragedy, opportunity) and trying to start a business, I have decided that the right thing to do is return your money so I can focus on dealing with pressing matters.

My passion and vision for (your concept or business field) has not disappeared. However, at a time when I should be giving 100 percent to both you and the business, my energy and focus are not there. That is not fair to you.

In this time of uncertainty, I cannot tell you what I will do in (one month, three months, a year), but I would like to believe that I will pick up on this idea and that you will still believe in me and let me try again. If you have any questions, please feel free to call my cell or e-mail me. You can reach me at (cell number) or (e-mail address).

Sincerely,

Jay Smith

Restarting the project at a later date

If life circumstances change again to allow you to focus on your startup or your plans for growing your business, you must be able to communicate with your former and new potential investors why you're worth the investment risk. Raising money in a new campaign will be a challenge — very likely harder than the first time around.

If you took all the steps we outline in previous sections — you returned every dime to your investors, complied with SEC regulations, and communicated openly with your investors — you should proceed with your head held high. But you aren't starting from square one here; you're starting from square *minus* one. You have to overcome two types of investor confusion:

✔ **The confusion of former investors:** Even if you communicated completely during your cancelation, some people won't recall exactly what happened. (You may hear things like, "Wait, didn't you do this before?" or "I thought I already invested.") As important as your business is to you, it's one of many important things in your former investors' lives, and they can't be expected to remember the details of the cancelation.

You have to reengage with them to explain again the who, what, when, where, and why of your idea. To do so,

- *Start with your family and closest friends.* These are the people who are with you in good times and in bad. You need them to invest in your new campaign to begin the process of generating traction. (Without the buy-in of your core network, your new campaign likely won't stand a chance.)

- *Organize the remaining list of your former investors into groups.* You may have groups such as work colleagues, friends, extended family, friends of friends, and people you don't know.

- *Within each group, determine who are the key influencers and/ or leaders.* These are the people you want to contact directly (by phone or e-mail, perhaps) to ask them to visit your new funding portal campaign page. If you can convince them to invest in you again and to publicly support you, they may pull additional investors back into your fold. Ask them directly for their help in contacting other prior investors in their circle. Tell them that you'll be reaching out to their friends and cc'ing or tagging them when you do so. That way, they can easily say "+1" or like the comment or reply to all saying "I have reinvested. You should review the offering at such-and-such crowdfund investing portal." (Be sure to thank them profusely when they help to spread the word of your campaign.)

✔ **The confusion of potential investors who knew about the previous campaign but didn't invest:** This group may be the most challenging because they weren't necessarily privy to your communication when you canceled the first project. As a result, they may not realize that you canceled at all, or they may have heard about the cancelation but not known that you refunded all the money to your initial investors.

To get them to consider investing, you have to fully explain what happened and why you're back. You may consider including a section in the written and video pitch on your funding portal campaign page that explains what occurred. The cancelation doesn't need to be your lead, but somewhere during the pitch you should make it clear that you succeeded with the previous campaign, something major happened in your life, you returned all the money to investors, and you complied fully with SEC regulations. You can point investors to a link that takes them to a section of the crowdfunding portal where you provide more details if you want.

Of course, you also want to take the opportunity to improve on your first campaign if possible by making your pitch even stronger this second time around. Consider what worked and what didn't work in the prior campaign, and try to learn from it.

As you map out where your investments came from previously, ask yourself some questions:

✔ Did certain sections of your social network invest more than others? For example, did you have greater success with your professional contacts on LinkedIn or your social contacts on Facebook?

✔ Can you identify common traits among people who chose not to invest? In general, were they people who lacked a professional connection with your industry? Or did geography play a role (meaning that people closest in location to you invested more often than those at a distance)?

This study doesn't need to be scientific, but if you can determine any possible investment influencer based on your prior campaign experience, you may be able to tweak your pitch to overcome it. (Or you may decide that you're better off focusing your time and energy on people who share traits with those who invested the first time around.)

Of course, your social networks likely have expanded since your previous campaign began, so you'll probably be reaching out to people who had no knowledge of the prior campaign at all. They'll have the same access to information about your previous campaign that everyone else does, so just be prepared to answer questions about what happened.

Interrupting a Campaign Midstream

For the same reasons that you may need to cancel a project immediately post-funding, you may decide that you need to stop your campaign midstream. If that happens, here's what you need to do:

1. **Find out the funding portal's policies and procedures for removing a campaign prior to its completion.**

   Follow all procedures as they're outlined by the SEC.

2. **Before you remove the campaign, send a message to all your investors.**

   Inform them that you're canceling the campaign, that their entire investment will be returned, and how the refund will occur (such as via the escrow agent).

3. **Provide the name and contact information for the escrow agent.**

   That way, investors can follow up if they have any questions.

4. **Make sure you have the contact information for every person who had decided to invest in your campaign.**

   That way, after it has been removed, you can contact these supporters directly (by e-mail, phone, or social media) to make sure they know that your campaign has been canceled and to thank them profusely for their support. If you know that you'll be able to restart the campaign in the future, go ahead and share that information.

5. **Make social media posts indicating that you're no longer seeking funding.**

   Be sure to thank everyone in your social networks for their support (whether moral or financial).

The SEC and the crowdfunding industry associations such as the Crowdfunding Professional Association (CfPA) and the Crowdfund Intermediary Regulatory Advocates (CFIRA) will be extremely focused on the issues of compliance with the laws and regulations regarding crowdfund investing. CfPA and CFIRA aim to ensure that online funding platforms comply with all SEC regulations. Consult with your funding platform to ensure you comply with all steps required to close down your campaign, and maintain records of all your actions in case there are questions you need to respond to.

Raising money via this new tool is not to be treated lightly, nor are the regulations. Lots of people (including us) fought very hard to make this funding method available to entrepreneurs everywhere. Please do all that you can to ensure that future generations of entrepreneurs are able to continue using it!

Extending a Project's Timeline

After you successfully raise your funding and start your company, you have a timeline that you've set for your company with goals that you want to stick to. But along the way, many things come up that you didn't plan on — that's completely normal. Some of these things may be good, and some of them take a lot more time and money than you expect.

Clearly, you want to follow through on your goals and stick to your timeline, but sometimes that's just not possible. Maybe your timeline was too aggressive, or maybe you just had too many unforeseen things come up that have delayed your progress. Evaluate your progress on a regular basis, and be honest with yourself about it. If you can see that you aren't going to meet a certain milestone or goal, you need to extend your timeline. This situation is not the end of the world. In fact, it's very common. Things come up that are simply out of your control.

Figure out what the main choke points are and how long it's going to take you to get them worked out. Some of your investors will undoubtedly be frustrated. How you deal with the situation will dictate how they react.

Set up a new timeline and be honest about it. If you thought a certain task would take a week, but you know you need a full month, be honest about needing a month. Don't underestimate your needs in the revised timeline; be realistic in your assessment. You want to tell your investors only *once* that a certain milestone or goal needs to be moved out; you don't want to make that same announcement multiple times.

Most investors know that starting a business always takes longer than expected. What they want from you is honesty. So be honest.

Revisiting your planned milestones and goals

When you decide to extend your timeline, you really need to dig into your planned milestones and goals. Some of your goals may have been too lofty. Now that you've been working on your business for a while, you have a better handle on what's possible. Take this opportunity to revisit your goals and decide which things you can drop and which are essential.

If you determine that a certain goal is no longer essential to the completion of your timeline, put it on the back burner. (Certain things that seem essential when you're in the planning stage become less so when you're actually up and running.)

For example, when Zak was starting his chain of olive oil and balsamic vinegar tasting stores called Pure Mountain Olive Oil, he thought that it was absolutely essential to have a big back office in each store. He believed that this office was needed for the success of the business. As he was working out the budget for the construction of his first shop, he had to cut out the back office. It was a hard decision for him to make. He now has a chain of stores, and none of them has a back office. Be flexible, and don't be so full of pride that you can't let some things go.

Explaining delays

As in any situation where you're making a *pivot* (a fairly significant change to your business plan), you must be honest and consistent in your investor communication. The sooner you can anticipate and communicate project delays to your investors, the better they'll handle the changes.

Think of it this way: You need to *sell* your investors on the idea of a delay. When selling anything to anyone, you want to talk about the benefits to *them* — not the benefits to you. Lest we sound like we're encouraging twisting information around, we aren't: We just want you to think about presenting the information so it's most appetizing to the person hearing it.

If you have multiple issues delaying your progress, you need to explain each one in a detailed but efficient manner. Consider creating a spreadsheet, and include the following information for each delay:

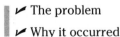 The problem

✔ Why it occurred

✔ What you're doing about it (how you're handling it)

✔ Why waiting for this problem to be fixed is important enough to delay the opening of your business or to extend your project timeline

✔ Why delaying your launch or your project will benefit the investor as a shareholder

After you create this spreadsheet, you can use it to keep your investors up to date on the progress of each issue. Add a column called "Progress Notes" or something similar. Let investors know that you'll be updating this list regularly so they can check on your progress with each item.

As an added bonus, you may find out that someone in your crowd has expertise that can help you come to a quicker resolution on one or more items. If they see that you've got a specific issue that relates to their field, they'll be more likely to offer help.

Asking your crowd to stick around

Say that your first year of business is coming to a close, and you're facing delays that will prevent you from hitting the goals you laid out for your first 12 months of operation. You know that, per the JOBS Act, your initial equity investors have to hold onto their stock for a minimum of 12 months. (If you chose to run a debt-based crowdfund investment campaign, chances are, your debt investors are obliged to stick with you for 12 months as well.) Should you fear that your crowd is going to run toward the exit as soon as the calendar reaches the 12-month mark?

As in so many situations, communication is your best weapon. If you follow the steps outlined in the previous section, you'll have already done a good job explaining the delay and setting up a solid plan for addressing each issue and informing your investors of your progress. Of course, as we advocate in Chapter 12, ideally you've been communicating with them consistently and clearly throughout your entire project so they trust you.

As the 12-month mark approaches, reach out to the crowd proactively, and ask them to stick around. You certainly don't want the distraction of major upheaval among your investors; the mass exodus of investors won't help you reach your goals any faster! Explain why their continued support is so vital, and request that they stick with you for a minimum of another three months or six months or whatever time frame you need to prove that you can meet your initial goals.

Give them solid reasons for why they should stick around. Create a list of bullet points that reflect your successes to date. Don't be humble! Show the value you've created for them by being detailed about your progress. If you've been collecting e-mail addresses of potential customers, for example, show your database to your investors. If you've been in talks with potential partners, disclose that fact.

Your investors will only want to walk away if they believe that you're never going to follow through on your plan and you'll never create a return on their investment. If you've extended your timeline six months, asking them to hold their exit decision until that time shouldn't intimidate them. Tell them that you're completely confident they'll have a change of heart when they see your progress (and, of course, make sure that your new timeline is honest).

Part V

Becoming a Crowdfund Investor

The 5th Wave   By Rich Tennant

"I've done some crowdfund investing. Right now I have some money in a struggling startup called Greece."

In this part . . .

If you aren't an entrepreneur or small business owner but you want to tap into crowdfund investing's potential, this part is for you! Many people have the opportunity to invest in small, private companies for the first time thanks to the legislation that legalized crowdfund investing. But before you put one dime into any project, no matter how well you know the players involved, you need to read this part.

You must be aware of the risks inherent in investing in small businesses and startups, and you have to make sure that this type of high-risk investment fits into your overall financial portfolio. You should also be prepared to do your homework by really studying the various opportunities available to you and knowing what investment limits the Securities and Exchange Commission has set. With that information in mind, you can consider how to commit your capital, how to become a valuable asset to any company you support, and how to map out your investment exit strategy.

Chapter 15

Evaluating Crowdfund Investing Opportunities

*I*f you've never invested in startups and small businesses before, crowd-fund investing may seem really exciting. After all, you have the chance — perhaps for the first time (because of the regulatory changes contained in the JOBS Act; see Chapter 2) — to put your money directly behind an entrepreneur's concept or into a small business that seems poised for great things.

But we're going to caution you right now to take your time, become very educated about the opportunities themselves and the risks involved, and stay on a strict budget if you decide to invest. Don't be surprised if we repeat these cautions about three dozen times in this chapter alone; we don't want you to lose your shirt — and lose your faith in every small business owner — because you don't become a millionaire on your first experience.

Chances are, you have a strong online social network. If you also have a group of entrepreneurial friends (or friends of friends), you may be hearing about multiple business concepts that sound really juicy. Perhaps you've received messages from your contacts asking you to check out an online investment pitch that outlines how you can buy into one of these concepts. If that's true, stop right now and repeat after us:

✔ I will invest only in people I know and trust.

✔ I will invest only in products or services I will use myself or believe will have real value for others.

✔ I will invest only in businesses for which I am willing to be a marketing engine or help out in some way.

✔ I understand that this is a long-term investment, I may never see my investment, and if I do, it may be a long time off and may not be the amount I put in.

✔ I am investing only as much as I can afford to walk away from or lose today.

Now wash, rinse, and repeat. And keep reading to find out why we want you to be so careful.

Knowing Your Overall Investment Goals

Making an investment decision of any kind starts with understanding what your investment goals are. If you have any net worth whatsoever, you likely have it broken up into savings and investments. Your savings generally cover your short-term needs, and your investments generally cover your long-term goals. When you make investments, you do so for your future benefit, whether that means a child's college education, your own retirement, or some other goal.

We don't claim to be financial planners, but we can tell you this with certainty: Crowdfund investing cannot and should not be your sole means of investment. If it is, you're risking that your long-term goals may never come to fruition. You absolutely must create a balanced financial portfolio that combines investment categories that represent different levels of risk and potential return. As long as you do so, crowdfund investing may very well play a role in your investment plans.

In this section, we walk you through the most basic basics of investment strategy. If you're coming to this book with little investment experience, we strongly encourage you to do additional reading to find out more about how to achieve a balanced portfolio that represents the type of risk you can handle and the potential rewards that correspond with that risk. The *For Dummies* series offers a full spectrum of reading options that may fill the bill, including: *Investing For Dummies,* 6th Edition, by Eric Tyson; *Stock Investing For Dummies,* 3rd Edition, by Paul Mladjenovic; *Bond Investing For Dummies,* 2nd Edition, by Russell Wild; *Mutual Funds For Dummies,* 6th Edition, by Eric Tyson; *Exchange-Traded Funds For Dummies,* 2nd Edition, by Russell Wild; and *Personal Finance For Dummies,* 7th Edition, by Eric Tyson (all published by Wiley).

Balancing risks and rewards

When you were a kid, did you ever climb a tree to the very top? If you did, you probably felt invincible. The reward was amazing, and you were oblivious to the risk.

We're guessing that no one could pay you enough money to climb to the top of that tree today. That's because no matter how great the reward may be, you're all too aware of the risk involved.

When you're young, you're much more likely to take risks than when you're older. You just don't believe that you can get very hurt. (And the reality is that if you do get hurt, you'll likely recover faster and less painfully than an older person would.) What's true for climbing trees is true for making investment decisions; the younger you are, the more risky you may be with your investments. You may truly believe that nothing will go wrong. (And if anything does go awry, you'll likely recover much faster and less painfully than an older person would.)

Young or old, we need you to be aware of this fact: Crowdfund investing is high-risk investing. You can't approach it with the assumption that because federal regulations allow it, this type of investing must somehow be immune from failure. It's not. As we point out elsewhere in the book, 50 percent of investments in early-stage companies fail. You're going to do your homework and follow the mantras we offer in this chapter's introduction, so you may be in better shape than some other investors, but you are not immune to failure. If you choose to put some money into crowdfund investing, you must be prepared for the worst.

Why invest in this type of venture at all, then? Ah, there's the rub. Because if — *if* — you put your dollars behind a concept and a management team that achieve their goals for growth, you stand to earn more than you would from a bond, a mutual fund, or most other traditional investments. The greater the risk you take, the greater the potential reward may be — *if* you choose wisely and (let's face it) get lucky.

Diversifying your portfolio

If we haven't scared you away from crowdfund investing yet, that means you probably have some tolerance for financial risk. How much tolerance? That's a question only you can answer (ideally with guidance from a financial advisor).

Creating an investment portfolio that meets your needs demands first assessing your level of risk tolerance. If you have nerves of steel and can withstand rocky financial times without selling every investment at the worst possible moment (when its value has fallen to the floor), you're pretty high on the risk tolerance scale. If you lie awake at night worrying that your stock index mutual fund ticked a quarter of a percent lower that day, you're in an entirely different risk zone.

Depending on how much risk you can stomach and what your long-term goals are, you should diversify your investments — spread them among various asset classes — accordingly. The term *asset classes* refers to groups of investments that share certain characteristics, including risk. Low-risk government bonds constitute one asset class, and high-risk junk bonds constitute a very different asset class. In between you have federal agency bonds, corporate bonds, international bonds, and more. Within the equity world, you have large-cap stocks, small-cap stocks, international stocks, value stocks, growth stocks, emerging market stocks, and more. (The word *cap* here refers to *capitalization,* which is an estimate of a company's value arrived at by multiplying its total number of outstanding shares by the current price of a single share.)

For every asset class, this truism holds: The lower the risk it represents, the lower the return (or potential return) it offers. Conversely, the higher the risk it represents, the higher the return (or potential return) it offers. That's why people don't get rich quick buying government bonds, and it's why people who take chances on risky stock classes have a fairly good chance of ending up either richly rewarded or completely broke.

Higher-risk asset classes also tend to be much more volatile than lower risk asset classes. If you buy a U.S. Treasury bond, you don't expect a lot of volatility from that investment; you know how much return you'll be getting. If you buy stocks in an emerging-market nation, on the other hand, you don't have a clue what your return will be in any given year. You hope to jump on the roller coaster while the car is pointing uphill, but you never know when you'll reach the crest and start rushing down the other side.

Many financial advisors make their living helping people determine how to craft a portfolio that fits all their needs, including their risk tolerance and need for returns. Most people (though certainly not all) find that as they get closer to reaching their long-term goals, such as retirement, their risk tolerance decreases. Therefore, a portfolio cannot be a static thing; as your life circumstances change, you and your financial advisor must be prepared to adjust your investments accordingly.

The beauty of diversifying your portfolio with a variety of asset classes is that you can still invest in some of the high-risk classes, including startups and small businesses, without risking your long-term goals. As long as you know that crowdfund investing is firmly planted on the high-risk end of the investment spectrum (see Figure 15-1), and as long as you maintain strict control over your investment choices, you absolutely can fit it into your portfolio. Just don't assume that all (or even *any*) of your crowdfund investments will turn into the next Google. Chances are very, very good that they won't.

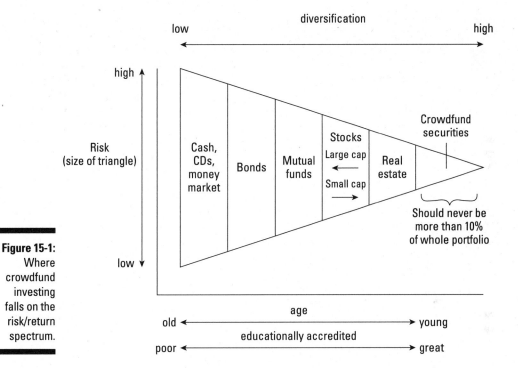

Figure 15-1:
Where crowdfund investing falls on the risk/return spectrum.

Realizing that crowdfund investing should be a small slice of the pie

You should *never* put more than 10 percent of your financial portfolio into crowdfund investments. (You may even consider something closer to the 5 percent range.) This limit is wise even if more than 10 percent of your portfolio is allocated to high-risk stocks. And if you and your financial advisor have determined that your allocation to high-risk stocks should be even lower (5 percent, for example), you don't want your crowdfund investments to push you over that limit.

Therefore, if you're considering crowdfund investing for your portfolio, you first must determine if you have any room for it. When you scan your entire portfolio and look at your spectrum of investments, find the total amount you already have in high-risk investments and figure out what percentage it represents of your total portfolio. (If you have most or all of your investments in one brokerage house, you may be able to put your finger on that percentage pretty easily. Otherwise, it's time to sharpen your math or spreadsheet skills.)

If you've already maxed out your high-risk investment percentage, don't put a dime into crowdfund investing unless and until you divest from another high-risk asset class. Either sell off another high-risk investment, or walk away from this type of investing. Don't play with your portfolio percentages by convincing yourself that "just 5 percent in this kind of investment isn't going to hurt." You need to be able to sleep at night if your investments hit the dirt. When and if that happens "just 5 percent" is going to feel like a *lot*.

A second — and equally important — factor that plays into your crowdfund investment limit is this: The JOBS Act limits how much investors can risk with crowdfund investing. We make this point several times in this book, starting in Chapter 2, but it definitely bears repeating: the Securities and Exchange Commission (SEC) won't allow you to invest every spare dollar in these types of ventures (and we agree with the SEC). The legislation was crafted carefully to avoid the prospect of investors gone wild. Here are the investment limits, which are based on annual salary:

If you make . . .	*You can make crowdfund investments up to . . .*
Less than $40,000	$2,000
$40,000 to $99,999.99	5% of your annual salary or net worth
$100,000 or more	10% of your annual salary or net worth up to $100,000

For a more thorough discussion of these limits, flip back to Chapter 4.

Protecting Yourself through Due Diligence

When you invest in a more traditional financial vehicle, such as a mutual fund, you depend pretty heavily on other people to tell you what to expect. The fund company creates a hefty prospectus (which, thankfully, is available in electronic format these days — let the trees rejoice!). This document outlines past performance, fund components, and management experience so you can get a decent sense of what you're in for when you part with your dollars. (Of course, you must actually *read* the prospectus in order for it to be of benefit; you can't let the sheer size of the document scare you off.)

If the people running a crowdfund investment campaign are doing their jobs well, you should be able to pretty easily put your hands on information that can help you anticipate what to expect from your investment. But seeking out that information is your job; no 72-page prospectus is going to magically appear in your mailbox or inbox when you express interest in a certain campaign.

In this section, we walk you through the fundamentals of familiarizing yourself with a crowdfund investment opportunity, starting with identifying how you know the person reaching out to you.

Pinpointing your connection to the entrepreneur or small business owner

The premise of crowdfund investing is that you put your money into ventures run by people you know and trust — or by people who have a secondary connection to you. What does a secondary connection look like? If people you know and trust have a connection with — and faith in — the people running the investment campaign, you have a secondary connection. You're just two degrees away from the entrepreneur or company owner. (Look behind you to see if Kevin Bacon is somewhere in sight.)

Why the desire for such a close connection between business owner and investor? Because it takes a lot more than a good idea to make a business profitable. It takes hard work, determination, and focus. (And did we mention luck?) Lots of people can come up with good ideas, and salesmen can make it sound like these ideas are going to be profitable for investors.

When you invest your dollars in people you know, you can make choices based on an individual's ability and tendency to follow through. You need to know enough about this person to understand his work ethic and be familiar with his past business endeavors.

Be cautious about investing in someone you may have met once but know very little about. (Laughing over drinks at a cocktail party doesn't give you the insight you need to figure out this person's business acumen.) And be cautious when friends forward information to you via social media about investment opportunities you should check out. If your friends have some financial sense, then be prepared to consider what they're sharing. But always follow up by finding out as much as possible about the entrepreneur or business owner. Here are some great questions to ask yourself as you do:

- Is this person trustworthy?
- Is she a hard worker?
- Does she have entrepreneurial experience?

✔ Does she have other business experience?

✔ Does she generally follow through on what she wants to do?

✔ Would I recommend her for a job to another friend or family member?

Always keep in mind that you are *not* evaluating people for friendships here. You're evaluating them for their ability to handle your money wisely. You can like someone a lot and not trust him with your money. (We have lots of close friends who fall into that category.) Therefore, if the answer to any of these questions is "no," you need to walk away.

Watching the pitch video

The pitch video that the entrepreneur or small business owner creates is your window into his business concept and plan. You can find this video by visiting the particular online funding platform that is hosting this person's investment campaign. (If you're curious what funding platforms do, check out Chapter 7.) You should view funding pitch videos *only* on SEC-approved crowdfund investing sites. That's because the SEC wants to insure that you have access not only to the video but also to the complete information about the company's offering, which is available on the same website.

When you visit the website, at the invitation either of the business owner himself or of someone in your social network, you should easily be able to locate the pitch video from the campaign home page. Watching this video is your opportunity to hear this person's passion and drive. It also gives you an idea how the business owner's mind is organized.

If the pitch video is scattered or wishy-washy and doesn't really say much of importance, chances are, the business itself is going to be disorganized and lack focus. After all, the entrepreneur or business owner should be well aware that the pitch video is his opportunity to sell everyone on the business. If he hasn't put a lot of time and energy into organizing it, this dearth of effort should be a major red flag.

On the other hand, a pitch video that is well thought out should give you a good sense of who the entrepreneur is, what kind of team he has created, and what his business model looks like. It doesn't have to be an Oscar-quality video to achieve these ends. The content is what really matters, and that content should include how investors' money is going to be used and why this entrepreneur is the right person for the job.

Pitch videos shouldn't be longer than five minutes, so don't expect a video to contain every bit of information you need to make an investment decision. Instead, consider it an advertisement that either piques your interest in the entrepreneur and the business or turns you off completely. The detailed pitch and financial information, which we explain in the next two sections, allow you to really dig into the business plan.

Reading the pitch information on the company page (and asking questions)

You should be able to locate the meat of the business model on the same funding portal where you find the pitch video. The entrepreneur or business owner should provide the equivalent of an executive summary from a business plan, which contains about three pages of information on the entrepreneur, her team, her competitors, and the business model. As you read this information, take notes and consider what questions you have.

If, after reviewing all the available information, you still have unanswered questions, you need to reach out to the entrepreneur or business owner directly. The online funding portal provides discussion forums that allow you to do just that. Don't be shy about asking questions, especially when the answers will help you determine whether to spend your money. Instead, assume that you're doing a community service here; if you couldn't find all the answers you were looking for, chances are, other potential investors are in the same boat.

Watching how an entrepreneur answers your questions gives you a very good glimpse into how she will relate to her investors after the investment campaign reaches a successful completion and she is growing her business. If questions are left unanswered in this phase, you may assume that it will be hard for you to get information from the entrepreneur down the road. (If the entrepreneur is busy now, just wait until she has launched her business!) This person needs to demonstrate that she can manage her time effectively, and this questions-and-answer interaction is a good window into her time management and communication abilities.

If the campaign is for an existing business and the business owner is looking for growth capital, the executive summary information should feel quite solid. After all, this person isn't just speculating about what the business will look like; he's in the midst of it and should know the company's strengths and weaknesses and its competitors. The pitch information section should address why this company is better than its competitors and how it's going to overcome any existing weaknesses.

Reviewing financial information

The financial information connected to the investment campaign is one of the most important elements for you to review and understand. That's because no matter how sound the idea for the business is, if the financials don't make sense, you're never going to see a return on your investment.

Not everyone feels comfortable looking at numbers, and the entrepreneur or business owner should understand this fact and keep things simple and straightforward. The financials should include clear explanations that walk you through what you're seeing. If that's not the case, don't get embarrassed and assume you should just trust that everything's fine. That's how people lose money! Instead, reach out to someone with an accounting or other financial background (*surely* there's an accountant somewhere in your family), and ask for help analyzing the data.

If you're looking at a campaign for an existing business, it should provide a good history of past performance. Consider whether its future goals mesh with that past performance; if there's a big leap planned and the owner hasn't explained how the leap is going to occur, be very wary. For example, say the company is a $100,000 revenue bricks-and-mortar store, and it wants to raise $50,000 for a new location. If the owner is saying that the combined revenue is going to be $500,000, send up a big red flag. Make sure you can locate a good explanation for every assumption the entrepreneur has made.

Applying Some Common Sense Tactics

When you're looking at lots of numbers, ratios, facts, and charts all whizzing by at 100 miles per hour, you may think, "Wow! This company can't lose! I gotta buy this now!" You experience the infomercial effect; you get so caught up in how amazing this business/product/spray-on hair is that your common sense flies out the window. You don't stop to consider how you would incorporate this business/product/spray-on hair into your daily life.

Consider exercise video infomercials. They all show amazing results in two to three months. Of course, all the people on-screen telling you how great their success is never really looked like most of us to begin with. But swept away by the promise of perfection, millions of people purchase the workout system. And in most cases, they never use the system more than once — if at all. That's because while they were viewing the infomercial, the realities of daily life, schedules, and diets weren't on their minds.

What's our point? When you run across a great pitch video and clear, concise online documents, you may immediately jump to the "Invest!" mindset. You begin, naturally, to look for reaffirming information and data for that investment or person. As you look at all the financials, for example, you may find yourself focusing on all the strong sales numbers and not asking as many questions about the unrealistic marketing plans to get to those sales numbers.

In this section, we encourage you to apply some common-sense tactics to avoid being swept up in your enthusiasm. You need to protect yourself from making bad decisions, and you have the means to do so if you just slow down, employ your gray matter, and take some additional steps.

Making sure you actually understand the business or project

Okay, this step is *really* fundamental. After watching and reading the pitch materials, answer these questions:

- ✓ **Do you understand exactly what the product or service is?** If someone asked you to describe it, can you give a 30- to 60-second description of what the product or service is and how it works?

- ✓ **Can you easily describe what problem this product or service solves for a person or a business?** We believe that most purchases are made either to stop current pain or to keep pain/discomfort from happening in the future. (Pain is not always physical pain, of course; it's often emotional or psychological pain.) No matter how cool a product may sound, until it solves a problem for a person or business, it's simply something that you pick up at a store, look at, and put back on the shelf.

- ✓ **Who is the customer for this business?** When we talk with entrepreneurs, a common answer is "Women will love this product!" or "Every dog owner is our customer." But a startup business *never* has the capital to sell to every woman or every dog owner. And even if it did, not everyone in those groups would buy the product.

  Make sure the entrepreneur has a *very* clear picture of the target customer. For example, "My customers are women within 6 miles of my store who work, have children, and want nutritious organic meals delivered to their homes twice a week so they don't have to cook. The age range for our product is women between 30 and 45." That type of answer indicates that the business has a good idea of its customer demographics, as well as what a reasonable geography is for targeting customers.

Asking a simple question: Would you buy it?

Also ask yourself these simple questions:

- ✓ Would you really buy this product or service?

- ✓ Would you really use this product or service? (Be honest! Buying is one thing; fitting this item or service into your daily life is quite another.)

- ✓ Would you really tell your friends about how great this product or service is and that they should buy or use it?

Maybe these seem like obvious questions, but many times in the rush of excitement, potential investors don't ask them. Of course, the answers to them depend on who the customer for this product or service is and whether the product or service actually provides a solution to a problem. (See how we're circling back to the fundamentals here?)

Discussing the opportunity with people you trust

Rushing to buy anything — especially stock in a company — is never a good idea. You don't necessarily want to wait for weeks or months to buy a stock; after all, crowdfund investment campaigns don't last very long (30 to 90 days, generally). However, you should take enough time to talk with trusted friends or colleagues who will either give you outside validation or ask helpful questions so that you have a second opinion about the quality of the investment and whether it's right for you.

In addition to having one-on-one conversations with people, you may consider starting a crowdfund investing club. Maybe some of your friends are interested in this small business investing space. If so, you each spend an hour or two of your own time researching companies every week or two weeks or month. Then you meet to discuss and debate whether companies that you like stand up to other members' scrutiny. At the end of the discussion, everyone makes her own individual investment decision. But you've had the opportunity to spend some time with friends and talk about interesting topics, and maybe you leave the meeting with some good input that helps you make better investment decisions.

Reading the crowd feedback online

Crowdfund investing is an online activity; the business owner or entrepreneur must use an online funding portal, and he reaches out to potential investors almost entirely online via social media. Of course, this means that you'll find potential investors discussing online the owner, the business model, the product, the financials, and anything else related to this opportunity. And that's a good thing; crowdfund investing as a whole can only benefit from vibrant, active crowds that parse these opportunities and determine which are worthwhile and which aren't.

Is it important to read online feedback about the product and the entrepreneur? Yes! Doing so can certainly move you closer to understanding the strengths and weaknesses of the campaign. Should you believe every single comment as fact? Probably not. Treat the feedback much like you'd treat a restaurant or movie review. After all, these are opinions, and you'll need to judge for yourself just how closely you think they track to the facts.

Avoiding impulse buys

Do not buy stock or invest in crowdfunded debt on impulse. Period. You are not buying an ice cream cone here, or even an exercise system you see on late-night TV. You're making an investment, and you should take it seriously. Making an impulse buy will almost certainly lead to regret.

Keep in mind that buying into a crowdfund investment campaign is *not* the same as buying into a publicly traded stock, a bond, a mutual fund, or another traditional financial vehicle. These other vehicles are *liquid,* meaning that markets exist for their trade, and you aren't locked into holding them for any length of time. As we explain in Chapter 4, as a crowdfund investor, you're locked into your investment for a minimum of 12 months. And even after that time, you may find it somewhat challenging to find a buyer for your equity or debt. (Secondary markets for these securities will emerge, undoubtedly, but the industry is brand new as of this writing so they don't yet exist.)

Therefore, you must do your research, talk with trusted friends, and carefully consider what to do. Then, and only then, should you make your decision of whether to invest.

Sniffing Out Fraud

The minute you start thinking about investing in a company through crowdfund investing, you assume responsibility to help watch for fraud. The power of the crowd — which includes you! — is precisely what makes crowdfund investing so great.

Historically, fraud has taken place one on one. In other words, one person (such as a crooked financial advisor) dupes one other person (such as a single investor). In crowdfund investing, for fraud to exist, one person will have to fool many, many people in a very public forum (the online funding portals and social media). Good luck, fraudsters!

As you're studying campaigns, asking questions, and monitoring crowd feedback on various business models, you may find that something raises a red flag. If that's the case, you have a responsibility to take action. In this section, we explain first why and then how.

Trusting that the crowd can spot signs of trouble

Before Bernie Madoff's name became permanently associated with a mind-boggling investment scandal, many people had major doubts about his claims. Some of them refused to invest because they knew what he was doing was a scam. But the primary outlet they had was to raise questions to Madoff's team, which meant (of course) that no other potential investors ever got to hear them.

Crowdfund investing changes the playing field. When one person has a doubt, it can quickly and powerfully become everyone's doubt. Mind you, this fact makes life tough for an honest entrepreneur who may have a paranoid potential investor in his crowd. One person can potentially raise lots of doubts about a legitimately good business plan being promoted by someone with the skills to make it a success. Is that fair? Maybe not. But it's not entirely a bad thing. Raising money from investors is not and should not be an easy thing to do.

We have faith that crowds are going to be able to spot signs of trouble shortly after they arise. The collective knowledge of the crowd is greater than the knowledge of any single person or small group of people. If 2,000 people have decided to invest in a business through crowdfunding investing and none of them has raised any serious concerns in the online discussion forums, let this be a good sign to you. However, if *you* see a problem — even if you're the only one to do so — you can't be scared to call it to the crowd's attention. If your concerns are unwarranted, the crowd will help you figure that out. If you've spotted something truly troubling, the crowd will thank you for stepping up to your responsibility.

Reporting your suspicions to the funding portal

If you've seen something in a crowdfund investing campaign that has raised your suspicions, you should first ask about it in the dialogue section of the campaign itself. But then you need to go a step further and report your suspicions to the online funding portal.

Funding portals should take every complaint and suspicion extremely seriously; they have a legal responsibility to do so. Funding portals are monitored by the SEC, and the SEC is always looking for any signs of fraud. If the SEC finds a problem and the funding portal knew about it (and failed to report it), that portal will suffer for its poor choices.

Plus, there's no worse press for a funding portal than allowing fraud to happen on its website. Everyone in the crowdfund investing community will hear about it, and potential investors will think twice before investing in a company listed on that website.

Chapter 16

Committing Your Capital

• •

• •

*T*hink of a time when you bought something that you couldn't return — maybe a nice pair of eggplant-colored pants on the "Final Sale" rack in the department store basement. Did you live to regret that decision? Did you wake up the next day wishing you could get your $7.98 back?

Making an impulse buy from a department store sale rack is risky enough. You definitely don't want to let impulse guide your decisions when it comes to crowdfund investing. If you do, you may live to regret those decisions, and they may cost you a lot more than $7.98.

As we discuss in Chapter 15, funding startups or small businesses via crowdfund investing is not the same as putting money into companies via the public markets. First, a one-year holding period applies to all equity shares you purchase via crowdfund investing. (The one-year holding period may apply to any debt you purchase as a crowdfund investment as well.) Second, as of this writing, while they're being created, secondary markets for those shares don't yet exist, meaning that even when your first year of investment is up, you may not easily be able to locate willing buyers. (The nature of the business you invest in will determine whether other investors are clamoring to get in.) Therefore, when you buy your shares, you'd better make sure you're happy with your purchase because you could be holding on to them for quite a while.

In this chapter, we first remind you why the JOBS Act limits what you can put into crowdfund investments each year. Then we discuss how you actually make a crowdfund investment and receive your security (either equity shares or a debt note). Finally, we cover what your rights as a shareholder are and help you figure out if you may benefit from any other investment perks.

Appreciating the Purpose of Investment Limits

The U.S. government doesn't often tell us what we can and cannot spend our money on. However, when it comes to buying stocks in private companies, the government makes an exception. We can hear your libertarian side shouting, "How dare the government tell me what I can do with my money!" We certainly understand that impulse. However, we encourage you to consider what prompted these investment limits.

As we explain in Chapter 2, limits on investment in private companies emerged as a direct response to the environment that created the stock market crash of 1929. In the years leading up to the crash, greedy salesmen took advantage of the average Joe, naïve to investing, by selling him shares in invisible or worthless entities. These smoke-and-mirror tricks created a massive loss of wealth for many people. The government's subsequent decision to restrict the sale of stock was a decision made with the intent of protecting the masses.

The unintended consequence of the government's actions was to shut the doors of private company investment even to people who *do* understand the risks and rewards of investing but aren't wealthy. Keeping these people out of the markets has slowed down our nation's innovation and entrepreneurship by making it harder for new and small businesses to access capital.

The JOBS Act signed into law in April 2012 represents a sea change. We got members of the federal government to understand that investment decisions shouldn't be based strictly on income or net worth thresholds. After all, consider the case of a finance professor or an accountant — someone who isn't a millionaire but clearly understands the risks of investing. Shouldn't that person, and anyone with similar investment knowledge, be able to invest in startups and small businesses?

The challenge is trying to figure out who knows enough to make sound investment decisions and who doesn't. To coin a new term, who is an *educationally accredited investor,* and who isn't? To help make this determination, each online funding portal (see Chapter 7) requires potential investors to take a quiz and demonstrate basic knowledge about the risks involved in these types of investments. In addition, the online funding portals must (per the JOBS Act) provide investor education materials that all potential investors can access in order to learn more about the risks.

For those who pass muster as educationally accredited investors, the JOBS Act provides an additional layer of protection by capping the amount an individual can invest each year on crowdfund investing campaigns. To be clear, the cap represents the *aggregate* amount an investor can spend on crowdfund investing each year — not the amount allowable per campaign. We outline the limits in Chapters 4 and 15.

Accredited and unaccredited investors: Breaking investment barriers

For many decades, U.S. investors have been divided into two categories: accredited and unaccredited. Federal law indicates that accredited investors meet at least one of two criteria:

✔ They have a net worth of more than $1 million (excluding their primary residence equity) either independently or with a spouse.

✔ They've earned more than $200,000 per year for the two most recent years or $300,000 per year with a spouse for the two most recent years.

Everyone else is considered unaccredited. Accredited investors can do whatever they want with their money and aren't restricted in their investment choices. Prior to the passage of the JOBS Act, entrepreneurs wanting to raise capital (and meeting certain criteria with the Securities and Exchange Commission) could do so by seeking investments from as many accredited investors as they wanted but from only (in most cases) up to 35 unaccredited investors.

To provide some context, according to 2009 Internal Revenue Service data, fewer than 3 percent of the 140 million tax returns filed reflected annual income of more than $200,000. Based on that data, we can broadly estimate that prior to the passage of the JOBS Act, as many as 97 percent of Americans were considered unaccredited investors based on the income criteria. (Some of the people in that 97 percent may have qualified as accredited investors per the net worth criteria.) And anyone considered an unaccredited investor had a fairly slim chance of getting involved in the funding of startups and small businesses. (With only 35 unaccredited investors allowed for most startups, the opportunities for widespread private equity investment just didn't exist.)

The JOBS Act changed the whole picture. Now, potential investors don't need to meet a minimum income or net worth threshold in order to invest in startups and small businesses. In other words, you can be an unaccredited investor and still have the opportunity to purchase private equity or debt. Someone making $25,000 could choose to invest $50 or $500 in a campaign she believes in. If you project this scenario out to the tens of millions of Americans who couldn't participate in private equity before, you can imagine the potential impact of crowdfund investing.

Money flowing into startups and small businesses will create demand for products and services that support these businesses (from copy paper to accounting software to automobiles), thereby creating the demand for jobs and stimulating the economy. This is a win-win-win, folks!

Keep in mind that although the legislation sets the limits on what you can invest, it's up to you (unless we usher in the era of *big* government) not to exceed those limits. This means that if you make $50,000 and the maximum you can invest in crowdfund opportunities is $2,500 (see Chapter 4 or 15 to figure out how to come up with your cap), you shouldn't invest $3,000 in crowdfund opportunities. You should respect the limits for these reasons:

- ✔ **Putting too many of your eggs in the crowdfund investing basket means that you aren't diversifying your financial portfolio well enough and you're increasing your risk of loss.** Your goal with any investment should be to balance risk and potential reward, and you don't want to tip yourself too far into the risk territory.

- ✔ **If you go over your limits, you're essentially proving to the federal government that people are irresponsible and can't be trusted with their own money.** Doing so could encourage people to lobby for truly *big* government in order to monitor these kinds of individual actions and decisions. Is that what you really want?

Making Your First Crowdfund Investment

This section walks you through what happens when you decide you're ready to become a crowdfund investor: You've considered the risks spelled out elsewhere in this book (including Chapter 15), you're prepared for the worst-case scenario (which is losing every dime you invest), and you can still clearly see the value of committing your capital.

With advice from a financial advisor, and keeping your entire financial portfolio in mind, you determine the (small) percentage of your total investments that you want to put into crowdfund investing campaigns. You know that the amount you invest in any specific campaign should be driven not only by the merits of the concept and business plan but also by how well you know — and how much you trust — the entrepreneur or small business owner. And, of course, the potential for return on your investment plays a role in your decision as well.

We'll add one more piece of advice to the pile we've offered throughout this book: Make your first crowdfund investment a fairly small one. Even if the campaign is being run by your best friend or your brother, don't max out your annual investment limit on the first campaign. After all, you don't yet know what being a crowdfund investor will actually feel like — even if you've read every word of this book. Give yourself this first opportunity to warm up to the whole process — to find out how much you like (or dislike) being on the business owner's marketing team and playing other supportive roles.

Preparing for a long-term relationship

After you've done your research into potential investments (with the help of Chapter 15) and you've reached out to someone you trust for a second opinion, you may feel ready to commit to an investment. But you have to be aware that committing your money to a crowdfund investing campaign doesn't lead to instant equity that immediately starts increasing or decreasing in value. Here's why:

If you want to buy stock in a public company, you can go to your online brokerage account (with Fidelity or Vanguard, for example) and purchase that stock in real time. You can also purchase *exchange-traded funds* (ETFs), which are bundles of stocks or other securities, in real time. You simply log in, do your research, and purchase the stock or ETF. When you buy stock or an ETF on the New York Stock Exchange or the NASDAQ, you're purchasing on the public stock markets: places where buyers and sellers know they can meet and trade stocks at publicly available prices. If you decide tomorrow that you no longer want that stock or ETF (it now reminds you of a certain pair of eggplant-colored pants hanging in your closet), you can sell it just as easily, although the price likely will have fluctuated even in the single day since your purchase.

Calling all accredited investors!

If you're an accredited investor and you've never made an investment in a private company, now is your chance. The first provision of the JOBS Act, Title II, deals with lifting the ban on general solicitation for accredited investors. What this means is that accredited investors will be among the first people to get onboard with crowdfund investing.

In 2011, in the United States, 600,000 accredited investors purchased $30 billion in private shares. By our rough calculations, that means that more than 85 percent of wealthy folks (hey, Britney Spears, that means you!) didn't. Clearly, when it comes to starting, running, and growing a business, cash is king. Without it, businesses can't hire people or purchase goods and services.

Imagine what could happen to our economy if we got just another 600,000 accredited investors to step up to the plate and inject another $30 billion into the economy. That would be huge! Encouraging private investment from the wealthiest citizens is important because when that happens, our government doesn't have to borrow money to inject into our economy (which in the long-term creates inflation). Instead, Americans invest in products or services that they would use themselves. So, if you have rich friends, tell them to start investing — wisely, of course — by following the same guidelines that everyone else should follow regarding creating a balanced financial portfolio.

When you decide to purchase equity shares or debt through a crowdfund investing campaign, the entire process is different. You aren't sending your money into a public stock market. You aren't interacting in a place where lots of buyers and sellers congregate, ready to do business. Instead, you're sending your money to one startup or small business. (As we explain in the following section, you're actually sending the money to a middleman called an *escrow agent* who holds the cash until the crowdfund investing campaign is complete, but we're getting ahead of ourselves here.)

In addition, you're taking this step knowing that you're making a commitment of at least 12 months (per the JOBS Act legislation). You're making an *illiquid investment,* which means you're putting your money into something that can't be turned back into cash quickly or easily. When you're completely comfortable with the level of commitment required here — you've got the engagement ring in hand and you're ready to bend your knee — it's time to invest.

Pledging your amount on the funding portal

When you're ready to pledge your funds to a crowdfund investing campaign, you log onto the online funding portal that supports this particular campaign. (See Chapter 7 for the scoop on what a funding portal does.) Here are the steps you'll most likely take next:

1. **Register with the portal.**

   You'll provide your name and preferred contact information

2. **Take the investor quiz.**

   As we note earlier in this chapter, this quiz determines whether you're an educationally accredited investor (translation: you understand what you're risking by pursuing a crowdfund investment). Don't stress: The quiz really isn't very difficult as long as you have realistic expectations about crowdfund investments.

3. **Accept the crowdfund investing portal's disclosure statements.**

   Doing so verifies that you understand the risks of investing in startups and small businesses.

4. **Input your checking account, savings account, or debit account number.**

   A credit card won't fly when you're making this type of investment. You can't use a credit card to buy public stock on an online brokerage account, and you aren't allowed to use a credit card to make crowdfund investments either. Why the restriction? See the nearby sidebar, "Cash only: Leave your credit cards in your wallet."

Cash only: Leave your credit cards in your wallet

A credit card purchase can be disputed, which can interrupt the business funding process. Using a credit card creates the possibility of a phantom transaction. You must buy stock with real money that you actually have in an account.

Think of this scenario: You're an entrepreneur, and you think that you've hit 101 percent of your crowdfund investing campaign target. The celebration begins — you're finally ready to move forward with your business! (As we explain in Chapter 3 and elsewhere in the book, the campaign target must be met or exceeded in order for the entrepreneur or small business owner to get a dime of the funding.) Maybe you're so energized that you immediately begin placing orders for supplies you're going to need in the first days of business operations. Then,

after your investors' credit cards are charged, you find out that 10 percent of them were not accepted. You're back down to having met only 91 percent of your campaign funding goal, which means you get nothing until you raise the remaining amount. What a huge disappointment and frustration (and cash flow problem!), through no fault of your own.

This type of situation would be bad not only for the business owner but also for the investor community. Imagine being a member of this entrepreneur's crowd and receiving conflicting reports: campaign completion one day, and campaign restart the next day because of the credit card fiasco. Investors like things to proceed in a tidy, orderly manner. To avoid the potential for chaos, the ban on credit cards makes perfect sense.

5. **Specify how much you intend to invest.**

   The amount you choose must be above the minimum established by the campaign and below your maximum allowed by the JOB Act. Where you fall in the middle of those two numbers is up to you, your financial portfolio, and your investment advisor (if you have one).

6. **Start signing.**

   Buying crowdfund investments isn't as easy as simply hitting the purchase button. There will also be documents like a subscription agreement, which summarize and standardize the offering. In other words, you're buying a certain number of shares at a certain price and those shares come with specific rights. You'll need to review and sign these documents.

Going into escrow until the campaign is complete

After you follow the steps outlined in the previous section, your money is transferred to what is known as an *escrow agent*. If you've ever bought a house, you're likely well versed in the concept of escrow. If not, escrow is fairly easy to understand.

In crowdfund investing, the escrow agent is a neutral third party — a company that holds investors' cash, as well as the shares of the company, in trust. When the conditions of the sale are met — in this case, the crowdfund investing campaign reaches 100 percent of its funding target — the escrow agent releases the cash to the seller of the stock and releases the stock to the buyers (the investors). If the conditions of the sale aren't met — the campaign fails to reach 100 percent of its funding target — the escrow agent returns the money to the investors.

The escrow process is a safety check: It eliminates the risk of paying for stock and not receiving what you pay for. The JOBS Act legislation states that a funding portal cannot be an escrow agent; it can't hold investors' cash. Funding portals don't carry insurance to guard themselves against potential fraud or failure with investor money; escrow agents do.

Assuming that the crowdfund investing campaign is a success, the last step of the process is for the escrow agent to transfer stock certificates or debt notes to the investors and wire the funds to the company's account. (These certificates or notes will be electronic; don't expect to receive hard copies in the mail.) At that point, you are officially a private equity or debt investor!

Knowing Your Rights as an Investor

You'll need to do a bit of independent research and reading to find out what your rights are as an investor in a specific company's campaign. For starters, your rights depend on whether you invest in debt or equity.

If you're an equity investor, your rights largely depend on the type of stock you purchase, such as common stock or preferred stock. You may have certain voting rights as a stockholder, for example. The online funding portal for the campaign is the best resource for this information; your rights and responsibilities as an investor should be spelled out in documentation associated with the campaign offering.

The same is true if you buy into the company on the debt side: There are many ways to structure a debt deal, and you need to know the specifics for your individual case. Here are some things you should make sure you know before you purchase private company debt:

✔ What is the payoff schedule?

✔ When will the company start paying down the loan: right away, or only after it starts producing revenue?

✔ Is there a time limit for how long the company has to pay you back?

✔ Are any contingencies built into the deal that would allow the company to postpone debt payments?

✔ Is the company allowed to pay off the balance early without interest (prepayment)?

✔ Is the payoff revenue-based financing (RBF)? RBF terms allow the company to pay off the loan based upon a certain percentage of revenue.

Although you should definitely do your homework to understand your specific rights, in this section, we cover two fundamental rights that apply to every crowdfund investor.

The right to be informed

Whether you own debt or equity, and no matter what type of debt or equity you own, you have the right to receive regular updates on the progress of the company. The entrepreneur or small business owner should send out reports to investors at least on a quarterly basis, if not more often. (The entrepreneur or owner should be very clear from day one about how often such reports will be released.) These reports should include the following types of updates:

✔ Problems encountered since the last report

✔ Successes achieved

✔ Revenue generated

✔ Major expenses incurred, including any major *unplanned* expenses (along with explanations of why they were necessary)

In addition, you should also receive an annual report that is more detailed and includes thorough financial statements that reflect the company's cash position, revenues and expenses for the entire year, and more. In Chapter 12, we spell out (for the business owner) what the Securities and Exchange Commission requires to be in those annual reports to investors. You may want to check out that information as well, just so you're aware if you fail to receive adequate reports from the company you invest in.

The right to sell

The biggest right you have as an investor is the right to sell your shares in the company after the 12-month holding period is complete. (If you're holding debt in the company, a similar holding period may apply.)

If things aren't going too well for the business, the entrepreneur or business owner will probably try to discourage you from selling your stock or debt. That's smart for him to do; the business needs all the financial stability it can get, especially when times are tough. But you must realize that no one can stop you from selling.

Anticipating Rewards for Your Investment

Your crowdfund investment can be structured in a variety of ways. You could be a debt investor, which means that you invest a certain amount of principal and, in exchange, you receive a certain amount of interest each month or quarter. If you're an equity owner, you could receive dividends quarterly or yearly, or you could receive no payment for your investment until you sell your shares.

Before you make the decision to invest in a specific campaign, you should know exactly how and when you can expect to have your capital returned. Researching that information is a key part of the due diligence we describe in Chapter 15, and the information should be readily accessible on the campaign's funding portal. You may very well find that your compensation comes only if the company meets and exceeds financial expectations; a lag in company performance could spell zero payoff for you.

Deciding (in advance) what to do with your payoff

Sometimes people's initial reaction to receiving money back from an investment is to treat every dollar that comes in as profit. This is not the case. The money you receive is not profit until your initial investment is covered with interest. Also keep in mind the time value of money; $1 that you invest today is not worth $1 a year from now.

If you're lucky enough to receive payments from your crowdfund investments, you should be prepared for what you want to do with that money. You may decide that you want to reward yourself with this money (a nice dinner out if the amount is small, a vacation if the investment has paid off nicely, or a new home if you really hit a home run!). Or you may determine that the smartest thing to do is use any proceeds from one company to invest in another startup or small business. If you've made good investment decisions, follow them up by making good decisions about how to put your payoff to good use. Most important, don't rush to make a decision. The best thing you can do is to put the money safely into your savings account, list your alternatives, and consult with a financial advisor if the amount is large enough.

Of course, there are tax implications to any decision of what to do with your gains. Be sure to prepare for April 15 by setting aside an appropriate amount in a savings account that you can use to pay the tax man. Speak with your accountant, or at least read about capital gains, to make sure you don't fall into a tax trap.

In this section, we discuss two types of rewards that you may encounter as a crowdfund investor: dividends and other perks.

Dividing up profits: Dividends

A common perk for owning stock in a company (whether a public or private one) is having the right to dividends. Dividends do not (usually) diminish the amount of stock that you own. Instead, they're a reward based on the amount of equity you own; you're given a certain percentage of the money in the dividend pool.

A startup or small business should pay you dividends only if it's making a significant profit. In the early stages of a business, its success depends on its ability to reinvest as much money as possible. Therefore, you likely won't see dividends in the first months or even the first years of a startup.

How dividends are paid varies widely; they could be issued monthly, quarterly, yearly, or not at all. For a small startup company, paying dividends can be very time consuming, so chances are, your dividends (if you get any) will be issued quarterly or — more likely — yearly.

As with all investments, there are major tax implications to money you receive from dividends. Be very careful not to spend every dime that you reap from your investments because you need a portion of it to cover your tax bill come April. Speak to an accounting professional, and don't get caught with your pants down (and pockets inside out).

Be careful that you don't fall into a trap that countless other people have fallen into: believing that your dividends are going to continue forever and most likely increase. When times are good, investors often believe that they're going to get even better. When someone makes an investment and starts getting dividends, she's riding a high that she may believe will never end. She may go out and spend all that money thinking that she can afford to spend the early dividends on luxury items (or nights out on the town) and use the dividends later in the year to pay for taxes. Then, in the fourth quarter of the year, the company takes a nosedive and has to stop paying dividends. When the tax man comes knocking on April 15, this investor is left with a huge bill that she can't pay. Save for taxes first before spending your dividends on unnecessary items. Don't make the same mistakes that others have made before you!

(Possibly) benefitting from other perks

Before the JOBS Act legalized equity- and debt-based crowdfund investing, crowdfunded investments existed that offered investors specific perks. (See Chapter 2 for some background on this type of crowdfunding effort.) Now that equity- and debt-based crowdfund investing exist, some companies may still choose to reward investors with specific perks.

The perks can vary widely depending on the company. If you invest in a restaurant or another bricks-and-mortar establishment, you may be given discounts each time you visit or on certain dates. In exchange for investing in technology-based companies, you could be given reduced fees for using their services.

If a company decides to give you perks, be grateful, but don't feel compelled to take advantage of them. Keep in mind that every discount you receive means that the company will have that much less revenue. In turn, this means your stock, as an owner of the company, will be worth less money. You want to support the business as much as possible without taking advantage of it and undermining your own investment. Remind yourself that you aren't *entitled* to discounts; the company that offers them is being generous.

If the entrepreneur or small business owner offers you and other investors very deep discounts, consider this action a red flag. Significant discounts for all investors and supporters will seriously affect the company's financial projections. If you sense that the perk is too good, don't be shy about letting the entrepreneur or business owner know what you're thinking.

The best reward systems are tied to current investors and customers bringing new customers to the business. That way, rewards are based on the company's existing supporters helping to increase its revenue and expand its customer base.

Chapter 17

Adding Value: Playing the Right Role as an Investor

In This Chapter

▶ Helping a company tap into your expertise or network

▶ Playing an advisory role

▶ Test-driving the company's product or service (if you can)

▶ Joining the company's (unpaid) marketing team and encouraging new investors

▶ Avoiding being a pest

▶ Responding to illegal activity

*W*hen you become an investor in a private company, you feel differently than you do when investing in a national or global public company. That's because you likely know the private company's owner or at least have a connection with this person through a friend or colleague. Crowdfund investing engages your heart more than public company investing does, and you want the company to succeed for many reasons — not strictly for your bottom line.

As a crowdfund investor, you may have opportunities to help the company beyond providing your financial capital. You may be asked to participate in product research and testing, in marketing the product or service being offered, or in advising the business owner on a specific area of your expertise.

Keep in mind that not every company that you invest in will make such requests. Let the business owner drive these decisions, and don't get offended if you aren't asked to participate. What you should want most is for the business owner to focus on making the business a success. Let him make the decisions about how best to use crowd investors to reach his business goals.

If you do get a chance to add value to the company, you have to strike the right balance with your participation. You don't want to act like an overprotective parent and risk smothering the business owner with your advice.

Instead, strive to be the smart, yet cool aunt or uncle who can offer help and then stand back and watch what happens. This chapter helps you understand how to achieve this balance, whether you're sharing your network, serving on a board of advisors, evaluating product or service quality, or playing a marketing role. In addition, we discuss how to handle a situation that we hope you never have to deal with: discovering that the company you invested in is breaking the law.

When investing in people you know, you need to enforce boundaries to separate your personal and financial relationships. You invest in someone because you believe in that person's vision, capabilities, and skills. Don't become so enmeshed in the day-to-day workings of the business that you hamstring the entrepreneur with second guessing, too much advice, or too much communication. If you do, you could risk hurting not only the business but also your relationship with its owner.

Sharing What and Who You Know

We believe that success in life is based on who you know as much as on what you know. As an investor in a small company, providing knowledge and introductions can be very helpful if done in the right way, and when the entrepreneur asks. Part of the reason that you've invested in a small private company may be your desire to feel more connected to your investments. One way to do that is to help connect the business owner with information, resources, and people who can help the company succeed.

Tapping into your professional experience

What professional experiences do you have in your background? Do they relate to the crowdfund investment you've made? How can you structure this information and deliver it in a way that's helpful and not distracting to the entrepreneur?

What may seem like common sense and very basic information to you as an experienced person in your field may be new and valuable information to someone who needs to gain that skill set. Don't underestimate what you may have to offer. For example, we have a friend who recently left a major national charitable and research society after being heavily involved in raising more than $500 million for the society. She began getting calls from individuals who had heard of her skills from their social networks. These people wanted to learn how she had raised all that money so they could apply her experience to their current needs. She didn't realize how much she knew about this very important topic and how happy people would be to tap into her expertise.

If you're willing to help, let the companies that you invest in know (in the manner they would like to receive communication) that you have skills in certain areas. When the business owner needs help in those areas, she'll very likely contact you.

How advice is received by others has a lot to do with how you deliver it. Carefully follow the entrepreneur's requests for how she would like to interact with investors. Regardless of how amazing the information you have may be, you're an investor, not a majority owner in the business. You need to respect the decisions of the entrepreneur, including decisions related to investor communication.

Connecting people who can benefit each other

The most powerful connections are two-way streets: They engage both parties in delivering and receiving value. When you become a crowdfund investor, try to identify relationships for the entrepreneurs or small business owners that can have bi-directional benefits.

Don't bombard the companies you've invested in with lots of communication about all the people you know. Instead, make this step a highly targeted exercise. No matter how great your connections, they need to match what the business needs at that time.

For example, say that you're investing in a small bakery that just started a year ago. It's located about 5 miles from the world headquarters of a multi-billion-dollar corporation. You know the head chef at this corporation, who just happens to be looking for a new bakery to supply his breakfast and lunchtime bread and pastry needs. Introducing the chef to the owner of the small bakery at this moment in time would be a recipe for failure because the corporation needs many times more bread than a small, new bakery can provide. When the bakery is a bit older, larger, and more experienced, this type of introduction could be truly valuable, but right now, the connection won't help either party.

When you do identify connections that can be helpful, make the introduction and step back. Don't try to micromanage the conversation. Let the two parties take it from there because your job — playing matchmaker — is done.

Serving on a Board of Advisors

On occasion, you may be asked to serve on a board of advisors for a new enterprise. This entity is different from a board of directors, which must represent the rights and interests of the stockholders and can take actions on their behalf as prescribed by the bylaws of the company. A board of advisors has no formal authority over the company or the CEO. Its function is to provide advice, know-how, connections, and (in some cases) additional financial support to the business owner. An advisory position is typically unpaid but is also very important to a new or small business.

Essentially, as an advisor you agree to be a mentor to the entrepreneur or business owner. You bring experience and a fresh perspective to whatever issues this person is dealing with. Your primary job is to offer honest, direct opinions in a respectful way.

A board of advisors also demonstrates to the outside world that the company is connected to people in the industry who are experts or powerful or successful. Affiliating with a board of advisors helps a company provide social proof to its customers or other investors that it's on target for success.

Keep in mind that not every investor can or will be invited to join the company's board of advisors. (The investment crowd is simply too large for that to happen.) You shouldn't expect to be asked or be offended if the invitation doesn't come.

If you're asked to join the board, make sure you have the time to commit to it. The time commitment usually isn't too intense, but during certain periods of time you may need to help in more active ways — when the business owner needs an introduction, for example, or is seeking access to angel or private equity investment. Being asked to serve on a board of advisors is an honor but also a significant responsibility. You're attaching your name and reputation to this company publicly, and you want to make sure that you want the public affiliation with the company, the owners, and the mission or brand.

Evaluating the Quality of What's Being Produced

These days, anyone who buys a product goes online to find out what other buyers say about it. It doesn't matter whether you're talking about a big-ticket item like a refrigerator, television, or car, or a smaller purchase such as a book or a pair of shoes. Online reviews (like online photos from a drunken weekend) seem to live forever, so a company wants to make sure that even its very first reviews out of the gate are glowing.

To get positive reviews, the company needs to offer good quality at a good price. Sounds simple, but achieving those two things from day one isn't always easy. That's why companies test their products or services prior to launching them to the public, and it's why you may find yourself called on to test a company's wares and offer your opinions. If that happens, this section can help you offer the most value for the entrepreneur or small business owner.

Getting a taste of the product or service early in the process

If you're investing in a startup or in a company that's aiming to grow by adding new products or services to its lineup, you may be asked to sample the products or services and offer your opinions on them. This step takes place shortly after the business owner has moved from planning to execution and — ideally — quite a while before the product or service is scheduled to be available to the public.

In Chapter 5, we discuss the stages of a new or growing business. Chances are, if you invest in a company at its earliest stage (when it has a great idea but hasn't yet executed that idea), you may be involved when the company develops its *proof of concept* (the period when the company moves its idea into reality, on a small scale, in order to demonstrate that it can work in the real world). Here are some examples:

✔ In the case of a bakery, the proof of concept phase could occur when the business owner starts producing small batches of the recipes she considers the best options for her market. If you live in the same area, you may be invited to a tasting party to offer your feedback.

✔ If the company is preparing to sell a new type of exercise equipment, it may offer its supporters and investors the chance to try the equipment and rate its ease and effectiveness.

✔ With an online retailer, the proof of concept may occur when the entrepreneur does a limited launch of his website so supporters and investors can test it before it goes live. You may be encouraged to visit the site, test its various features, and place a mock order to see what customers will experience and identify any barriers they may encounter.

Elsewhere in this chapter, we encourage you to take a step back and let the entrepreneur or business owner determine when and if he needs your input. But when it comes to testing a new product or service, we encourage you to be more proactive. Based on the communication you receive from the business owner, you should be able to determine when a product or service is getting close to public release. If you've invested your money but you haven't actually seen or experienced the product or service being created, you likely want to request the opportunity to do so before it's made public. You have a huge incentive for wanting to make sure this product or service is polished and ready to go before the public launch date. If the business owner doesn't offer the opportunity to sample it, you should probably ask.

Why "probably" and not "definitely"? Because not every type of business can offer you the chance to sample the product or service being offered. If you invest in a company that offers its services to a narrow market niche that you don't belong to, you're out of luck. If the company is developing software for the biotech industry and you know nothing about biotechnology, you likely can't offer helpful feedback in the proof of concept stage. In a situation like this, you just have to keep reading the company's communication, including its descriptions of trials it has run to test the product or service effectiveness. If you aren't satisfied with the type or extent of testing being done, you can certainly say so. But at a certain point, you have to accept your limitations as a participant in this phase and let the business owner be the business owner and make the final decisions. ***Remember:*** You're the cool aunt or uncle — not the mean parent.

Offering constructive feedback

When you do have the chance to take the product or service for a test-drive, your job is to offer constructive feedback that will enhance the company's reputation and chances for success. You can and should do so in a way that is kind and helpful. The entrepreneur or business owner is emotionally invested in this product or service and likely is scared that the crowd will tear it apart. Don't assume that you know everything and the entrepreneur or owner knows nothing. Instead, even if your interaction with the product or service is problematic, try to think about why it was developed in this specific way and what the entrepreneur or owner is trying to accomplish. Then consider how you might ask questions or offer comments that can elicit improvements without bruising egos.

Avoid using the word *you* when offering your feedback. This may seem like strange advice at first, but *you* statements or questions can feel like personal attacks. Often, questions that start with *who, what, where, when, why,* or *how* can take some of the sting away from negative criticism.

Consider an example of a software program that you don't think is up to snuff. If you're truly concerned because the public release date is looming and you think the quality is subpar, you may find yourself wanting to say something like, "You shouldn't have outsourced the programming to India." But that's the kind of statement that leads to defensive responses instead of careful consideration of your point. Instead, think about how you can reword your concern as a question that avoids the word *you.* For example, "Help me understand: What makes programmers from India better than others?" This type of question allows the entrepreneur to explain why she made a certain decision and may open your eyes to issues you hadn't previously considered. It may also open up a conversation about a programming resource the entrepreneur hadn't previously considered.

Another great tactic is to offer feedback from your first-person perspective, grounded in your own similar experiences (if you have any). For example, "I had similar trouble when I was working with XYZ Company a few years ago. We debated whether to hire a local programmer or to outsource the job. When we made the decision, we considered these factors. . . ."

By reframing the discussion into the first-person perspective and removing the word *you,* you remove the element of attack from your communication with the entrepreneur. And the chances of your being able to share your wisdom increase greatly.

Allow the business owner to make the decisions he thinks are best for his business. Don't expect that every piece of advice you offer will be used exactly as you wish. You invested in the management team, and you have to allow them to do their jobs as managers and business owners.

Becoming an Ambassador or Evangelist for the Company

If you aren't willing to become an ambassador or evangelist for the company you're investing in, you probably shouldn't invest. The foundation of crowd-fund investing is putting your money into someone you know and believe in — and something you would buy and use and be proud to discuss with everyone around you.

When you become a member of a company's investment crowd, you also become a marketing engine for that business. You can do so by asking the entrepreneur how she specifically needs help getting the message out, or you can make marketing this company your own personal mission. In this section, we explain how you can promote what the company is creating, as well as the company itself (as a great investment).

Conducting grassroots marketing

Grassroots marketing involves organizing and motivating volunteers to engage in personal or local outreach. It requires that you develop relationships with other stakeholders or representatives to make them enthusiastic about the entrepreneur's product or service so that they become advocates, spreading the word about it and becoming an additional sales force. And it means that you do all this without being paid (because entrepreneurs are cash poor).

Why grassroots? Because this is the earliest stage of marketing and, if planted correctly, it has the ability to grow wild like grass. The planting can take place via blogs, Twitter, Facebook, Google+, LinkedIn, or any other social networks, as well as face to face when you talk about this new product or service with your friends, business associates, and people you meet at a bar.

A specific kind of grassroots marketing is called *buzz marketing*. It's word-of-mouth marketing among potential consumers and users of a product or service. Buzz marketing works because individuals are easier to trust than organizations that may have a vested interest in promoting the product or service.

This word-of-mouth marketing among peers amplifies the original marketing message, creating a vague but positive association, excitement, or anticipation about a product or service. Positive buzz is often the goal of viral marketing, public relations, and social media. The term refers both to the execution of the marketing technique and the resulting goodwill that is created. Here are just a few examples of buzz marketing: the Pebble Watch, Harry Potter, Beanie Babies, and the hundreds of Carly Rae Jepsen "Call Me Maybe" spinoff videos. (Google this last one, and you'll see what we're talking about.)

Encouraging other investors to follow your lead

In addition to promoting the specific product or service being created, you may find that you want to promote the company itself to other potential investors. Can you do so without breaking the law? Yes, if you read this section.

If the business is still raising capital, the entrepreneur or owner is very restricted regarding how he can market the investment opportunity. He can market it only through the online funding platform he's using (see Chapter 7). He can't send out an e-mail telling people what they'll get by investing a certain sum of money, and he can't make phone calls describing the specific investment opportunity. If he breaks these rules, his entire crowdfund investment pitch can be shut down by the Securities and Exchange Commission (SEC), whose regulations govern this new type of investment.

An entrepreneur will have trouble hitting his funding target if he has to rely solely on his first-degree connections for investments. (See this book's website, www.dummies.com/go/crowdfundinvesting to learn more about what investors can and can't do to support the companies they invest in.) Based on what the SEC will allow, he needs you — and other investors like you — to spread the word about why investing in him is worth considering. This may include your using your own Facebook, LinkedIn, Twitter, or other social networks to direct your contacts to the crowdfund investing portal where the offering is being made; there, they can learn more about what the company is doing and why you wanted to invest. You can share the URL of the online funding portal and encourage your networks to check it out.

If you're an ambassador for a business in which you have an equity investment, unless you're a broker-dealer (see Chapter 7), you *can't* receive a commission for bringing investments to the entrepreneur. You can't say to the entrepreneur, "Hey, if you give me 5 percent of the money I bring in, I'll go out to my network and get as many of them to invest in your business as possible." **That's illegal!** The percentage in question is called a *finder's fee,* and it's absolutely not allowed per the JOBS Act. The only way you can promote an offering is to do so out of your true desire to help the entrepreneur and the business to succeed.

Serving as a role model for other investors

We want you to encourage other investors to follow your lead, but only if you're setting a good example. Therefore, we hope you follow our sage advice about how to be a role model for other investors. (Hey, we're writing the book — we're allowed to call our advice sagacious!)

It's important to understand that the entrepreneur or business owner may be new at communicating with investors. If people start giving tons of advice or making demands on the entrepreneur, he may have a very difficult time figuring out how to deal with the crowd (on top of trying to deal with his business plan and financing and everything else involved in getting a business off the ground). The worst thing that could happen is the entrepreneur or owner tries to follow *all* the advice he's receiving and gets distracted from his mission.

As an educated investor and a true ambassador for the company, you have the opportunity to set a very good example for other people to follow. Doing so could provide the best help possible to the entrepreneur. When you're on the funding portal, be vocal in the dialogue or chat rooms. Explain that you're there to support the entrepreneur and that you understand the decisions are his to make. Direct your comments to the entrepreneur in this way:

✔ "I know you must be getting a lot of advice from a lot of different people. If you'd like some help performing market research, I've done market studies in the past and I'd be more than willing to lend some hours."

✔ "I'm here to support you. I know sometimes dealing with investors can be a big headache. If you need any help communicating with people, feel free to post your needs, and I'll be here to help where I can. I'm sure you're extremely busy, so if I don't hear back from you I understand you're busy building the business."

When you post comments like this that other investors can read, they may think twice before pestering the entrepreneur. Some investors undoubtedly will never before have invested in a company where their voice can be heard. This experience is completely new to them, and they won't be sure how to act. If you present yourself confidently and professionally in your comments, some people are very likely to follow suit.

If you read comments written by another investor who's setting a bad example by being demanding and disrespectful of the business owner's time, try your best to share with that person what you know about how to be the best possible investor. Encourage patience, but try not to offend. Let the investor know you understand the desire for immediate answers, but the entire crowd needs to trust the entrepreneur or owner and respect the communication timeline he has established.

Walking a Fine Line: Participating without Becoming a Nuisance

You may be so busy with your own life that you don't have any interest whatsoever in providing help to the business other than your financial investment. If that's the case, it's completely fine. However, if you do have some extra bandwidth and would like to add additional value, do so carefully.

As we say elsewhere, the best thing you can do is let the entrepreneur or business owner know what your strengths are and where you can provide value. Be a resource for this person to tap into when and how she sees fit. By participating in this manner, you're walking that tightrope between providing value and becoming a nuisance.

 Try to limit your communication to the entrepreneur or business owner. Before you write a post in a dialogue room or send an e-mail to the entrepreneur or owner, make sure that you gather your thoughts. Include everything about the topic in one communication, and write as clearly and concisely as you can. If possible, use bullet points to separate your ideas.

Taking these steps is even more important if you have a personal relationship with the entrepreneur or business owner. Avoid the assumption that because this person is your friend or part of your family, you have carte blanche to reach out whenever you have a thought about the business. Try to restrain yourself from doing this. The closer your connection to the entrepreneur or business owner, the more that person feels obligated to listen to what you say and to respond to all your posts. What's the problem with that? Say the entrepreneur or owner has 300 investors, and 60 of them are first-degree contacts. If even half of those 60 people are writing constant and disorganized e-mails, the poor entrepreneur or business owner is going to be dealing with a *ton* of distractions.

A good rule to follow is to write an e-mail or conversation post and then leave it for the night. Come back to it in the morning and ask yourself three questions:

✔ Do I really need to send it?

✔ If I do need to send it, is there anything else I should add?

✔ If I do need to send it, is there anything I can remove?

If you do send a communication, be patient. The entrepreneur is extremely busy. If you don't hear back immediately, it's because either she decided not to take your advice or she's so busy taking your advice that she doesn't have time to write back. Either way, you've had your say, and we recommend you let the business owner move forward as she sees fit.

Taking Action If You Believe the Company Is Breaking the Law

We wish we didn't need to write this section, but unfortunately, people do break laws. In the case of a startup or growing business, you may find out that the entrepreneur or business owner is doing one of these things:

✔ Soliciting investments on the phone or by e-mail instead of via the online funding portal

✔ Paying an employee under the table

✔ *Cooking the books* (fudging the company's financial reports) in some other way, whether big or small

When an entrepreneur or business owner breaks the law, he puts not only himself but also your investment at risk. Therefore, you need to take action right away if you believe something illegal is happening.

Weighing the appropriate action

Depending on what exactly is happening, you may want to start off by contacting the entrepreneur or business owner directly to explain what you know. (Presumably, if you know about something illegal going on, other investors may know as well, so the sooner you act the better.) This course of action may be best if you suspect the entrepreneur or owner is simply making a mistake or misunderstanding the law. (Maybe you overheard him explaining the investment opportunity to someone in person, for example, and you suspect he just doesn't realize the ramifications of what he did.)

If you have bigger concerns about what's going on, and you suspect the entrepreneur or owner knows exactly what he's doing and chooses to do it anyway, you may need to notify the SEC, which polices the rules governing crowdfund investing (see this book's website, `www.dummies.com/go/crowdfundinvesting`). The best way to do so likely is to contact the online funding portal, which should have a system in place for handling this type of complaint. (Funding portals will take such complaints very seriously; they don't want to stain their own reputations.) Send an e-mail to the portal first, and then follow up within a day or two with a phone call. The funding portal is on your side, so don't be shy about bringing a problem to light.

Of course, there are options in the middle of these two courses of action, so seeking advice from an attorney is always a good idea. Maybe *you* are the one misunderstanding the law; you need to rule out that possibility before blowing the whistle publicly. But if the attorney confirms your suspicion, you have to take action of some kind; you accept that responsibility as a member of the crowd.

Making sure the crowd is informed

If you have completely confirmed that illegal activity is occurring, the funding portal should notify all investors of what's happening. If you've reached out to the funding portal with a complaint, you have the right to ask how and when the portal will send this notification. As long as the funding portal does its job correctly, your work is done.

But in the worst-case scenario, if the funding portal drags its feet about notifying investors of the problem, your work isn't done. You have a responsibility to inform the rest of the crowd of what you know. Of course, you want to exercise extreme caution when posting a message that alleges illegal activity; you don't want to put the company in a terrible position based on unconfirmed suspicions. Only if and when you are 100 percent certain of the facts of the situation should you take this step and share your concerns with fellow investors. Just think how horrible it would be if you published a statement about wrongdoing, only to discover afterwards that you were wrong and the company went out of business due to your allegations.

Chapter 18

Exiting a Crowdfund Investment

· ·

· ·

*I*s this the chapter where we tell you how to get rich quick? No! It is not! Instead, this is the chapter where we help you think ahead regarding how you want to cash in on your investment.

As we hammer home in Chapters 15, 16, and 17, you need to make careful, informed decisions about where to invest reasonable amounts of your money in private companies. You need to commit yourself to long-term investing (a minimum of 12 months, per the JOBS Act, if you're an equity investor). Finally, you need to think proactively about what kind of outcome you desire. Do you intend to hold on to your investment indefinitely? Are you going to hold for exactly 12 months and then move on? Will you sell only when the company reaches a certain level of success (or bail out when it hits a certain level of failure)?

Only you can make the decision, but it's well worth considering even before you invest. Just as you set goals for yourself in other aspects in your life, you should think about what success in this investment looks like to you. In this chapter, we discuss some ways to think through these issues, and we also explain how the laws are written to protect you from unscrupulous individuals or uninformed decisions.

We've said it before, and we'll say it again: Crowdfund investing is not a way to make a quick buck. It's a way to invest in the communities you're a part of, whether they be communities of geography, communities of origin, or communities of interest. It's also a way of investing in businesses you know and entrepreneurs you believe in. You want to have reasonable expectations of your exit from all investments, including crowdfund investments.

The long-term success of your community can be a very rewarding outcome for an investment. Therefore, you may determine that a crowdfund investment will be, in part, a form of giving back to your community instead of a more traditional investment. Obviously, the vast majority of your investments should be made based solely on the expected financial outcome. But if you choose to (and you can afford to), you may want to make one or two small investments in your community that are driven by your desire to give back. Make those investments in businesses that you believe will create an improved life for you and others in your community.

Entering the Investment with the Right Attitude and Expectations

"Begin with the end in mind." This truism holds for many aspects of life. It speaks to the need to plan what you want to achieve before you take action. How can you know when you've succeeded if you haven't decided what success looks like?

When the subject is investing, you need to ask yourself *why* you're investing in the first place. What are your end goals? What is your time horizon? Do you need to earn a certain percentage on your investments within a year? Five years? Twenty years? Consider these questions:

- ✔ **Are you looking for a quick gain?** If so, crowdfunding investing is not for you. In addition to the legislated 12-month holding period for equity crowdfund investments, these types of investments are less liquid (meaning very likely more difficult to sell) than more traditional investments. Unlike with a mutual fund or a public company stock, you can't necessarily count on being able to sell a crowdfund investment on the exact date you determine would be best for your goals.

- ✔ **Are you looking to hold and then sell in the two- to five-year time frame?** Maybe you'd like to help a company get started, and then you want to find a way to sell your shares. This outcome is permitted by the law and seems very possible. Nothing is guaranteed, but you should be able to find buyers for your shares (especially if the company is performing well and meeting its goals). See the upcoming section "Knowing your options if you want or need to sell" for tips.

- ✔ **Are you expecting the company you invest in to have a huge initial public offering (IPO) that will turn your shares into gold?** Reality check: Of all the possible outcomes for your shares, an IPO is the least likely. Only a tiny fraction of companies ever make it to an IPO. The process of turning a private company into a publicly held company is very expensive; the IPO itself costs a bundle, and the ongoing regulatory compliance measures are very costly as well. Consider the likelihood of an IPO happening to be akin to the likelihood of your being struck by lightning. Yes, it does happen on rare occasions, but chances are, it won't happen to you in your lifetime.

✔ **Are you buying the shares for a mixture of reasons?** Are you investing in your community via crowdfund investing, and are you looking for a nontraditional exit? Are you willing to take some form of dividends from a community-based business instead of getting a big payout by selling your shares?

Maybe you're making a crowdfund investment decision because the business is right for your community. For example, maybe you live in a small town that needs a grocery store, and the community gets together to raise money to get it started. Will you see a huge financial windfall in a handful of years from this type of investment? Probably not. But will you be able to get milk, eggs, bread, and vegetables when you need them without having to drive 30 miles to the next larger town? Yes . . . and that has real value for you and your community. In very real ways, you'll benefit every day from this type of investment.

Whatever your desired or planned outcome is, make sure you're clear about it at the beginning. That way, you'll be more likely to feel at peace with the actual outcome because you understand not only what you want but also how likely that desired result may be.

Also, keep in mind the portfolio strategy that we touch on in Chapter 15, which involves making investments in a variety of asset classes that offer payouts on a variety of time horizons. Even within your crowdfund investing allocation, you may be better off making multiple investments that reflect a variety of possible exit strategies. (As any good financial planner will tell you, diversity in your portfolio is a good thing.)

Planning Your Exit Well in Advance

The way to exit a crowdfund investment is similar to the ways you can exit any other investment in the private capital markets. Until 2012, only a very small number of people were allowed to make these kinds of investments. Now, with crowdfund investing, most people have this opportunity. With this opportunity come rules — rules that make good sense and that protect investors and small business people.

Respecting why you're stuck for one year

In Chapter 2, we offer a very broad overview of how U.S. federal securities laws came to be in the early 20th century. Those laws remained relatively unchanged until the 1990s, when Congress relaxed the security laws to make it easier for entrepreneurs to generally solicit investors for money. The legislation changes in the 1990s included zero restrictions regarding how solicitation could take place and the amount of time investors needed to hold on to the shares they purchased.

The unintended consequence of this legislative change was that shysters entered the market and began selling worthless stocks to the naive masses. (If you read Chapter 2, you'll realize that this scenario mirrors pretty closely what was happening in the United States in the years leading up to the stock market crash of 1929.) Using accomplices to pump up their fake or worthless securities, they would dump these worthless stocks on people and take off with the profit. Because the law didn't require a minimum holding period, investors were left high and dry. Many people lost a lot of money in the process. The legislation also didn't require that investors go through a background check to remove repeat offenders.

We mention this problem because it explains why, as a crowdfund investor, you must hold your company stock for a minimum of one year. (If you hold a company's debt instead, you may or may not be subject to the same holding period.) The SEC doesn't want you (or anyone else) buying a stock in a company and then immediately trying to inflate its worth. For example, say that you buy equity in a company via a crowdfund investing campaign. As soon as the campaign closes, you go onto your social networks and write a message like this: " I just bought a piece of the next Facebook. No more shares are available, but I'm willing to share some of mine at the right price." (Of course, the "right price" is going to be twice what you paid for the shares, or more.)

If you and other crowdfund investors acted in this way, the whole crowdfund investment opportunity would sink. Potential investors would be looking to get rich quick instead of investing in companies they really believe in. The entire process would get a bad reputation, and entrepreneurs and small business owners with solid business plans in plain-Jane industries would watch their funding opportunities dry up.

Requiring crowdfund investors to hold on to their stocks for a year creates more transparency in the marketplace, and transparency is a great thing. After the year period is up, if an initial investor decides to sell her stock, other potential investors will be able to evaluate whether the company in question is really worth the price she paid for the stock — or more, or less. Twelve months' worth of information about the company (including an annual report that the company files with the Securities and Exchange

Commission [SEC] and sends out to its investors) will be available for review, and anyone willing to do his homework should be able to avoid getting duped.

Need more convincing that the one-year holding period is valuable? Consider this: The majority of the trading that takes place in the public markets is short term. This rapid buying and selling of securities creates uncertainty in the value of any stock. (Why are so many people selling it? Why are so many people buying it?) This uncertainty is otherwise known as *volatility*. The more volatility that exists, the more the price of a stock will move — both up and down. Volatility makes the owners of a business react to the movement of the stock, which isn't always the right thing to do and isn't always in the best interest of the shareholders.

Holding on to a stock for a minimum of a year decreases the stock's volatility, thus allowing entrepreneurs and business owners to focus on what they should be doing: running a business.

Considering whether you want to commit for multiple years

If you opt for crowdfund investments, you should consider holding on to your stock for longer than the required year. That's because entrepreneurs and small business owners are committed to crowdfund investing for the long haul. Their return is tied to the long-term productivity of the company, and that productivity can increase if the company's funding base is stable.

Think of committing to a company in terms similar to committing to a personal relationship. Just as in your personal life, you'll run into bumps along the way, and the key to long-term success is communication from both sides.

If you're doing your part as an investor — using the product or service that's sold by this company, acting as a marketing engine for the company, and driving sales — your investment should be increasing over time, which should keep you committed. After all, exiting a company that's on a growth trajectory eliminates your future returns.

New businesses take a long time to scale and almost always take longer to reach their goals than originally planned. You need to understand these facts about startups so you aren't disappointed when your $1,000 investment doesn't turn into $50,000 in a couple years. Even if you're looking for the next Facebook (good luck!), you should remember that an early investor in Facebook waited years to cash in. To give you some perspective, Facebook was launched in 2004, and the company didn't go public until 2012. Manage your expectations, be patient, and be realistic about the results you're hoping for.

Want to look like a smart investor? Consider going into a crowdfund investment the same way venture capitalists go into an investment. When venture capitalists look at an investment opportunity, they don't look at it from a short-term point of view; they look at it from a five-year point of view. They understand that investing in a business requires a combination of money and experience. Money may come from a quick injection, but experience comes only with time. Entrepreneurs will only benefit as the business grows.

Knowing your options if you want or need to sell

If you want to exit your investment after the first year, you can. No chain tethers you to the entrepreneur or business owner after this point. Here are your options:

- ✔ **Selling on the secondary market:** A *secondary market* is akin to one of the public exchanges, like NASDAQ, that exists for buying and selling public company stocks. Of course, a secondary market for a crowdfund investment needs to allow for the sale of private shares. It operates under the same principles of supply and demand that a public exchange does. In other words, you have to wait until the demand exists (a buyer is available) before you can sell your shares.

  To be clear, secondary markets for crowdfund investments are *not* the same as NASDAQ. Don't misunderstand what we're saying and think you'll be able to go to *The Wall Street Journal* and see what's going on with your stock. Instead, secondary markets for crowdfund investments are private exchanges that act *similar* to the public exchanges. It's important for you to understand that it's much harder to sell your crowdfund investment stock on the secondary market than it is to sell the stock of a public company on a public exchange. There simply aren't enough buyers available to make shares on the private secondary market very liquid. This fact is especially true if you own shares in a local business (think about a bakery or a dry cleaner, for example).

- ✔ **Being bought out by a professional investor:** This option could arise at any time, or it may never happen (depending on the specific company you're invested in). The majority owners in the company may vote on allowing a buyout, and you then have the opportunity to sell your shares. If this scenario occurs, you may consider your work done and allow someone with stronger hands to take over, or you may stick around for the ride if that option is available to you. (Who knows . . . the company's performance may get even better!)

We discuss these two options in more detail in the following sections.

The secondary market

First, a little background. The term *primary market* generally refers to the place where securities are bought directly from the issuer. For example, when a purchaser buys shares directly from a company having an IPO, that purchaser is buying on the primary market. Buying treasuries (bonds and notes) from the federal government is another example of a primary market.

Secondary markets, in contrast, do not involve the issuers. Instead, the sellers on secondary markets are securities owners (stockholders). The most well-known secondary markets are the major U.S. stock exchanges: the New York Stock Exchange (NYSE) and NASDAQ.

The secondary market for crowdfunded securities is in its nascent stage. As crowdfund investing grows, so will this marketplace. It's very possible that websites may emerge that specialize in the resale of crowdfunded securities. As these websites and the marketplace grow, we'll surely see SEC regulations forming around them. Make sure you're following the letter of the law! If you use a secondary market, make sure it's registered with the SEC and the Financial Industry Regulatory Authority (FINRA) and is allowed to help you sell your shares.

After the 12-month holding period expires, if you want to unload your shares, the secondary market will generally be the first place you go. Keep in mind, though, that if you're trying to sell your shares because you're not happy with the progress of the company, you probably aren't the only investor thinking that way, and you'll most likely get only pennies on the dollar for your shares (assuming you can find a willing buyer at any price). The integration of social media with crowdfund investing is crucial here; chances are, if investors in the same company are bothered by its performance, they've shared their dissatisfaction with their social networks. Any such public comments can and will be read by potential investors, which will affect your ability to sell.

A buyout from a professional investor

If this scenario happens, you may experience a gain on your investment. Different types of professional investors exist, but they fit into three main categories, which we define in Chapter 3:

- Angel investors
- Private equity investors
- Venture capital investors

Historically, professional investors don't like having lots of small investors in the companies they buy into. When they look to invest in a crowdfund-invested company, they may want to buy out all the crowdfund investors.

This is likely good news for you! It means that you're getting an *exit* (the buzzword that all investors dream of).

Many private investors were very excited when we successfully carved out the exemption for companies to be able to raise money through crowdfund investing. Savvy investors look to hedge their bets as much as possible. Crowdfund investing is seen by many people as an onramp to institutional investors. It allows businesses to flesh out their ideas, develop a proof of concept (see Chapter 5), and get some initial traction. When crowdfund-invested companies approach professional investors, they'll be showing that they offer much more than just an idea. They'll have proof that their idea can create revenue and that the entrepreneur or small business owner has what it takes to run a business.

Here's an example of how a professional buyout may work: When you purchase your security in the company, you receive a percentage of the company's entire stock. This percentage was calculated based on the valuation of the company. For instance, if you invested $10,000 and received 1 percent of the company, that means the company was valued at $1 million at the time. (Reversing this calculation, the formula to calculate a company's value is this: a $10,000 investment divided by 1 percent of the company received equals the company value of $1 million.) A normal starting point for professional investors is to purchase 20 percent of the entire company. To figure out how many dollars equal 20 percent of the company, the investors will do an updated valuation of the company.

If a company is attracting professional investors, that probably means the company has significantly increased its value. If the same company is now valued at $4 million (four times what it was worth when you first invested), a professional investor looking for a 20 percent stake will need to invest $800,000. Because the investor is buying out the crowdfunded investors, a portion of this money could go directly into the crowd's pockets. If you owned 1 percent of the company, you would expect a check to the tune of $40,000. Not bad, huh?

Check out this book's website, www.dummies.com/go/crowdfundinvesting, for more information on exits.

Your job as a crowdfund investor is to help promote the business. Promoting the business leads not only to more customers but also to more revenue. More revenue (while keeping expenses in check) leads to a higher valuation. So, unlike when you invest in a public company, you can actually help drive a private company to a higher valuation by being a marketing agent for it. (You should be aptly motivated to market the business!)

Holding Out Hope for an IPO

An IPO occurs when a company goes public — it lists its shares with a stock exchange for the general public to be able to purchase. IPOs can be the exit of all exits. They're what some investors dream of when they invest in startup companies. Many entrepreneurs and startup companies talk about getting an IPO, and they try to hype up their team and investors with talk of an IPO as the goal. No doubt, an IPO is a great goal to have, but it's a very unlikely one.

The chances of your crowdfund-invested company getting an IPO are extremely small — minuscule, in fact. To give you an idea of how small the chances are, according to *Forbes* magazine, in 2011, there were a total of 153 IPOs. That's right, 153. Compare this to the 500,000 businesses that incorporate each year. (Granted, a company can't go from zero to public in one year, but these numbers illustrate the fact that an IPO is rare.)

Furthermore, the chances of your investing in a company at the startup stage via crowdfund investing and being able to keep your investment to the IPO stage are even smaller. The company will likely need much more growth capital along the way to get ready for an IPO. As we mention in the previous section, if the company raises professional capital, the chances of these investors buying out your stock are very large.

We don't mean to be negative, but we want to put things in perspective. If you do get an IPO exit, *woo-hoo!* Start planning out how you're going to use the boatloads of money you get. But if your investment plan is to hold out for the IPO, you may need to rethink your plan. We're not telling you not to do it; some companies do go public, and some crowdfund investors may gain a great deal when this happens. We just want you to be realistic in your hopes.

If you have an opportunity to exit with a gain on your investment, that's a great exit — even if it isn't an IPO.

Waiting for a Merger or Acquisition

A merger or acquisition is another common way for an investor to have an exit. It occurs when a company combines forces with another company (merger) or when a company gets bought out by a larger company (acquisition). These deals can be structured in many ways, and the details are beyond the scope of this book.

However, we can offer some generalities. Usually, when a company is bought out, investors are given cash or stock — or a combination of both — as compensation. The value of the company buying out your shares will dictate which one (cash or stock) is better for you. For instance, if your crowdfund investment company is a specialty food shop selling pasta and cheese with one location, and a larger company that has six locations buys you out, you'll likely be better off if you get cash for your shares and not stock. On the other end of the spectrum, if your company makes high-tech widgets and Apple buys you out, it very well may be much better if you get stock.

Of all the ways you can exit your investment, the only option that offers you a degree of control is selling on the secondary market. All the other options, including mergers and acquisitions, are decided by the majority stockholders. This fact could frustrate you, so you should think about it upfront. Consider this example and how you would've reacted as an investor: Groupon, the well-known group-buying website, was offered $6 billion to sell the company. Amazingly, the majority shareholders turned down this offer. We have no doubt that many minority shareholders were furious with this decision, but they had zero control over it. As with all things related to crowdfund investing, you have to manage your expectations and understand the lack of control you may have over how you exit your crowdfunded investment.

Part VI
The Part of Tens

The 5th Wave   By Rich Tennant

Being Dracula's slave didn't pay much, but Renfield always found extra money to invest.

In this part . . .

This part is a staple in the *For Dummies* series. Here, we offer four short-and-sweet chapters that cover best practices for a crowdfund investing campaign, reasons that other nations should pay attention to what the United States is doing with this type of investment, cases from the crowdfunding world that illustrate the power of collective investments, and stories that will tug at your heartstrings.

Chapter 19

Ten Best Practices for a Crowdfund Investing Campaign

In This Chapter

▶ Giving your investors what they need

▶ Striving for sanity — and happiness — in your work

*I*f you follow the Golden Rule — "Do unto others as you would have them do unto you" — then you'll be living by the tenets of crowdfunding and won't let down either yourself or your investors. This chapter outlines ten specific principles to follow to help you do just that.

Set Realistic Expectations

No one expects you to climb Mt. Everest in a day — especially if climbing a mountain is new to you. Your investors *do* expect you to set reasonable expectations based on your experience and set milestones to achieving those goals.

Look at what you want to accomplish. Define the stage at which you'll accomplish your goal. (Remember the three stages of a business that we explain in Chapter 5: idea, working model, and growth.) Set expectations that will help you get to the next level.

Take the time to map out a business plan. (No matter what type of funding you're using to finance your idea, you can't skip this very important step; see Chapter 5.) Break your plan into milestones, and make sure each milestone is achievable based on time and resources. Doing so is critical because during fundraising, potential investors will question your expectations, and you want to be able to provide solid answers.

If you set your expectations right, you'll win the confidence of the crowd, and your chances of meeting your funding goal will increase.

Work for Your Investors

When you take on investors, you take on a responsibility that's greater than just performing at a job. You actually have a legal responsibility — a *fiduciary responsibility* — to do right by your investors and act in their best interest. This means that you work for your investors and not for yourself.

Your investors want to make sure you're making sound decisions with their money, and they want to hear about what you're doing — communication is crucial! You may be the president and CEO of your enterprise, but when you present your annual report to investors or seek additional rounds of financing, your investors will give you your performance review.

We've all seen examples of how a business owner's irresponsibility affects investors. Don't add fodder to investors' concerns by taking audacious steps (buying a BMW as soon as your funding campaign is successful) or keeping secrets (drawing a huge salary and failing to inform investors about the size of your paycheck). Before you make any business decision, ask yourself, "What would my investors want me to do?" or "If something goes wrong, what will my investors think about this decision?"

Don't Be Evil

In 2008, the financial system in the United States (and, later, throughout the world) collapsed. Many factors contributed, but a big one was this: People were being evil. Certain people were looking out for only themselves and were thinking very short term. They wanted (and got) short-term gains at the expense of billions of other people.

Crowdfund investing is a brand-new industry that allows entrepreneurs and small businesses access to capital to start and grow their companies. Many people stand to benefit from this funding source — including the American people, who need the jobs it can help to create — *if* the industry maintains a great reputation. If it becomes tainted, even by a few individuals' poor behavior, the industry as a whole will be constrained. Therefore, everyone involved in the industry — from funding platform owner to investor to entrepreneur — has the responsibility to make sure things are done right.

Anyone who tries to game the crowdfund investing system is going to get caught and will weaken the entire industry. The Securities and Exchange Commission (SEC), Financial Industry Regulatory Authority (FINRA), and many other government organizations are watching the industry closely, so make sure that everything you do is aboveboard. Not a big enough deterrent for you? Keep in mind that we've worked closely with the federal government to make sure that anyone who partakes in fraud on crowdfund investing platforms will become an example for why fraud doesn't pay.

Thank Everyone — Constantly

Most people genuinely like being helpful, but they also like to be appreciated for their efforts. Showing your appreciation to your supporters is simple and powerful. Throughout the process of starting your business and raising money, you're going to get help from many people. Thank them often, and thank them genuinely.

When your campaign is live (meaning that you're courting investors via an online funding portal; see Chapter 7), be grateful for every investment pledge you receive — no matter the size. Thank people in your online forums, via e-mail updates, and on your Facebook page. Doing so not only tightens your connection with the people who have pledged but also is an unobtrusive way to nudge people who haven't yet invested.

When a friend, family member, or another close supporter invests in you, take the time to call and say thanks. Doing so emphasizes your appreciation and helps turn these supporters into your promoters. If they feel appreciated, chances are, they'll start talking about you and your business to other people.

This type of investment is all about engaging a crowd. One of the easiest ways to do so and get your business to go viral is by thanking your supporters.

Give Credit Where Credit Is Due

Entrepreneurs often like to think that they do everything themselves, but that's simply not true. Any successful entrepreneur will tell you that you need the support of countless people. The quickest and surest way to get people to stop helping you is to take credit for their work.

If someone helps you, give him credit in an open format. Your investors don't expect you to be a one-man show, so share the spotlight. For example, if you have a team of people working for you, and someone is managing all the comments on your crowdfund investing campaign (see our discussion of community managers in Chapter 6), make sure the rest of your team knows how important that person's contributions are. Showing such appreciation can get the rest of your team to work even harder.

Engage with Investors in Regular and Scalable Ways

Say that you've raised the capital you need for your business from 400 investors. Congratulations! Now what? How can you communicate with those investors so they know what's happening with their investment at the same time you're trying to run your business?

The word *scalable* is very important here. Chances are, you're already putting in 60 to 80 hours (or more) each week to achieve your business goals. You simply can't respond to individual e-mails or calls from your investors. If you did, you wouldn't have any time to run your business.

As we explain in Chapter 7, you need to select an online funding portal that helps you manage investor relations. Make sure the portal provides an integrated solution and/or works with a partner to support ongoing communication. You want to be sure you can utilize social media, e-mail, live chat, and other tools to keep your investors connected to their investment and to you on a regular, scheduled basis. Create a *communication cadence* (a pace and pattern of communication) that works for you, and tell your investors what this cadence will be so they can set their expectations. Then meet those expectations! If you say something like "I'll publish a monthly investor update that will go out via e-mail," then do it. As long as you communicate regularly and on schedule, most investors will appreciate it and will respect your time.

Create Ways to Include Your Supporters

Your supporters are worth more than just money. They bring wisdom, knowledge, and marketing power to your venture. Take advantage of the fact that you have a group of backers with a vested interest in your success, and figure out ways to include them. Here are a few suggestions:

✔ **Create an informal board of advisors, and establish subgroups for sales, marketing, public relations, graphics, design, operations, and finance.** After you hit your funding target, send a thank-you e-mail to all your supporters. Let them know that your venture is a team effort and you're looking for their help. Ask if anyone wants to help out on one of the committees you've created. Let folks know this is a short-term assignment until you can hire full-time resources. Most investors will love the fact that you want to include them.

- ✔ **From your board of advisors, pick a few seasoned entrepreneurs — preferably ones who have raised capital before — to be your mentors.** Mentors are wonderful because not only do they share experiences on what *not* to do but also they can help connect you with people who can move your business to the next level. They could even be connections to more traditional forms of financing (such as angel investors or venture capital firms; see Chapter 3) down the road.

- ✔ **Create an online dropbox to store information that will be valuable for your business.** Invite your supporters to upload news clips, links to websites, competitor information, photos, and so on. Create folders within the dropbox so people know where to put their various items of interest.

- ✔ **Use social media to stay in touch.** Create a LinkedIn Group for your investors and publish quick updates to it. You can also ask for input and create polls via this group. Doing so reinforces an ongoing dialogue with your investors.

  You can use Facebook to do the same thing, but you want to draw a firm distinction between your business and personal activities. If your brand is fun and lighthearted, Facebook may actually be the best way to go for this interaction. Create a private Facebook group for your investors.

- ✔ **Create an e-mail inbox for questions from investors.** Once or twice a month, review the questions and create a video of your responses to five to ten of them. Use whatever video function you have on your laptop — the goal is to keep this activity quick and easy. (With a bit of practice, you should be able to accomplish this activity in an hour or less.)

Make Your Vision and Goals Transparent to Your Investors

To gain investors, you must clearly communicate your vision and goals. The same is true for growing and leading your team. People want to belong to a group and contribute to something larger than themselves. They want to know where they're going and that their leaders are truly leading them somewhere with purpose and planning. So, whether you're talking to your investors or employees, you must communicate your vision and your goals over and over and over and over and over and over and over. At some point, you'll think, "I've said this a hundred times already. Why do I have to say it again?" You have to constantly repeat your vision and goals because that's how culture is formed and how investors know you're on track and that they're aligned with you.

Even if you have to change your strategy or direction, that's okay (all startups pivot their plans to one degree or another). The key is to do so in a fully transparent way. The best way we've found to create and execute effectively on a vision and goals is to use the Rockefeller Habits. We highly recommend the book *Mastering the Rockefeller Habits,* by Verne Harnish (Gazelles). This book is just 126 pages long and gives you a logical and easy-to-follow road map to ensure that you know your vision and goals and that the strategies and tactics you execute every day are fully aligned with your vision and goals. It features practical exercises and a one-page strategic plan that will save you a huge amount of time and energy.

Understand Why These People Are Investing in Your Company

Investors, especially early-stage investors, are supporting you and your team (if you have a team at this point) more than they're supporting the exact details of your plan. They believe you have skills and abilities, and they want to give you the opportunity to succeed (with their money). They see something in you that they want to support. When you run into rough times and wonder why you ever decided to start this company, let their faith in you inspire your own confidence.

Work with People You Like

We can't stress this point enough. As you're building your company, nothing is more important than the team you create. No matter what skills people have, if you don't like them, you shouldn't work with them. Paul English, the co-founder and chief technology officer of KAYAK (one of the largest online travel sites in the world) says that the difference between an A team and an A+ team is the difference between a million-dollar company and a billion-dollar company. We couldn't agree more.

Chapter 20

Ten Reasons Every Country Should Consider Crowdfund Investing

. . . .

In This Chapter

▶ Igniting economies, creating jobs, and enhancing political stability

▶ Opening up local investment opportunities

. . . .

*E*very government in the world is focused on how to grow its economy. Elections are won and lost based on the strength of the plans of politicians who promise prosperity for their people at every level of the economic ladder.

But how does a government create jobs? How does it effectively grow the economy? We believe governments do so by making it faster and easier for businesses to start, grow, and (in some cases) fail. Small business and entrepreneurs are the driving force behind every successful economy across the globe. We believe that cultures and governments that embrace and celebrate the entrepreneur are more likely to succeed in both the short and long term.

We spend a great deal of time traveling outside the United States meeting with governments, nongovernmental organizations, banks, development organizations, entrepreneurs, and investors. The constant theme we hear is this: We need to expand our entrepreneurial capacity. We must cultivate risk capital and a culture of entrepreneurship. We must make it easier for businesses to form and grow. We're working to build innovation centers and incubators . . . how can we make them successful?

Although crowdfund investing is not an economic cure-all, it can be an important part of the solution. It allows significant numbers of citizens to make modest investments in high-growth and/or Main Street businesses. In this chapter, we discuss ten reasons why crowdfund investing is already becoming, or will become, a trending topic in financial industries and entrepreneurial ecosystems around the world.

Ideas Go Where the Money Is

With the proper care and feeding, businesses and entrepreneurs can flourish. Fostering an ecosystem that encourages entrepreneurship and innovation requires capital. If the financial markets or regulations in a particular country are such that capital isn't flowing, businesses can't get the money they need.

Entrepreneurs who are passionate enough about their ideas will go where the money is available to fund them. This is why many Canadian entrepreneurs head to the United States: because capital is more readily available to fund them. That was true prior to 2013, when only about 2 percent of the U.S. population could legally provide funding to entrepreneurs. And now, with the advent of crowdfund investing, anyone in the United States can help fund someone with a good idea. This is a game changer!

Countries that wait to update their securities laws will create "brain drain" as skilled entrepreneurs head to other countries where they can fund and launch their businesses. An idea that is successfully funded in one country generally stays there and rarely returns back to the entrepreneur's country of origin.

Ideas Can Turn into Job-Producing Businesses

Ideas launch businesses. Businesses require people to grow. Good ideas can turn into great job-creating businesses. According to the Small Business Administration, all *net new jobs* (new jobs minus the newly unemployed) in the United States in the past 30 years were created by small businesses. Big businesses employ thousands of people, but tens of thousands of small businesses provide the products and services within a community and create a much larger number of jobs.

Crowdfund investing allows a community to fund local businesses and, in doing so, to create its own jobs. Local jobs provide wages that are spent on goods and services to provide for livelihoods. According to Amy Cortese, author of *Locavesting: The Revolution in Local Investing and How to Profit From It* (Wiley), every dollar invested in a local business has a 3x multiplier. What does that mean? The money goes from the business to the employee, from the employee to the local grocery store, and from the local grocery store to staff (as well as to the purchase of more products, which may or may not be created in the community).

Focusing on community businesses keeps capital within the community. Leveraging crowdfund investing to do so takes the burden off the traditional sources (banks and governments) and lets the community — the people who will use the products or services — play the funding role.

Job-Producing Businesses Are Tax Revenue Generators

Businesses pay salaries to employees. Employees pay payroll taxes to the government. U.S. payroll taxes fund both Social Security and Medicare. The more jobs there are, the greater the tax receipts. The greater the tax receipts, the more money the government has to cover these expenses and pay for the future health of its citizens.

In addition, businesses are for-profit entities, meaning they aim to drive profit to the bottom line and provide a return to their investors. Profitable businesses pay taxes on their profits to help support the infrastructure (roads, electricity, water, and so on) without which a business could not operate. Crowdfund investing will encourage more profit-seeking businesses that will generate more tax receipts for governments.

Economic Stimulus Is a Byproduct of Entrepreneurship and Innovation

Entrepreneurship and innovation are about creating and sustaining ideas — ideas that provide solutions to problems and are purchased by consumers domestically and globally. The cash that consumers pay to a business is used to purchase goods to make the product or service, to hire employees, and to pay for things like lawyers, marketing services, and rent.

This flow of capital is a boost to an economy. The more a government can do to encourage entrepreneurship and innovation, the more capital will flow, and the better off its economy will be. Crowdfund investing encourages the flow of capital into productive businesses that can create jobs and provide tax revenue.

Local Investing Keeps Money in the Community and Country

One of your authors, Zak, owns a chain of olive oil and balsamic vinegar tasting shops (www.puremountainoliveoil.com). His company imports products into the United States from about ten different countries; it's truly an international business. However, the vast majority of capital that his company spends stays in the local communities where he has his bricks-and-mortar shops. That money is spent on chamber of commerce dues, tax attorney services, lawyers, general contractors, landlords, business services (phone, Internet, trash pickup), local advertising, and so on. The business also employs more than 30 people who live close to the shops. All these people make a living from the revenue Zak's company generates and, in turn, support the local communities further via grocery stores, gas stations, restaurants, and other everyday expenses.

Many state and federal governments understand this multiplier and try to make their regions as attractive as possible for entrepreneurs to start businesses. Governments that don't understand this multiplier need to pay attention to the flow of capital generated by businesses in their communities. The easier it is for businesses to raise capital and start operations, the more money will stay in the local community and be paid in taxes to the local governments.

If a government makes it difficult to invest in businesses, people with money are still going to look to invest; they'll just look outside their borders. Money will go where it can grow. If a government makes it hard for people to grow their money within their borders, money will flow to other countries. For people with small amounts of capital to invest who may not have the opportunity to invest their money in other countries, a likely option is for the money to sit in a bank account at no interest or, worse, stuffed under the mattress. This money is not generating a return for its owner, nor is it generating economic output for the community.

Consider the example of Kiva (www.kiva.org), a web-based company based in San Francisco that helps people with money make loans to entrepreneurs in the developing world. Since its inception, people from all over the world have invested hundreds of millions of dollars through micro investments. Investments start at $25, and the projects funded usually fall within the $300 to $1,200 range. Because of regulations in the United States, Kiva has mainly helped people in the developing world to raise capital. If the United States would've had regulations making it more attractive for people to invest in American entrepreneurs, just imagine the millions of dollars that could have been put to work in domestic businesses!

Crowdfund Investing Leads to a Larger Middle Class and Greater Stability

The global financial crisis of 2008 caused deep and lasting destruction to economies in both the developed and developing world. Many people who considered themselves middle class (and who had benefited from the growing global economy) found themselves out of work entirely or underemployed. Two stark examples from the developed world show the gravity of the situation: Italy's unemployment rate is over 25 percent, and in Spain, almost 50 percent of people under 30 are unemployed. This is a dangerous situation for political stability. When you have over 15 percent unemployment in a country, and when that unemployment is particularly pronounced in citizens under 30 (who are educated and frustrated because they followed the rules, went to school to get a good job, and now are unable to work), you have a recipe for unrest.

Crowdfund investing provides communities with a way to support their own members in building businesses that add value and create jobs. When entrepreneurial individuals have access to capital (from crowdfund investing or from more traditional sources), their businesses can grow.

Recently, Jason was in Italy speaking to groups in Milan and Rome about this exact topic. While he was there, Madrid was erupting in violence that was fueled by educated young adults who were frustrated by their lack of access to jobs or the ability to use their skills productively.

Countries must create ways to grow the size of their middle class. Having a "barbell" economy with a large underclass, a large wealthy class, and very little in the middle is unhealthy. A barbell economy doesn't offer people in the underclass models for how to improve their circumstances or create better lives for their families. Crowdfund investing can be a part of the solution to create paths to development and prosperity.

The Number-One Source of Net New Jobs Is Small Businesses

Many economic studies show that the number-one source of net new jobs is small businesses. If you want to create new jobs in your country, you need to help small businesses to start and grow. Historically, in the United States, we've gotten out of recessions in large part via the jobs that small businesses create. One of the reasons we had such a tough time getting out of the recession that started in 2008 is that capital markets dried up, which meant many small businesses couldn't get bank loans or even credit cards. With the legalization of equity-based crowdfund investing, small businesses will have a new spigot of capital that they can use to grow their businesses and create jobs.

What about big business? Doesn't it drive the country's economic engines? Well, during an economic slowdown, big businesses tend to implement hiring freezes and layoffs. They tighten their belts and get rid of excess. This situation often leaves a lot of talented and smart people without jobs. And even when big companies experience growth during an economic downturn, they often hold off on hiring as much as they can. They don't want to overextend themselves, so they go through restructuring, freeing up human resources to focus their energy on new projects. Workloads become heavier, and people work longer hours.

Small businesses simply don't have this option. People working in small businesses are already oftentimes wearing multiple hats (sales manager, salesperson, marketing manager, social media marketer, advertising manager, and so on). When small businesses grow, they have to hire more people.

The Web Can Get Capital Flowing

Before the Internet, banks or other third parties were the only way for individuals to pool their resources and then provide them (via the banks and their lending guidelines) to other individuals to build businesses. Now, individuals can use the web to connect people who have capital to people and businesses that need capital. Other than face-to-face communication, there is no more transparent communication channel than the Internet. The web supports many-to-many communication that enables people to communicate their needs and allows other people to evaluate those needs and determine whether to provide the requested resources.

People Want to Support Their Countries

Don't underestimate the power of national pride. During the Olympics, people cheer on their fellow countrymen even though they've never met the athletes and oftentimes have never even heard their names. People want to support the country and culture they know.

Likewise, people want to invest in people, products, and services they know. If you're a potential crowdfund investor and you don't have a tight connection with someone running a crowdfund investing campaign, where are you likely to put your dollars? Chances are, you're going to invest in someone from one of the communities you belong to.

In many countries today, people have a hard time investing in businesses that their fellow countrymen are starting and growing. If countries allow for crowdfund investing to occur within their borders, cash will begin to flow from the people who have it to the people who can use it to create jobs and grow businesses — instead of that capital being invested in other countries where it's easier to make seed/early-stage investments.

National pride is one reason cash will be invested locally, but savvy and successful businessmen and women also understand that the better off their country's economy is, the better off their own businesses will be. This is also one of the reasons we believe crowdfund investing will create interesting opportunities for diaspora investment, because people who live outside the countries where they were born have a natural affinity to their countries. Today, literally billions of *diaspora remittances* (money sent by people living in another country back home to friends and relatives to help provide for their basic needs) are transmitted every year. With crowdfund investing, you create the opportunity for additional capital flows to not only support basic needs but also to make real investments in high-value and potentially high-growth businesses in the countries to which people feel deeply connected.

You Don't Want to Be Left Behind!

Crowdfund investing is the dawn of Web 3.0, where the social web meets capital formation. It's a true disruption of the private capital markets. For the first time, both existing Main Street businesses and startup businesses can seek capital via the same channel and can leverage the power of their communities. More and more countries are exploring this opportunity and working to legalize versions of crowdfund investing that are appropriate for their cultures and capital markets. This is another step in making the world a smaller and more connected place. Don't be left behind!

Chapter 21

Ten Crowdfunding Cases

● ●

In This Chapter

▶ Growing a small business with crowd support

▶ Getting a brand-new venture off the ground via crowd investment

● ●

Crowdfunding and crowdfund investing aren't the same thing (see Chapter 2 if you need clarification on that point), but donation- or perks-based crowdfunding provided the proof of concept necessary to get crowdfund investing off the ground. The ten stories in this chapter demonstrate how powerful a crowd can be by illustrating what can be done when a good idea meets up with hard work and widespread financial investment.

We believe that, thanks to crowdfund investing opportunities, more people will support great ideas because now you can own a piece of a business and feel connected to the results of the business because you become a brand ambassador for that business. Keep this fact in mind when you review the pitches that follow. Ask yourself, "Could this have been a company I would've invested in?"

Dessert Truck, Inc.

If you live in New York City, you've probably heard of Dessert Truck. This food truck has a passionate following and is famous for its chocolate bread pudding, Nutella brioche donuts, and crème brûlée. When you start winning awards from food truck reviewer *Vendy*, appear on the Food Network, and are featured in articles written in *Food & Wine* magazine, it only makes sense to think bigger.

That's exactly what Jerome Chang, owner of the Dessert Truck, did. Unfortunately, access to capital for perishable goods isn't plentiful, which is why he turned to Lucky Ant (www.luckyant.com), a hyper-local crowdfunding platform for small businesses. The goal was small: Seek donations to the tune of $3,900 to help cover packaging costs for a grocery label. In exchange, people received perks that included free desserts. However, the end result was much bigger.

Not only did Dessert Truck hit its funding target, but also its enthusiastic following gave the company enough confidence to take the plunge and open a storefront. By starting with a food truck, building a following, and crowdfunding, Chang was able to launch a retail location knowing that the risk of failure would be less.

Escape the City

The potential for crowdfund investing is global. For an example, just look to the United Kingdom's equity-based crowdfunding platform called Crowdcube (www.crowdcube.com) and a company called Escape the City. Escape the City is a London-based company on a mission to help ambitious professionals make exciting career transitions. It's a matchmaking service helping people find their dream jobs, and it has helped a community of 65,000 escapees find exciting jobs, start their own businesses, and go on big adventures because "Life is too short to do work that doesn't matter to you." But they needed capital to expand and grow.

Escape the City was founded by Dom Jackman and Rob Symington, who quit their management consultancy jobs in order to set up the business. Given that "leaving the city" was part of the company's philosophy, Jackman and Symington were reluctant to have to rely on the city for financing. Therefore, the company turned down two offers of venture capital funding. (Not many companies can make that claim.)

Instead, to accomplish its goals, Escape the City set out to raise £600,000 via Crowdcube. In less than 14 days, it hit that funding target from 394 investors. In exchange, it gave up 24 percent equity in the business. The funds were used to pivot the company, to create an "aspirational alternative to a LinkedIn profile," shifting from being a site that focuses on content to one that focuses on networking. The best part about Escape the City is that these two entrepreneurs didn't create jobs just for themselves but for everyone else using their platform!

The Asian Resource Center

The Asian Resource Center (ARC) in Oakland, California, was established in 1985 to celebrate and promote the rich diversity of the Pan-Asian and broader communities. It's part of the nonprofit East Bay Asian Local Development Corporation (EBALDC).

Various organizations in ARC address a range of social issues in the areas of affordable housing, healthcare, youth programs, environmental justice, and more.

As a nonprofit, resources are limited. Figuring out how to better utilize resources means that more can go back to the community. For over ten years, ARC had tried to tap into the benefits of alternative energy by going solar but had found doing so cost prohibitive. Now, thanks to a funding campaign on Solar Mosaic (`www.joinmosaic.com`), a renewable energy crowdfunding platform focused on solar energy, 134 investors provided $98,000, and ARC is proud host of the first community-funded solar project in Oakland. The project started with 12 solar modules, and eventually there will be 120 installed on ARC's roofs. The project is expected to save ARC more than $100,000. And the best part is, the $100,000 is invested right back into the community!

TikTok+LunaTik Multi-Touch Watch Kits by Scott Wilson and MINIMAL

This is one of our personal favorite stories. Scott Wilson and his design team, MINIMAL, loved the iPod Nano — so much so that they believed that, given a sleek band, it would make a great watch. The only problem: They needed $1,500 to manufacture and start selling a watch band with a clip to which someone could attach the iPod Nano.

The team decided that they wanted to do pre-sales of their watches on Kickstarter (`www.kickstarter.com`). They would offer the watch bands at a discount compared to what they would sell for when they were complete. The team set up six different levels of investment, the lowest of which was just $1. At that level, 128 people participated and got a thank-you from the company. The magic really started at $25, for which the backer would receive a watch kit. People started streaming in, and more than 2,400 people backed the company at this level. As the dollar amount went up, Wilson's team slightly increased what they were preselling. At the $500 level, 100 people backed Wilson and his design team, and they got to throw a party and give away ten watches to their friends and family.

All in, when the campaign closed, they had raised $942,578 from 13,512 people.

Amanda Palmer and the Grand Theft Orchestra

For all you music lovers out there who think you need a major record label in order to make an album, think again.

Amanda Palmer was the lead singer of the band Dresden Dolls, which had a cult following in the early 2000s. Hers is far from a household name, but Palmer was very active with her fan base online. She decided that she wanted to make an album by getting direct support from her fans. The album would be titled *Amanda Palmer & The Grand Theft Orchestra* and would cost about $100,000 to make.

With the aid of a crowdfunding website, Palmer reached out to her online community. People came out in droves, and she raised $1,192,793 for the album.

This story fits well in this book because it highlights how essential it is to leverage your online social networks when you set out to do an equity-based or debt-based crowdfund investing campaign. Palmer wasn't shy about asking her fans to support her, and you shouldn't be either. With that said, you must keep in mind a key difference between crowdfunding and crowdfund investing: Per the JOBS Act that opened the door to crowdfund investing, you *can't* seek investments directly on social media outlets such as Facebook or LinkedIn. Instead, you can use those outlets to direct people to your investment campaign on an SEC-registered funding platform (see Chapter 7).

Sedation Wars: Battle for Alabaster

Growing up, one of your authors, Zak, spent his winters sitting in front of a crackling fire with his brother and parents playing board games. Not as many people play board games these days, but Zak's love of board games led us to this case study.

Renowned game designer and miniature figurine designer Mike McVey set out on Kickstarter to raise $20,000 to design a board game called Sedation Wars: Battle for Alabaster, a two-player survival horror game. Mike planned for this game's success to fund further games in the same board-game series. But Mike raised plenty of capital to design more than just his first game. Other people besides Zak seem to be nostalgic about board games. More than 4,000 people came together and invested $951,254.

Cheer

Time for some shameless self-promotion! In addition to being an entrepreneur, one of your authors, Jason, is also a documentary film producer. His first feature film, *Cheer,* was created primarily in Bangkok, Thailand, and in Orlando, Florida. After bootstrapping the filming and original edit of the film, and after the film had its world premiere at the Bangkok World Film Festival, Jason and his director decided to raise money on Kickstarter to do more post-production work on the film. The goal was to raise $19,999. (The number 9 is very lucky in Thai culture.)

Jason and his team worked very hard to spread the word among Thai people both in Thailand and in the United States and to promote the film itself. Through their efforts, they were able to raise almost twice their goal amount.

Kone Coffee

A barista in Portland, Oregon, had an idea. He wanted to create the best coffee filter possible — one that would create amazing coffee, be environmentally responsible, and have a great design. He worked with friends in Portland who helped him to create the Kone Coffee Filter. This stainless steel filter is both beautiful and functional. But he didn't stop there! He also worked with a local pottery shop to create a drip mechanism and pot for the filter so that it fit perfectly and so that it had the same aesthetic as the cone filter.

When he created a pitch video asking for funding for producing these items, he used visuals, music, and his own words to tell a compelling story of why he wanted to do so. His goal was to raise $5,000. Instead, he raised more than $155,000!

For us, the most interesting part of this story is what happened after his hugely successful campaign. He experienced problems in creating his product and challenges in finalizing his production run. He fell behind schedule and had to redesign his pot due to production issues. But through it all, he communicated regularly (via e-mail updates and photos) with his contributors, and they stuck by him and trusted that he was doing the right thing. Heed the lesson of the importance of communication (the topic of Chapter 12)!

Lockitron

When entrepreneurs saw how effective arts crowdfunding sites like Kickstarter were, they began to use the same channels to find funding for their companies and products. But as more and more people joined the crowdfunding parade, problems began to arise with order fulfillment. Some entrepreneurs encountered production issues that led to shipment delays, and customers found themselves having paid for items that weren't delivered in a timely manner.

After a number of reports in the news regarding these issues, a company named Lockitron created a solution. Over the course of a long weekend, it put together a crowdfunding site of its own, but with an important twist: It used Amazon Payments as a sort of escrow agent to hold customer funds until the product had shipped. That way, customers had the assurance that their funds would be transferred to an entrepreneur only *after* their orders had been fulfilled.

Lockitron hoped to raise $150,000 within one month to support its venture. Instead, within the first two days it raised five times that amount. Clearly, its product was interesting and had broad appeal.

Forage Kitchen

The Forage Kitchen project is about breaking down barriers to entry so people can launch their own restaurants. Based in San Francisco, it's a co-working space for food. The brain child of Iso Rabins, the whole idea behind Forage Kitchen is to help small food makers get their start. This incubator provides all the things people need to get their start in the food business. They have access to everything from cooking space and utensils to office space and business support.

This project needed to raise $150,000 to build its space. More than 1,600 people thought this was a great idea, and Rabins successfully raised $156,502. The next time you're in San Francisco, check it out!

Chapter 22

Ten Stories That Inspire

In This Chapter

▶ Funding great ideas in nontraditional ways

▶ Growing hope and inspiration via crowdfunding

When you take actions that combine the mind and the heart, wonderful things can happen. This is why we put these ten stories in the book. They're meant to inspire you. They show you how people are willing to part with their hard-earned dollars, without expecting a return, when they believe in someone else's idea. What we'll see when crowdfund investing is in full gear is thousands of such heart-warming ideas that will launch businesses, and the crowd will invest not only because there's a chance for a return but because they feel good about the idea.

Ubooly

Consumer-related products are historically hard to fund. Such was the case with Ubooly (pronounced oo-boo-ley). The website www.ubooly.com describes Ubooly as a cuddly orange marsupial that loves to go on adventures and a voice interactive toy powered by your iPhone or iPod Touch. Ubooly is the brainchild of husband-and-wife team Carly Gloge and Isaac Squires, founders of design agency Warb.

The company, based in Boulder, Colorado (an example of great ideas that reside in areas that are considered "good for capital" but "hard to access"), first tried its hand in the venture capital world. With no luck, the two took to crowdfunding site Kickstarter (www.kickstarter.com) to prove that their idea had legs and that a toy that uses Apple's mobile devices to provide interactive games, as well as speech recognition features, could fly with consumers. Their goal was to raise $25,000. They raised $28,000 from 161 backers. The funds were used for the initial production run and the company's participation in an entrepreneurial contest called TechStars 2012 Boulder. At TechStars, they were able to secure $335,000 in additional venture capital and a spot on a web reality series, the Internet's version of reality TV.

With their funds, Gloge and Squires want to create an entire thriving ecosystem around their toy, with apps that not only learn and grow with a child but also suit specific use cases. For example, there's a GPS-tracking app in the works that provides a virtual tour guide experience for kids on vacation.

Since the success of their initial campaign, they've raised $1.5 million in seed funding from venture capital funds. Perhaps the VCs will think twice about such products the next time around.

Project Homophobia

You can't help but cry when watching the video about this project at Indiegogo (www.indiegogo.com), another perks-based crowdfunding platform. It opens with a young adolescent named Jamie telling gay youth, just like him, via his own web video to "hold your head high" despite being bullied. Unfortunately, Jamie just couldn't take the bullying any longer. Four months after filming his "it gets better" video, Jamie committed suicide.

Screenwriter and director Gregor Schmidinger decided to use his filmmaking talent to do something rather than sit idly by. He launched a crowdfunding campaign with the goal of raising $6,000. The goal was to film a story about a young boy coming to terms with his sexuality and having to deal with the social pressures as well.

By the time the clock ran out on his campaign, he had raised $10,067 from 141 backers. People from all over the world funded the project, and comments came from people of all walks of life. With his funds, Gregor made a 23-minute short film that has already received over 100,000 views since June 2012.

One of the commenters from Germany said, "Is there a category for short films in the Oscars? They should nominate you." What this campaign shows us is that crowdfunding can both empower and inspire people to make a difference.

The First Crowdfunded Baby

Struggling to have a baby is stressful. Such was the case for Jessica and Sean Haley. They tried for three years to conceive a child naturally, and their doctor gave them a 1 percent chance of success. Their insurance would not cover the cost of in vitro fertilization (IVF), so they turned to the Internet.

Unfortunately, their first try with Kickstarter wasn't a success. Kickstarter rejected their application because it doesn't accept health or medical projects.

Then in June 2011, just months away from their fourth wedding anniversary, in an act of desperation, the couple from Melbourne Beach, Florida, posted their story on Indiegogo.

In her campaign, Jessica detailed her challenges and life changes, including taking pills and daily injections, and how, after 16 eggs were harvested, their family hopes lay with three embryos.

Through Indiegogo they asked for $5,000. Their story touched many, ultimately raising $8,050.

On September 2, 2011, the couple learned that their 1 percent chance of successfully becoming pregnant had turned into a 100 percent certainty. Jessica was pregnant! She continued to detail her journey on Twitter and, on April 7, 2012, gave birth to baby Landon, who spent his first few days in intensive care.

As Jessica says, "He's here because of hundreds of people that believed in us and wanted us to become parents. Our dream came true. We have a baby, one that comes with an amazing story that we hope and pray inspires others who are facing infertility issues, too."

Crowdfunding Hope

Dustin Dorough is a Superman fan who decided that he wanted to bring a little hope to children across North America. He launched a crowdfunding project on Indiegogo to raise money to pay for his trip. On September 6, 2012, his campaign successfully reached its goal of $6,500. Dustin set aside three months of his life for a trip that will take him over 15,000 miles. He's planning on going to a children's hospital in each of the lower 48 states in addition to several provinces in Canada. We love this story so much because it shows someone crowdfunding hope.

Dustin didn't stand to make anything out of this project himself. He was simply a fan of Superman who thought sick kids needed a little lifting up. He wanted to bring comfort and hope to sick children. The passion began when a friend of his who worked in a children's hospital invited him to come and visit in his new Superman uniform. He wasn't able to make the trip, but he decided that he would visit a hospital in every state instead. He plans on giving each child a signed picture of Superman as a symbol of their strength in fighting their own battles.

The Annual Clock

Scott Thrift was tired of life passing him by too fast. He often wasn't able to realize he was having fun and creating good experiences until months after the experience happened. He would look back and say, "Wow, I loved that."

After talking with his friends about his experiences, he realized that he wasn't alone. Time is moving so quickly that people aren't sure of the value of a day, a week, or a month. You can't live in the moment when the moment changes every second. Scott wanted to create a new way to look at life, a way that would make us slow down and enjoy things. He set out to make an annual clock.

The clock would take an entire year to make a full cycle. The clock's face would represent the changes in seasons, from white (winter) to green (spring) to yellow (summer) to red (fall). He believed that the meditative simplicity of the clock would help people enjoy the present moment.

Apparently, Scott wasn't alone in his belief. He was able to recruit 837 backers on his Kickstarter campaign for a total of $97,567 when the campaign closed in November 2011. His goal was only $24,000, so he blew it out of the water. Maybe his clock will help us all slow down, enjoy our coffee, and make time matter.

From Nothing to World Cup

Jay DeMerit had a dream. He wanted to be a professional soccer player. Being from the United States, however, he faced some hurdles. Professional soccer is a much bigger sport in Europe and South America, so Jay got on a plane and moved to England with $1,800. After the first year, he came back to the United States with no money to his name. He was trying out for teams but wasn't making it anywhere, and then he got a break: He made it into the English Premier League.

Once on the field, Jay tried even harder. He went from making £40 a week in England in the mid 2000s to starting in the 2010 World Cup for the United States.

One of DeMerit's college friends, Ranko Tutulugdzija, decided that this story needed to be told. The only problem was he wasn't a filmmaker and he didn't have a budget to get a film made. Nevertheless, Ranko believed people wanted to hear this story, so he turned to the crowd to raise $215,000 to create a documentary telling the Jay DeMerit story. The project was successfully funded in July 2011 with over 1,900 backers and raised a total of $223,422. The film was released later that year. Now Jay DeMerit's story will be able to inspire athletes worldwide because his story had the support of the crowd.

A Photographic View of Breast Cancer

Cancer touches everyone, and in 2008, it touched Angelo Merendino in a horrible way. Five months earlier, he had married Jennifer, the woman of his dreams, and then she was diagnosed with breast cancer. She fought it off, but in 2010, the cancer came back.

This time, they didn't want to go through the experience alone. They wanted people to understand what they were going through and set out to make a photo exhibit. Angelo wanted to raise $8,500 to cover the costs of prints and to travel to show exhibits. In 2011, he was able to successfully raise over $15,000 on Indiegogo. Because of this crowdfunded project, people will have a better understanding of what people go though when they're battling cancer. The exhibit is called *The Battle We Didn't Choose* and it was touring in 2012. Thank you, Angelo.

Vivian Maier: Photographer

If a photograph is taken and no one sees it for almost 40 years, does it still have an audience?

A young man named John Maloof attended a furniture auction that included boxes from storage facilities that had been unpaid for years. He purchased a few boxes, and inside he discovered prints and negatives of 100,000 photos that had been taken by a female photographer between 1950 and 1990 on the streets of Chicago. Her name was Vivian Maier. (You can see her work at www.vivianmaier.com.)

At first, the photos appeared to be simple street life images. However, they're amazingly rich with detail, emotion, and elegance. The photos inspired Maloof to take up photography himself. In that process, he discovered just how difficult it was to capture street life with the depth and completeness that Maier had. When he shared Maier's photos with friends, he saw how they moved everyone who viewed them. It inspired him to preserve the photos, create a high-quality photo book about her work and life, and create a documentary film to honor her.

The story started to get attention locally and then nationally. What began as a quest to raise $15,000 ended when they raised $105,042 from 1,495 backers. Now a woman who created her art in total privacy, who was a nanny in Chicago for almost her entire life, will receive recognition for her stunning achievement — all thanks to crowdfunding and a lot of hard work from the people who are executing this campaign.

The Cheer Ambassadors Film

A story about cheerleading in Thailand? Really?

Yes, really. One of your authors, Jason, was sitting on a beach in Thailand talking with a group of friends, and friends of friends, about their work and passions in life. During the conversation, one of the Thais said his passion in life was cheerleading. Jason learned that cheerleading (the acrobatic style of cheerleading that you see in championships on ESPN) is the fastest growing sport in the world, with more than 4 million athletes from over 100 countries competing each year for the world championship title at Disney World in Orlando, Florida.

These friends told Jason the story of a coach and his team from the streets of Bangkok, who created a national championship team with no money or outside support. This team raised the equivalent of $100,000 so it could travel to the United States to compete in the world championships in 2009. Even more amazing is that this team, in its first showing on the world stage, placed second in the world and shocked the entire sport.

When he heard this story, Jason knew that it was a movie that needed to be made, and he and his friends had to make it. With no experience in filmmaking, they purchased equipment, taught themselves how to use it, and filmed and edited the movie. They needed finishing funds for post-production of the movie and were able to successfully raise almost 200 percent of their goal. Jason can tell you from firsthand experience that it was a challenge, but without crowdfunding they never would've been able to finish the film and be invited to show in five film festivals around the world.

The Break: Surviving the Recovery

New York writer Louise Rozett volunteered in the dining hall at Ground Zero after the 9/11 attacks. She cleared trays, handed out food, and listened when people needed to talk. For her it was the most profound experience of her life. She found that people who worked at the site were changed in subtle and not so subtle ways — some even not being comfortable in their own homes because it felt so different from their daily experience at the site.

As a writer, Rozett was compelled to create a fictional story based on her experiences. She submitted a play script to the New York Fringe Festival, and it was accepted. That was the good news. The bad news was how expensive it would be to put on even the most basic of productions. So, she and her creative team turned to Kickstarter, where they were able to raise over $25,000 to tell this amazing story to a wider audience and honor the sacrifices of those who worked for weeks or months in the aftermath of 9/11.

Appendix

Resources

. . . .

Advisory Services

Crowdfund Capital Advisors; www.crowdfundcapitaladvisors.com: Provides advisory services to professional investors, governments, non-governmental organizations (NGOs), development institutions, and corporations to create early-stage finance strategies that include crowdfund investing. It also provides consulting services to brands, corporations, entrepreneurs, and investors in how to maximize the benefits of crowdfund investing.

massolution; www.massolution.com: Wrote the first Crowdfunding Industry Report. Also created the first certification program for crowdfunding portals to establish best practices. Crowdsourcing.org (www.crowdsourcing.org), an online news source on crowdfunding and crowdsourcing, is a product of massolution.

Industry Groups

CrowdFund Intermediary Regulatory Advocates (CFIRA); www.cfira.org: The industry advocacy group working with the Securities and Exchange Commission (SEC) and the Financial Industry Regulatory Authority (FINRA).

Crowdfunding Professional Association (CfPA); www.crowdfunding professional.org: The trade association for the crowdfunding industry.

Small Business Administration (SBA); www.sba.gov: A government association full of information related to starting and growing a small business.

Small Business & Entrepreneurship Council; www.sbecouncil.org: The industry association representing the interests of small businesses and entrepreneurs in Washington, D.C.

Startup Exemption; www.startupexemption.com: The group of entrepreneurs and supporters who rallied around the framework to legalize crowdfund investing in the United States.

Perks-Based Crowdfunding Platforms

Indiegogo; www.indiegogo.com: A perks-based platform that has also funded small businesses.

Kickstarter; www.kickstarter.com: The most well-known crowdfunding platform. Pitches must be art- or design-related.

Rock the Post; www.rockthepost.com: A perks-based platform that specializes in helping small businesses, entrepreneurs, and nonprofits raise capital.

RocketHub; www.rockethub.com: A crowdfunding platform with a broad array of pitches.

Crowdfund Investing Platforms

As of this book's publication, the following sites are preparing for launch but will not be able to offer securities via companies until the SEC says, "Go." Check back with the CfPA (see "Industry Groups," earlier in this appendix) for updates.

Crowdfunder; www.crowdfunder.com: A debt- and equity-based crowdfund investing platform.

Crowdnetic; www.crowdnetic.com: Consider it the Bloomberg of the crowdfund investing space for all data related to trends in crowdfund investing.

EarlyShares; www.earlyshares.com: An equity-based crowdfund investing platform.

SeedInvest; www.seedinvest.com: An equity-based crowdfund investing platform.

SoMoLend; www.somolend.com: A debt-based crowdfund investing platform.

Crowdfund Investing Legal Expertise

Ellenoff, Grossman & Schole LLP; www.egsllp.com: The leading law firm globally focused on crowdfund investing. These guys have more than 30 years of experience in small business capital formation and SEC regulations.

Crowdfund Investing Secondary Market Provider

GATE Impact; www.gateimpact.com: A broker-dealer focused on the crowdfund investing ecosystem. Also a secondary market platform for trading crowdfund invested shares after the 12-month holding period is up.

Crowdfund Investing Due Diligence Service

CrowdCheck; www.crowdcheck.com: A background service provider to the crowdfund investing industry.

Regulatory Bodies

Financial Industry Regulatory Authority (FINRA); www.finra.org: Oversees investment banks and broker-dealers that perform financial transactions. Will also be the gatekeeper to the funding portals offering crowdfund investments.

North America Securities Administrators Association (NASAA); www.nasaa.org: A conglomerate of the individual state security administrators that patrol the securities offerings in each state.

Securities and Exchange Commission (SEC); www.sec.gov: Oversees the securities markets in the United States and sets the regulations that govern the crowdfund investing industry.

Online Services for Small Businesses and Startups

Business Plan Pro; www.businessplanpro.com: A program that helps you create a business plan. A great tool for both startups and ongoing entities.

Crowdfund Mafia; www.crowdfundmafia.com: Helps companies raise funds for their crowdfund investing campaigns.

Funding Roadmap; www.fundingroadmap.com: An online business planning to crowdfunding program that can walk you through the step-by-step disclosures with which you'll need to comply.

LegalZoom; www.legalzoom.com: The one-stop shop for everything you need from incorporating to intellectual property protection.

Leverage Public Relations; www.leverage-pr.com: A leader in the crowdfund investing space.

Quickbooks; www.quickbooks.intuit.com: An easy-to-use accounting program that will keep you compliant with the Internal Revenue Service (IRS), SEC, and your investors. A must for startup businesses!

The Rockefeller Habits; www.gazelles.com/implement_rockefeller_habts.html: Running and growing a hyper-growth organization can be a challenge. This site can help you stay organized and focused on your goals.

Index

• V •

• W •

• Y •

• Z •